# DON'T CALL ME *GRINGA*

*A Memoir*

*BY*

SALLY CANTÚ

Cover and Book design: Vladimir Verano Third Place Press

Front cover image "Sally & Gloria in the labor camp," © 2015 Sally Cantú.

Author contact: sriccobono@hotmail.com

ISBN: 978-0-692-46888-3

*Printed by Third Place Press,*
*Lake Forest Park, Washington*
*www.thirdplacepress.com*

For My Family

In Loving Memory of: *Apá*, Mom, and Lydia

To:
Triana + Family,

Enjoy the book. Best
Wishes always.
Triana, I'll always think
of you as being so special +
Loved by my mother :)
Thank you! Love,
Sally

# The Cantú Family

PARENTS

Valentin & Beatrice Cantú

CHILDREN BORN IN TEXAS - *Listed by Age*:

Efrain

Lydia

Viola

Elida

Hector

Imelda

Maria Celia (Mary Sally)

CHILDREN BORN IN WASHINGTON

Gloria Ana

Valentin Omar (Rudy)

Norma Linda

Alfredo Rogelio (Freddy)

# Contents

# Prologue

Just north of the Texas-Mexico border lies a tiny place in South Texas known as La Blanca. Not big enough to be an actual town or city, it was more appropriately referred to as a *Rancho.* It was on this *Rancho* that I drew my first breath on the 26th of February, 1952. Like my grandparents, parents, and siblings before me, I was born a US citizen, although I like to boast that I was "almost" born in Mexico.

Regardless of where I was born, however, I will always be as Mexican as I am American. Even if—because of the Mexican economic, political and social situation that has people fleeing to the US seeking survival and a better way of life—I must affirm my relief and good fortune at having been born an American citizen, I am still proud of my Mexican heritage.

It has always amazed me that a simple little line on a map might determine one's destiny. Almost by geographic accident, I was born an American citizen. But what if La Blanca had been located just a bit farther south? What if the border had been just a little bit farther north? My family has lived in that area for generations, even before it became US territory and the border lines were redrawn.

All my life I have known people who have fled poverty and unemployment in Mexico. The perils they face in surreptitiously crossing the border into the US are difficult to imagine. Many lives have been lost in this attempt, yet Mexicans try and try again to get into the U.S. What they seek is a basic human right, something that most of us take for granted daily.

Growing up, I often heard the word *Gringo* used to refer to White or Caucasian people. As an adult, I realized that, as a rule, Mexican people consider Latinos from the US to be *Gringos.* When I visit Mexico, I am often told that I am a *Gringa*—that I am not Mexican because neither I nor my parents were born in Mexico. I still beg to differ. Who better than I can judge what's in my own heart and soul?

As far back as my family can trace, my parents' families lived in Texas. It is common knowledge that Texas was once part of Mexico. Thus, my Mexican roots are undeniable. My father did not speak English, and he was *Mejicano,* heart and soul. Unfortunately, not much more than this is known about my father's ancestry: My paternal great-grandparents were landowners who lost their land when Mexico lost her northern territory to the United States. Later, my dad's siblings were proud, yet humble and honorable people who worked the land for their *patrónes.* Through generations, they retained their *Mexicanismo,* even as their homeland was lost to the United States. My family has always maintained that we did not cross the border—on the contrary, the border irrefutably crossed us.

My mother, her parents, and her siblings were fluent in English, as well as Spanish. Her background was diverse, including Mexican, Caucasian and Spanish ancestry. There are many Caucasian names in her lineage, including Campbell, Johnston and Weaver, but more than that I do not know.

Having lived in Washington State my entire life, I may be very much Americanized, but my family has preserved its Mexican culture, language and traditions—and they are still central to our way of life. We are a mixture of Mexican and American, and I feel extremely fortunate to be both. I embrace the fact that I am Chicana, I am Mexican, and I am American.

I ask only one thing from everyone—for it is indeed my greatest vexation: Please, Don't Call Me *Gringa.*

stration by Raul Cortés Monroy

# Part I

# Chapter 1

For over 200 years Mexicans have played an essential yet unsung role in U.S. history. In 1775, Mexican and Spanish explorers first set foot on what we now know as the Washington Coast. Immigration has been ongoing ever since.

By the 1950's, the Yakima Valley in Washington State saw a great influx of migrants from southern states and Mexico. Drawn by the age-old promise of a better life and stories of abundant farm labor and agricultural work, families arrived in droves. News spread about the good life and fortunes to be made.

A common adage among Mexican people was that money could be shoveled off the streets en los Estados Unidos, the United States. The belief prevailed that there was money to be made en El Norte, as well as many other opportunities for advancement. It was rumored that in the north, segregation and discrimination were not as prevalent. Public restrooms were not marked "White Only" or "Colored Only" as they were in the south.

Segregated restrooms were quite a dilemma for my family, as we are all very fair-complexioned. We are not "Colored," but we are certainly not "White" either. The segregated public restrooms posed quite an ordeal for Mexican people, but my family had long since made the decision to avoid using either white or colored restrooms as much as possible. When absolutely necessary, we were to use the "White Only" restroom, acting as nonchalant and indiscreet as possible. This decision was based on the simple fact that, given the two choices, we could more readily pass for "White," whereas we could never pass for "Colored." In an effort to prevent problems either way, the safest choice was made in the hopes that we would go unnoticed. Yet, the underlying fear of being accused of using the wrong restroom was always with us. We were all too familiar with the outrage that could be unleashed upon us if we were caught using the wrong restroom. To our dismay, fear, and discomfort, there was no such thing as the right restroom for us.

Ironically, our birth certificates indicated that we were "White." This was not just a debatable issue—it was a blatant, out-and-out lie. How could such an important document contain such a grave error? This was something I would eventually come to question, but not until much, much later.

There appeared to be many valid reasons for families to make the daring move to El Norte. My parents knew people who, in prior years, had made the move and were working in Washington State. Others had made the move to California and were already working steadily and sending money to family members who had stayed behind. Just about everywhere, the dominant topic of conversation was about how much better life was in the north. Dad came home with bits and pieces of conversations he had overheard or been involved in.

Mario Mendoza, who owned the local cantina, was convinced that moving north was the best thing a family could do. "Si, compadres," he said, standing behind the bar drying beer mugs. "Dicen que la familia Garza is doing very well over there in the north, and there is never a lack of work. I myself think it is a wise move. Oh, and of course there are young Diego and Rodofo, who left together last year. I hear they both send money home to their families on a regular basis. What more proof do we need, eh? Everyone earns money enough to send home."

Mario Mendoza always knew the latest chisme, both from his regular customers, and from the many drifters who passed through the little border town of La Blanca, Texas.

"Well, all I can say is that I, too, have heard nothing but good news about the ones who have gone north," chimed in Juan José Castillo, who was a regular at Mario's Cantina. "More and more people are talking about making the move. I'm all for it, and my wife and family agree. We plan to make the move within the next month."

"En serio, Juan José, you are really going that soon?" someone asked. The men at the card table all looked up. This was a topic of interest to everyone.

"Claro, we have everything ready to go. We have been saving money for a while now, and I signed up with one of the drivers I know. We will be leaving next month. Everything is set."

"Miren compadres," Angel Morales added, "I like the idea of the men going first and sending for family once we are settled and doing well. I'm thinking of taking that route. It seems safer as long as you know and trust the driver and make arrangements ahead of time."

After hearing all the talk, Mom and Dad started planning the great move north. As time drew near, the family met regularly to discuss the move. Mom, Dad, and the two eldest children, Efrain and Lydia, were seated at the kitchen table to discuss the idea of moving north to Washington State. Mom reported that Comadre Chita, from across the street, had received a letter from her son full of good news about his new life in Washington.

"We've heard nothing but good news about El Norte," Mom said to the family. "I like everything I've seen and heard about Washington State. I say if we're going to make the move, let's go that far north. I hear it's beautiful and green, with mountains and rivers all around."

"Yes, I agree that it should be Washington State," Dad added. "Most of the good news we've heard comes from there, and the pictures we've seen are beautiful. People look happy. Besides, we have some contacts there already. I've also been asking around about travel arrangements," Dad continued. "I think that going by truck will be best. I've already arranged to go with Oscar Mendez, from work, to look into it more and talk to some of the drivers. We have enough money saved to make the trip and get settled once we get there."

"Hija, bring the money so we can count it," Mom told Lydia, pointing towards the kitchen pantry, where the money can was hidden.

"Okay, Mom," Lydia replied excitedly, rushing towards the pantry and pulling open the curtain. Down on her hands and knees, Lydia reached back into the bottom shelf and pulled out the tin coffee can that served as the family bank.

"Here it is, Mom. Efrain and I will count it," she said, sitting next to her older brother.

"Write down today's date on this page," Dad said, placing his pencil and a small notebook next to the can in front of Efrain.

These round table discussions had been going on for some time now. My parents considered and weighed the options, until finally the decision was made. La Familia Cantú would soon embark upon an astounding journey that would change the course of our lives forever.

La Familia Cantú consisted of my parents, Valentin Cantú y Beatrice Cavazos Cantú, and their seven children. We were headed for a place called the Seedless Hop Ranch, located in Grandview, Washington, where living quarters would be provided. The patrón of that ranch expected our arrival, and there would be work enough to make a decent living.

Mom and Dad made arrangements for the trip and paid the deposit for our passage in a huge truck that would be transporting other families as well. Mom was concerned that we would be traveling like cargo or livestock and that among our traveling companions would be many whom we did not know.

"Valentin," she said to Dad pensively. "No estoy segura. ¿Y si las cosas no salen bien?"

"Si, Bea, tienes razón," Dad replied. "But didn't we agree that the move is necessary? That it will mean a better future for all of us?" he asked. "Y no te preocupes. Voy averiguar más sobre el viaje."

Now that the decision was final and money had actually exchanged hands, Mom was thinking more and more about the safety and security of her family. Her anxiety and concern continued to mount. Dad tried to reassure her, and as promised, made further inquiries about the trip. He inspected the passenger list and was assured that our traveling companions would be decent families like ours—in search of work and a better life. Many of the names on the list were familiar, and it was a relief to see that most of the travelers were family groups.

"Okay," Mom told Dad, "I'll try to stop worrying. I know it doesn't do any good." She thought a moment and said, "With God's help, everything will work out for the best."

Time passed ever so quickly, and soon moving day was upon us. As our belongings were loaded into the truck, Mom looked back nostalgically at the home we were leaving. With her hand on her heart, she turned to Dad, saying, "Bueno, que sea lo que Dios mande." With that, she commended herself and her family to God.

By the time the driver picked up the last of the passengers, the truck was jam-packed with people, children, and belongings.

"Oh, Mom," Lydia whispered, "these people are so noisy, and the kids, I hope they're not this bad all the way."

"It's just the uncertainty and excitement of the trip. Don't worry," Mom responded with a reassuring smile. "I think things will settle down in a bit."

To make matters worse, the truck was not fully enclosed. It had a floor and walls on each side, but instead of a permanent roof or top, it was covered by a heavy tarp.

At the beginning of the trip, some of the men and older boys pulled back the tarp so they could stick their heads out to get some fresh air and view the scenery. Women, girls, and children were not allowed to do so, however, as it could be dangerous.

"Mom, I want to look outside, too," Lydia said. "You know I can do anything Efrain can do. It's not fair that they let him and not me just because I'm a girl."

"I know, Hija," Mom assured her, "but they don't know you and are just trying to keep some order. Don't take things personally. We don't need to prove anything here. It's only temporary. Besides, I need you with me so we can keep an eye on the children."

After a moment, Lydia smiled. "Okay, Mom, it's no big deal anyway."

The trip from Texas to Washington proved to be exceedingly difficult. It was crowded and uncomfortable from the beginning, but even more so because we knew that the trip would take a number of days. The rules were clearly laid out beforehand: there would be no stopping for sleep; the truck would continue day and night, with drivers regularly changing shifts; the only stops would be for food, gas, and restroom breaks; but as time was of the essence, all stops would be as few and far between as possible; all travelers were advised to stock up on water, food, and drinks at each stop, as it would be some time before another stop was made.

In March, 1953, during this ride, I was one year old, and my mother was pregnant with my sister Gloria. Suffering the symptoms of her pregnancy, Mom often nibbled on a cracker and sipped Kool-Aid or water to settle her nauseous stomach. With rosary in hand, she spent most of her time silently reciting prayers for a safe trip and good luck upon arrival.

It didn't take long for people to get restless and cranky. Putting up with other people's personal hygiene, or lack thereof, was bad enough, but the cramped quarters only intensified the problem. The smell in the truck was a mixture of mold, sweat, and overall griminess. Mom and Dad exchanged an apprehensive glance. Dad whispered, "It's only for a few days. Just think about being there."

"Pull the tarp back," someone yelled. "Let's get some fresh air circulating."

"Si, si por favor." The passengers agreed fresh air would make all the difference.

The faces of the riders were uniformly grim. Some whispered back and forth, looking around nervously. Everyone understood that this was not a pleasure trip. Mom and Dad kept close watch on their children, who had all been instructed to stay put and behave. But the same could not be said for other children in the truck.

The uncomfortable, cramped quarters made it extremely difficult for people to rest, much less sleep. Children lay on quilts and blankets, but adults only caught snippets of sleep where they sat among all the clutter. Always on the lookout, Mom and Dad took turns dozing.

The truck we traveled in was old and lacked adequate ventilation or heat. Onward we traveled over rough and bumpy roads. Often, a child was sent tumbling from one spot to another causing undue chaos. The screaming, crying, scolding, and comforting that followed were exasperating and only added to the discomposure of these untimely disturbances.

In March, weather in the southern states wasn't so bad, but as we moved northward, the weather cooled considerably until it was freezing cold. The children shivered and complained. All too soon, the lack of sleep and cramped quarters gave way to exhaustion and irritability, as parents did their best to maintain some semblance of humor and good spirits. But that was not always possible.

Weather conditions went from bad to worse as we traveled on icy, snow-covered roads. Car troubles—flat tires, a lose tarp—made the trip all the more grueling. Luck was not on our side.

The worst by far was when the truck hit a patch of black ice and ended up skidding sideways into a little ditch. Everyone was throttled and shaken. The children were screaming and crying, their belongings strewn throughout the truck, yet by the grace of God there were no serious injuries. Sensing fear and apprehension, Dad addressed my mother in a voice loud enough to be overheard, "Podría haber sido mucho peor. Gracias a Diós tenemos un buen conductor."

"Si, tiene razón," many of the riders agreed, and soon everyone was singing the praises of our driver and discussing how much worse it could have been. People crossed themselves and thanked God for his mercy.

The realization of our narrow escape had everyone talking about how lucky we were to have come out of the situation in one piece. Miraculously, the accident served a useful purpose. Thankful that it hadn't been worse, everyone readjusted their temperament, and the overall mood in the truck changed for the better. This was one instance when a few bumps, bruises, scratches and scrapes were a small price to pay.

Even so, everyone was more than ready for the long, arduous trip to be over: The riders on the truck repeatedly asked, "When will we get there?" "¿Cuándo llegamos?"

In spite of everything, according to my mother, I took my first steps in the back of the truck. Mom held both my hands in hers as I tottered and took a step or two. Apparently, this accomplishment overjoyed me, and I kept stepping busily, from my mother to my big sister Lydia's hands. "Come on, stand up, Baby Sally," Lydia said, laughing and holding both my hands in hers. She carefully guided me forward as I stood on my wobbly little legs and giggled. A step or two was all I managed before plopping down, overjoyed by my new experience.

"Ven, Mijita," Mom continued, "Otro pasito, one more little step." Happily, I obliged until I tuckered myself out and was ready for a nap.

# CHAPTER 2

Before my family relocated to Washington State, we lived in La Blanca, Texas, a small border town where the primary language was Spanish. But even prior to that, before Mexico lost its northern territory to the United States, we originated in Mexico.

In the late 1800's Feliciano Cantú married Gregoria Rodriguez. Los Cantús were landowners in northern Mexico, but by the 1850's Mexico had lost considerable land to the United States. As the U.S./Mexican border moved south, La Familia Cantú was displaced. Having always been Mexican citizens by the very nature of their birthright, they suddenly found themselves in the United States and eventually lost all legal rights to their land. So it was that my ancestors went from being landowners working their own land, to farmworkers working the land owned by the patrónes.

Before the Cantú land was lost to the US, however, my great, great grandfather, Don José Cantú, experienced an ordeal he almost didn't live to tell about.

"What a beautiful evening this is turning out to be, Hijo," José Cantú told his eldest son Salvador as they put away the horses for the night.

"Si, Apá," Salvador responded. "It was a hot day, but it looks like we have a nice breeze coming in for the evening. I'll finish with the horses. You go on into the house."

"Thank you, son," Don José smiled. "I am very tired. Don't forget to lock the hacienda gate, eh. I'll see you and your brothers back at the house."

Later that night, as the family prepared for bed, they were startled by the sound of many horses running, followed by shouting and shooting. Don José yelled out to his wife, María, and their daughter Guadalupe, as he herded them into the kitchen. Opening the trap door under the table, he shouted, "Get downstairs and hide. Do not come out until one of us comes for you."

"Si, Viejo," María answered shakily. "What's going on?"

"Todavía no sabemos, pero suena mal," Don José responded hurriedly. He had a bad feeling.

With the women safely hidden, and the table back in place, Don José and his four sons collected their guns and ammunition.

Ready to face the intruders, they gathered in the front room. Suddenly, amid the rowdy yelling and laughing, they heard a loud voice, "Ey, come outside and don't try anything. We have you covered, and you are seriously outnumbered. We don't want to hurt anybody but we won't hesitate, if we have to."

"Stay away from the windows!" Don José said anxiously as he signaled his sons to stay back. "Hijo, did you forget to lock the hacienda gate?"

"No, Apá," Salvador answered quickly. "I swear I locked it."

"Come out now or we're coming in," the leader yelled again.

Don José crossed himself whispering, "Lord, please protect us." He opened the door and stepped out onto the porch with his arms up, still clutching the rifle in his right hand. At least thirty armed men stood in front of the house. Covered in dirt and dust, the men looked tired, as did their horses. Their clothes were in tatters, but they were all heavily armed with pistolas and rifles. Most of them wore carrilleras across their chests. Some wore Mexican sombreros, others vaquero hats.

These men are a dangerous lot. Best to deal with them carefully, Don José thought to himself as he yelled, "How can I help you, señores? I am José Cantú at your service."

"First, you can drop your rifle and tell anyone inside to do the same. They call me El Alacran. We don't want any trouble. We just need a place to rest for a bit, some food, and drink. Then we'll be on our way and nobody gets hurt. Understand? Who else is in the house?"

"Yes, I understand. It is just me and my sons, and we will give you what you ask. Just please...."

"Eyy, we could use some clothes," one of the men hissed, pulling at his sweat-stained shirt, which was in rags.

"And maybe a bath." El Alacran laughed loudly. He sniffed at his armpit and made a face. "The horses need rest, water...."

"Please," Don José interjected, "we will give you what you need. There is plenty of room in the barns for sleeping and we...."

"Gracias, compadre. Muy amable." El Alacran smiled, tipping his hat. "But I'll decide who sleeps where. From this moment on I give the orders. Understood?"

"Dismount, men," he yelled over his shoulder. "Tend to the horses." A few of the men searched the house for weapons and liquor, but most stayed on the grounds.

In the kitchen, El Alacran helped himself to the bottle of mezcal he found under the sink. Walking back to the front room, he dropped himself heavily onto a large cushioned chair. "Excelente mezcal, señor." He smiled after swallowing a big swig. As he grunted and wiped his mouth on his dirty sleeve, El Alacran gestured to Don José, "Please, have a seat. Mi casa es su casa," he laughed.

Don José sat in the chair El Alacran pointed to. Glancing guardedly at the intruding bandido, he sensed the mounting tension between them. Don José felt El Alacran's glare, but he kept his eyes downcast so as not to appear to challenge this unwanted guest.

"Where are the women?" Growled the bandido, staring intently at his subservient host.

"My wife's sister is ready to give birth, señor. So my wife and daughter are staying with her for the time necessary. My sons and I are on our own for now," Don José replied.

"Well, I don't care who does it, but someone get in that kitchen and start cooking," El Alacran responded with a grunt, as he kicked off his boots and relaxed back into the chair. "I want some meat and strong coffee. And I want it fast!" he added with a glare.

The men outside were rowdy and drunk and they took what they wanted. Some gathered around campfires while others slept. Livestock were slaughtered and the storerooms raided for drink and other staples. All the while, Don José and his sons took orders from El Alacran and his group of bandidos while praying that the women would not be discovered.

Finally, after two torturous nights, El Alacran announced that he and his band of bandidos were leaving. "We've enjoyed your hospitality too long already, Don José, and as much as we would like to stay, we must move on."

Don José nodded at El Alacran, "Si, señor. Whatever you say."

"Pedro, see that the eggs are gathered, and feed the livestock, Hijo," Don José said with a sigh of relief. "I'll join your brothers in the cornfield."

While Don José was working in the field, Segundo, El Alacran's right-hand man, suddenly yelled out, "Hey you, José! El Alacran wants to see you. Right now."

"Yes, Segundo, where is Alacran?"

"Follow me," Segundo said motioning with his head. The two men walked to the house.

"Señor," Don José greeted El Alacran with a nod and a tip of his hat, "what can I do for you?"

"Well, I have good news, and I have what you may perceive as not so good news," laughed El Alacran. "I know you and your sons are anxious to get back to your normal routine, so we will be leaving you today. However, you, sir, will leave with us. You see, we don't know this rugged territory. Your sons have informed me that they were born on this hacienda. If this is the case, you must know the area well. You will serve as our guide."

Don José could only think of putting distance between these bandidos and his family. Thinking of his wife and daughter, he quickly assured El Alacran that he knew the territory better than anyone. "With your permission, señor—I mean Alacran—I'll have Salvador prepare my horse."

"Yes," Alacran nodded. "We leave within the hour. And I hope your sons realize there will be dire consequences if they attempt to follow or try anything at all. If they want you back safe, they will heed this warning. Understand?"

"Yes, of course. They will not disobey my orders. Of that I can assure you, sir." Segundo followed Don José to the barn, but only long enough to give the boys a stern warning. Soon, he was distracted by one of the men and left Don José's side.

Relieved and grateful for the opportunity to speak to his sons without supervision, Don Jose instructed his youngest son, Lencho, "Quickly, son! Saddle El Rey for me while I fill the canteen." He handed Lencho El Rey's saddle with a wink. The boys all knew that El Rey was their father's best and fastest horse. El Rey was a champion.

"Don't worry, Father. We'll see to our mother and sister...," whispered Lencho, glancing around.

"Yes, but wait until..."

"¡Ya!" shouted El Alacran. "Is the food packed? The canteens filled?"

Soon, all that remained of the bandidos was the dust their horses stirred up as they rode off. Don José lead the bandidos through the rugged territory as the sun blazed down upon them. He wanted this group as far away from his hacienda and his family as he could get them. And he wasn't going to make it easy for them to find their way back to his familia.

"How far before we reach water? Our canteens are getting low," El Alacran yelled out. "Isn't there an easier route than this one? I warn you, Cantú."

"Don't worry, Alacran," Don José yelled back, wiping his face and neck with his bandana. "We reach the river before nightfall. No danger of running out of water." The rugged group rode on in the sweltering heat.

After an hour or so, Don José saw the landmark he had been looking out for, a tall cactus he planned to use for his escape. There was no way around the cactus. One could go right or left, but the cactus and the huge, immoveable rocks surrounding it on either side blocked any possibility of going straight ahead. Don José whispered to El Rey, rubbing his trusty stead's ears and patting his neck.

Suddenly, Don José yelled out and dug his spurs into El Rey. They charged straight ahead. All the other horses reared and bucked as the bandidos tried to regain control of them. El Rey raced toward the cactus at record speed, hurdling over it. Horse and rider ran relentlessly on as bullets flew past them. The valiant steed and rider, though riddled with cactus needles, rode for their lives.

A few days later, El Rey sauntered into the Cantú courtyard with Don José slumped over his saddle. "Mom! Mom! It's Dad, and he's hurt," Guadalupe called. The rest of the family ran out to El Rey.

Rushing to her husband's side, María yelled, "Sons! Hurry! Help me with your father. Dear God! He is covered in cactus needles! José! Salvador! Pronto! Ride into town for the doctor and tell him about the cactus needles. Hurry, son. Tell Doctor Moreno that your father is burning up with fever. Ricardo, you ride out for Don Mario. Maybe he can save El Rey. They are both gravely ill."

María assisted Doctor Moreno as he extracted hundreds of cactus needles from her husband's swollen, inflamed body. "José, come back to us," María pleaded. He lay in a fever for days, lingering between life and death. Unwilling to leave his side, María sat at José's bedside night after night, cooling his forehead with a compress and tending to his swollen body.

"El Rey? How is El Rey?" Don José asked weakly, slipping in and out of consciousness.

"Ay, Doctor," María said with a worried look. "We must not tell him El Rey did not make it, not until he is stronger, until he is better."

Little by little, Don José was nursed back to health. The Cantú family was finally safe, yet they mourned the loss of their beloved champion El Rey, burying him in a special grave. They never forget the magnificent stallion and his great sacrifice.

Feliciano Cantú recounted the story of the bandidos to his new bride, Gregoria. He wanted his wife to know more about his family history, and she was eager to learn. Over the years, Feliciano and Gregoria had five sons and one daughter. One son, Pedro Cantú, would become a U.S. Marshal, attributing his career choice to an intense desire to help bring justice to a world of corruption and discrimination. Valentin Cantú, their fourth son and my father, was born February 14, 1906. His birth was a blessing for which I am eternally grateful.

# Chapter 3

I was born the seventh child in a Mexican-American, Catholic, farmworker family. My parents, Valentin y Beatrice Cantú, had six children. Imelda, the youngest, was five years old. One would think that they were a complete family already. Nonetheless, after that five year drought, I came along and was welcomed by my parents and siblings as the blessing they believed me to be.

As the last of my siblings to be born in Texas, I was also the last child to be born at home, although my mother did have an attending physician, rather than a comadrona or midwife. Perhaps it is a bit hasty to proclaim my miraculous arrival as such a joyous occasion for all concerned. If truth be told, Imelda, who had been the baby of the family for five years standing, suddenly felt pangs of jealousy and envy, very unfamiliar and disturbing sentiments. The unhappy child watched in confusion and anger, as her mother and father adored and fussed over the new baby sister, leaving poor little Imelda feeling discarded and neglected.

All of a sudden, Imelda couldn't keep her parents' attention due to their focus on the new baby, who, by the way, was no angel. Por lo contrario, the screaming, red-faced infant was rather hideous—not to mention annoying.

For Imelda, each passing day only seemed more and more hopeless. The novelty of the new baby showed no indication of wearing off. Imelda had been replaced, dethroned, and life would never be the same. Day after day, the whole family focused their attention on aquella… that intruder. ¡Tanto wato! So much commotion over this fussy, insignificant, yet thunder-stealing infant!

Shortly after my birth, Imelda was outside playing when she came across a hammer that had been left carelessly unattended. It was lying at the foot of the big tree in front of the house. She had seen her brothers, Efrain and Hector, using it earlier that day. Suddenly, she had a wonderful idea, the perfect solution to her problem. She picked up the hammer and rushed to my crib side. There I lay, in all my splendor, cooing and making those annoying baby sounds.

Imelda's little brain raced with fear and excitement as she tried desperately to hold the hammer steady and maneuver it between the bars of the crib. Just as she was in position, ready to hit me with the hammer, she heard screams of confusion and hysteria. Imelda jumped back and screamed in fright, desperately trying to pull the hammer back—but it was stuck between the bars of the crib. Mom grabbed the hammer out of Imelda's hand yelling, "¡Dios Santo! ¿Hija qué estás haciendo?"

"¡Ahh, Amá!" Imelda shrieked, startled out of her wits. "¡Me asusto!"

Now I, Baby Sally, was wailing and Imelda was trying to rationalize her actions. With Mom in hysterics and Baby Sally bawling, poor little Imelda hopelessly burst into tears. Mom held me tightly but managed to give Imelda a pat on the head and a one-armed hug, trying to calm her down. Still, Mom's attention was fully focused on me.

Poor little Imelda! I give up, she thought. Her failed assault had relegated her to a sorrowful existence as second chair.

"Mom and Dad don't love me anymore," Imelda cried sadly with deep ragged breaths. "They don't care!" Running to Lydia for comfort and reassurance, she continued her sobbing. "With aquella around they've forgotten about me. They're so busy they don't even notice me anymore."

"Who doesn't care about what?" Lydia asked, smoothing Imelda's hair, wiping her tears, and giving her a big hug. "Don't cry. Come on, what's wrong?"

Imelda buried her head into Lydia's breast and reveled in the comfort of her hug. This was too much for her to bear. She had to do something. But it would have to be something significant, something that would make Mom and Dad take notice.

After giving the matter considerable thought, Imelda came up with the perfect solution. Hurriedly, she grabbed a bag from the pantry. Racing to her room, she picked out one of her pretty Sunday dresses and her favorite doll. Running to the kitchen, she took a tortilla, a hunk of cheese and an apple, just in case the family took too long to find her.

Imelda ran out the front door, jumped off the landing and onto the dirt yard, where she had often happily played. Clenching her fists and wiping away her tears with the back of her hand, she braced herself as she walked out to the dirt road that lead to Tía María's house. She could feel her heart thumping hard in her chest.

"Okay," she whimpered. "They're gonna miss me right away and then they'll be sorry." Although she had a strong conviction that she would soon be missed and everyone would be out looking for her, she still couldn't shake a nagging fear.

"One last look," she sighed, pausing to glance back at her home nostalgically. The thought of abandoning her rash plan flashed through her mind, but only momentarily.

"¡Ay no! No," she told herself, thinking that this was a sure-fire way to accomplish her goal.

Although apprehensive, her determination was greater. She had walked to Tía María's house so many times before, but she now realized that she had never gone by herself. She thought, I know the way by heart; it's straight to the corner stop sign then a turn and three houses down. Yeah, pretty close.

In a matter of minutes, Imelda arrived at Tía María's house, fully prepared with an explanation. She quickly told her cousins that she had run away from home, due to her unbearable situation.

"Me escapé de mi casa porque ya no me quieren," she explained sadly. "Todos están muy ocupados con aquella." Suddenly, she couldn't go on through her tears, but none of the cousins seemed surprised, and they didn't protest. In fact, the family welcomed her as if nothing out of the ordinary was going on.

Quickly drying her tears with the skirt of her dress, Imelda tried to regain her composure. She didn't want to cry in front of anyone, and besides, none of the cousins seemed concerned. Their reaction was a bit unsettling. Not only had she expected resistance, but also insistence that she return home straight away. Not knowing quite what to make of this situation, she thought, surely mom and dad must be missing me by now.

Tía María was hanging laundry out to dry. Noticing Imelda, she called over, "¿Imeldita, con quien veniste? ¿Qué estás hacienda aquí solita?"

Oh good, Imelda thought, somebody is concerned about me. Tía María will do something. But, upon hearing Imelda's explanation, Tía María simply told her not to worry, and assured her that she had a place to stay, here with them. "Ay, mijita, no te preocupes, te puedes quedar con nosotros. Aquí tienes tu casa con tus tíos y tus primos. Ya verás, vas a estar bien."

Imelda's eyes opened wide as she realized that Tía María wasn't a bit concerned—instead, she said, "Mi casa es tu casa, you are welcome here with your aunt and cousins." Imelda got a funny feeling in her tummy. Her plan was not turning out right. She looked at Tía María sadly, but managed to force a smile. Walking over to play with her cousins, she felt anxious and uneasy. She was trying hard to hold up, but felt so sad. It seemed that she'd been gone from home for such a very long time.

She felt an inexplicable emptiness inside, and she greatly missed her mom and dad. This was not what she had bargained for. In the midst of her fear and anxiety, poor little Imelda burst into tears and sobs. She couldn't help herself; she just did not know what to do.

The next thing she knew, her cousins were yelling and Tía María came running. After much commotion and embarrassment, her cousins took Imelda home. So much for her big plan. "Oh well, ni modo."

She was very relieved to be home again, where mom's welcome was a big, tight, warm hug. Cousins are fun to visit, but there's nothing like being safe and secure at home, even if it means putting up with that fussing, screaming, aquella.

At the age of four months, my ears were pierced—in keeping with tradition. Plans commenced for the essential sacrament of my baptism. With the date finally set, my family still had much to do to prepare for this sacred event.

Finally, on July 6, 1952, the day of my baptism arrived. The mass was held at the Sacred Heart of Jesus Church in Elsa, Texas. I was a sight to behold and looked adorable in my christening gown, cap, and booties. I wore my little gold earrings. As usual, family and friends fretted and fussed over me, little María Celia Cantú, (aka Mary Sally) the most beautiful baby in the world. At least that is how my mother tells it and why would I doubt my own saintly mother?

After the baptism mass, the celebration fiesta began. Along with my family, many friends, relatives, and neighbors—including Padre Frans and my godparents—attended. Tables and chairs had been set up in advance. The churchyard held quite a crowd.

"Pongan la comida en esta mesa, por favor," my mother instructed as she brought out casserolas, bowls of food, and baskets of tortillas. The main dishes were pollo en mole, carne asada y tamales. Side dishes included frijoles, arroz, ensalada, salsa roja y salsa verde. During and after the meal, musicians played traditional Mexican tunes as the fiesta went on for hours.

As daily life continued, my mother's fulltime job was housewife and mother. Meticulous in her work, she set high standards. She kept our home immaculately clean and made sure we were always well dressed. She even ironed my father's work clothes—quite a chore, especially because my father worked very hard in the hot, dusty Texas fields.

Mom's appearance was also always up to her standards. Even though she stayed home all day—caring for her children, cleaning, cooking, sewing or doing laundry—she always wore makeup, kept her hair combed neatly, and wore a fresh, crisp cotton dress and apron.

"Niño's, get up and get ready for school," Mom called. Efrain and Lydia were always up first. They got dressed and saw to it that Viola, Elida and Hector were also clean and ready for school. Although she was too young to attend school, Imelda got up with her siblings and joined everyone at the table for breakfast. Dad had always already left for work—before the children were up.

"Mom, remember that I need a special notebook for school." Efrain reminded her.

"Yes, I told your father last night. Be ready when he gets home from work today, so he can take you to buy it. And all of you be sure to ask your teachers if there's anything else you need."

"I think we have what we need, Mom, but we'll check. Since this is the first week of school, there might be a few more things," Lydia added.

"Okay, finish up. Don't be late!" Mom said with a flip of the dishtowel in her hand.

"Cleanliness is next to Godliness" was number two on my mother's personal list of commandments; second only to, "Thou shalt not lie, EVER, especially to thy parents." We kids learned these maternal rules early. Mom enforced them the same as she did the biblical decalogue.

Anyone who knew my mother knew only too well that La Señora Cantú would never tolerate a lie. I grew up thinking that people don't lie, that people are good and trustworthy. I was so conditioned to this conviction that it never even entered my mind that someone might not be telling me the truth. This naiveté would prove to be the source of much disillusionment later in my life. Our childhood lives were very protected. We knew no evil, and within the sanctity of the family, life was good.

My mother cooked real meals—she made everything from scratch, including the best homemade flour tortillas ever. We were raised on those flour tortillas, although sometimes Mom would make corn tortillas, which were also scrumptious. She ground all her spices in the molcajete.

Nobody cooked like my mother. She could cook anything, and it was always delicious and spicy. She could make an extraordinary meal out of the simplest ingredients, and there was always plenty for everybody. The aroma in my mother's kitchen was mouth-watering. The scent of fresh ground spices filled the air and enhanced the richness and flavor of each dish. Visitors never left our home without being fed—either a full meal or simply café con leche accompanied by pan dulce o taquitos. Mom graciously offered whatever she had on hand or could quickly whip up.

"Oh, come in, Comadre Chita. Come in out of the heat and rest for a while." Comadre Chita was an elderly neighbor from across the street. Her husband had passed away years before, and her only son had recently left home to seek his fortune in Washington State.

Comadre Chita was not really a comadre to my parent's—she had never been a sponsor for any religious ritual involving any of the Cantú children. But all the adults who knew her addressed her with the honorific Comadre, a title bestowed upon her out of respect. Comadre Chita was a good-natured, sweet and generous woman, well-liked by all of her neighbors and the larger community. She had a dark complexion and her skin was weathered by years of work, but she was always bright-eyed and smiling. She loved children and they loved her in return. Comadre Chita was a good woman.

"Oh, gracias, Comadre Beatice," Chita replied and added excitedly that she had received another letter from her son. "Mi Diegito esta encantado de la vida, ganando buen dinero en Washington. He is working steadily for his patrón. He doesn't have to go around looking for work with different patrónes. He has security now. What a blessing."

"Ay, Comadre," Mom responded with a smile and a hug, "What good news. I'm so happy to hear that your Diego is doing so well. May God bless and keep him in His care."

Mom was very fond of Comadre Chita. Every day, the elderly lady worked in her garden, and she would often walk across the street to say hello and visit with my mother for a bit. She loved Mom's café con leche, and she found comfort and solace with our family.

Since Diego's departure, Comadre Chita had established a habit of stopping by for a visit with Mom just about every day, usually around mid-morning or mid-afternoon. This was a good diversion for both of them and a much deserved break from the daily work.

"Buenos Dias, Comadre Bea. I think it's time for a little break, if you're not too busy, of course."

"Never too busy for a nice break and conversation with you, please come in and sit for a while.Pásele a la cocina, Comadre Chita. El cafécito está recién hecho."

We were poor, but we lack nothing. Dad worked tirelessly to provide for his growing family and dear wife. He enjoyed job security, a good wage, and respect from his patrón, Walter Rabe, for it was an established fact that Dad was an expert tractor driver. El Patrón Walter knew the value of a hardworking, dependable and expert worker and he paid Dad accordingly. Valentin Cantú, was the highest paid tractor driver in the entire area and beyond.

One evening after dinner, there was a knock at our door. Efrain opened it and was greeted by a tall, rugged looking, middle aged Gringo. With a friendly smile, the stranger took off his hat and held out his hand saying, "Hello, son, I'm Dan Rogers. I'm here to see Valentin Cantú. Your father, I presume?"

"Yes, I'll get my father," Efrain replied, shaking hands with the man at the door.

As it turned out, Dan Rogers was one of the more prominent farmers in Brownsville, Texas. He was seeking an experienced tractor driver and had also heard about Dad's expertise with horses. He was here to offer Dad a job on his ranch. Of course, the job came with higher wages, as well as paid expenses for the move to Brownsville.

After much discussion and contemplation, Mom and Dad sent a letter to Mr. Dan Rogers, thanking him for his consideration and trust, but declining his generous offer.

"Si, Valentin," Mom assured Dad, "this is the right decision. We have a good life here with family and good friends nearby. The children are doing well in school, and your job is steady and secure."

"Besides," Dad replied pensively, "Walter Rabe is a good man and a good boss, he has earned my loyalty. It would not be right to leave him and drop the work just like that. No, it would not be just." Dad continued working for Walter Rabe for many years and the Cantú family lived well.

"Apá," Imelda yelled, running out to greet Dad as he came home from work. They walked into the house hand in hand, to the aroma of fresh flour tortillas cooking on the comal. Dad sniffed the air with a smile. Hot, tired, and dusty, Dad's first priority was to clean up. After his bath, he would always walk into the kitchen looking refreshed. "Que bueno huele," he said taking his place at the head of the table while the rest of the family gathered around. Dinner was always the meal where conversation brought everyone together and the family shared news about the events of the day.

For my parents, their mission in life was clear—to love, provide for, and protect their familia. This was a passion they took to heart.

We were raised with an unconditional belief and faith in God, Christ, and the Blessed Mother, La Virgen de Guadalupe. A strong Catholic faith, strict morals, respect for and consideration of others—and, above all, respect and appreciation for our elders—these values were an ironclad code of honor in the Cantú household.

Mom and Dad loved music, and Mom sang often while tending to her household chores. As a baby, I loved being held by my mother as she sang lively Mexican tunes.

"Andale MiCeli (My Sally), vamos a bailar con las manitas," Mom laughingly encouraged me, twirling her hand and singing: "El piojo y la pulga se iban a casar, y no se casaron por falta de maíz. Lo tiro, lo tiro, lo tiroliroliro. Lo tiro, lo tiro, lo tirolirola. Upon hearing her singing voice, I would light up and laugh, twirling both of my hands in time to Mom's singing, as she danced around with me in her arms. When she stopped singing and dancing I pleaded for more, cooing, smiling, and holding up my hands. As she commenced again, I'd laugh some more and happily twirl my hands.

"Ay, Ay, Ay, Ay, canta y no llores. Porque cantando se alegran Cielito Lindo los corazónes." Mom continued, with me enjoying every moment in her arms. Finally tuckered out, I would drift off to her soothing nightly lullabies. In the morning, I came alive to her animated daytime tunes. My mother's songs could sooth the savage beast and rock her babies to sleep.

On a beautiful, sunny, South Texas Sunday, Dad drove the family home from church. It was 1952, and many people still rode horses or used horse-drawn carts for transportation. My father owned a car. On this day, my oldest sister, Lydia, sat between Mom and Dad, while my brothers and sisters were in the back seat. Baby Sally, however, held the place of honor in Mom's lap.

The whole family dressed up for church. Dad wore slacks, a nice lightweight shirt and a tie. And he always wore his hat, which, of course, he would remove upon entering the church and put right back on upon exiting. His shoes were polished to a high-gloss shine.

Mom wore a nice dress with matching hat, high heels, and purse. With curled hair under her hat and makeup and lipstick applied precisely, she always looked picturesque. All seven children, from Efrain down to Baby Sally, were just as neatly and meticulously put together, with careful attention to every detail.

"I'll stop at La Tiendita to gas up," Dad said to Mom. La Tiendita was the local grocery market and gas station, now under new management.

With the car parked in front of the store, I was motionless as my mother stood me on her lap. I was seven months old. Pink ribbons adorned my soft brown curls, while the white cotton dress I wore was accented with eyelets and pink lace.

Suddenly, a lady ran out of the store yelling, "Is that a doll or a child? Oh, my goodness, what a beautiful baby!"

As the story goes, the owners of La Tiendita were a Caucasian couple who desperately wanted a child of their own. They had tried for years, before accepting the sad fact that they would forever remain childless. Yet, here, before their very eyes, was a couple who had been blessed repeatedly with many beautiful children.

"Surely, it must be quite a hardship to provide for a family of this size," the woman said to my parents. The proprietors continued talking with Mom and Dad until finally they surprised my parents by offering their most valuable possession, their store, in exchange for the beautiful baby.

"Por favor, por favor!" the lady implored. "We offer you our most valuable possession, this store, La Tiendita. I guarantee you will have a good life. This store brings in a very good income, doesn't it, Bill?"

"Absolutely. You'll make a good living with this store. We've done very well and wouldn't think of giving it up—except for the fact that we want a child more than anything in the world." The couple pleaded with my parents, to no avail. Huge tears ran down the woman's cheeks as she petitioned my mother.

"You have so many beautiful children", she cried. "I promise you, Baby Sally will be loved and cared for, she will never want for anything. She'll be educated in the finest schools...."

Needless to say, as bad as my parents felt for the childless couple, they were not about to give up Baby Sally. As we drove away from La Tiendita, Dad shook his head, saying, "Que cosas, pobre gente; pero como pueden pensar...."

Lydia broke in, "Oh, that lady scared me! I thought she must be crazy, but now I just feel so sorry for her."

Mom added, "At first I was angry and upset but, yes, it is sad, que Dios los bendiga with a child of their own."

My mother first told us this story when I was a young adult in the 1970's. I had come home for the weekend, from Seattle, to visit Mom and Dad. As we sat around the dining room table, laughing and talking, Mom relayed the story.

"Oh my God, Mom! You're making this up, aren't you?" I laughed.

"No," my mother answered gravely, "It's true, it really happened."

"Seriously? They really wanted to buy me?" I asked in disbelief.

"Yes, they really wanted you. They couldn't have children, and they thought you were so beautiful. Ask your dad or Lydia. I'm sure they remember. Ay, MiCeli (my Sally) how could I make up something like this?"

"Wow, that's incredible," I beamed, feeling rather special.

Gloria, the sister who came along a year and nine months after me, laughingly interjected, "But Mom, why didn't you trade her? We would've been rich. Imagine how different our lives could have been. And Sally would have been raised with Gringo parents, thinking she was White. No one would've been the wiser, not even Sally."

Everyone laughed as Gloria continued her rampage against me adding, "We all could've been rich Tiendita owners, with franchises and everything. Mom, you blew our chance!"

Everyone, including myself, got a big laugh out of it. I gave Gloria a hard time, telling her how mean she was and pretending to be deeply hurt, but I couldn't keep a straight face. My poor mother stood up for me. She said she couldn't have lived without MiCeli. "¡Ni lo mande Dios!"

En fin, I added, "You guys wouldn't have been rich anyway. The Kids would have eaten all the edible merchandise, the store would have gone bankrupt, and you'd be back where you started… con nada… in addition to losing the most precious family member—Mom's favorite, I might add."

This conversation went on and on, with everyone throwing in their two cents worth. We all laughed and debated how different things might have been. Shaking her head, Mom rose from her seat at the table. "¡Ay niños! You're impossible," she said.

"Mom, wait—tell us another Texas story. I'm liking those Texans," I said, smiling, as I glanced at Gloria.

"I'll tell you about my Uncle Charlie Johnston, mi Tío Chále. He was my mother's brother, and he lived in La Villa, Texas. But, not right now, it's late. I'll tell you that one another time."

# Chapter 4

In 1953, when my family arrived and settled in Grandview, Washington, I was one year old. What awaited us was far worse than anyone could have imagined.

The cruelty of migrant life slapped my parents in the face with an all-consuming sting. They both gasped upon seeing the labor camp that was to be our new home. My mother stood staring in disbelief at the ramshackle brown wooden shacks that housed the migrant farm workers. With her hand over her heart, she whispered to my father, "Valentin, no puede ser. It just can't be." Dad was speechless, looking at his children and then back to his wife. He took a breath, straightened his slumping shoulders and calmly reassured her that things would work out. The look between them seemed to say, "Don't scare the children."

The intense pain and anguish of this new reality would remain our cross to bear for a very long time. In Texas, we had a decent home. Here, to my family's utter shock and dismay, the farmers house their workers in campos or labor camps. Inconceivably, whole families were assigned one-room shacks with splintered wooden floors and no running water. A tiny woodstove in the corner, y di que te fue bien (and say that you did well). This was our new reality, a reality that all the great stories of El Norte somehow failed to mention.

One outhouse serviced the entire labor camp, along with two rickety old showers—one for men, one for women—enclosed in a wooden space that looked ready to collapse under a heavy breath. We all hoped that Washington, particularly Grandview, was not a stomping ground for big, bad wolves.

Shocked and devastated, my parents whispered to each other and tried to hide their distress, but a solemn feeling seemed to have swept over the entire family. My mother whispered to my father, "Valentin, esta situación es inhumana." My father was stern and deep in thought. Amid the chilling tension and bewilderment, the family worked in silence, unpacking our belongings from the truck and hauling them into one of the shacks. The magnitude of our new reality was more than traumatic.

My parents and two oldest siblings, Efrain and Lydia, seemed to be in deep, hushed conversation for quite a while. Oblivious to our troubles, I happily played with my big sisters. It didn't take long for my parents to make a decision regarding our new, unacceptable living arrangements. Leaving Efrain and Lydia in charge of the children, they walked over to the patrón's house to announce our arrival and have a talk with the new boss.

After a brief but polite introduction, my mother proceeded to explain to the new patrón that her husband Valentin, did not speak English but he did understand a bit. Mom did the talking, but she left no doubt that she spoke on behalf of her husband and entire family. Our new living quarters were simply not acceptable.

"We're so sorry to bother you Mr. and Mrs. Mears, but there are a few things my husband and I need to discuss with you, if you can spare the time."

With a surprised look on his face, Mr. Mears replied, "Oh, uh, yes, of course, Mrs. Cantú. Come on in, Mr. Cantú."

"Thank you," my mother smiled with a nod, "But would you mind walking over to the camp with us?"

"Why, um, yes, of course," Mr. Mears replied, rubbing his face, "Just let me grab my hat." He looked puzzled as he wondered what this was all about. Then the three of them—Mom, Dad and Mr. Mears—headed towards the camp.

"Mr. Mears," Mom commenced, "I don't know an easy way to say this, so I'll just come straight to the point. We don't want to be rude, and we don't mean to offend, but I'm afraid that the living quarters simply won't do." Mr. Mears' mouth dropped open in surprise, as Mom continued. "In the correspondence between us, Mr. Mears, you lead us to believe that suitable housing would be provided for our family. Surely you'll agree that a one-room shack is no place for a family with seven children to live."

Rubbing his face and chin, Mr. Mears shifted uncomfortably from one foot to the other. He toke off his hat and wiped his forehead with his bandana. "Well, I see your point, Mrs. Cantú, but to be perfectly honest, I've never had a complaint like this before."

The three of them stood together in front of the shack our family had been assigned. After an awkward moment of silence followed by a deep sigh, Mom pointed to the shack, saying, "Honestly, Mr. Mears, would you live in this with your family? And I understand that you and Mrs. Mears have only two sons. Please consider that we have two sons, four daughters and a baby."

Mom and Dad spoke in Spanish, and then Mom turned back to address Mr. Mears. "Valentin, my husband, says we would invite you in, but as you know we have no room, not even a chair to offer you.

They had a lengthy talk and word has it that my mother, very politely, but in no uncertain terms, informed the Patrón that the family was not about to live all bunched up and sleeping together like animals. She firmly stated that it is only common decency for boys and girls to have separate sleeping quarters. One room is not a decent or humane way for a family to live.

Heaven only knows what else my mother said, but she was not one to be taken lightly. As furious and upset as she may be, Mom knew how to restrain and compose herself. My mother had a dignified level of class. She presented herself as cool and in control, knew how to defend herself and to state her point firmly, clearly, and precisely. She was defending and protecting her family, her number one priority in life.

Within a short time, my mother returned to our shack. Dad, the patrón and several other men commenced to work and by the time their task was complete, we had acquired another room. The men moved two of the labor camp shacks together facing back to back. The next day, a doorway was built between the two, thereby connecting them into one home. La familia Cantú now had a two-room home and a separate shack for my two brothers.

My dad and oldest brother, Efrain, along with other men in the labor camp, continued working, building another outhouse. They also improved the shower facilities. The patrón, who provided materials, agreed it was a beneficial arrangement for all concerned. The labor camp men would provide the free labor, the camp would see improvements, and the people living in the camp would reap the benefits. People at the camp worked together, and before long, life in the camp was a bit more tolerable, although far from easy.

"I know, I feel the same way," Dad said to Mom, "but we can't fight our own and everyone else's battles as well. At least we can be glad that we did something to improve the toilet and shower situation for everyone."

"Yes, you're right," Mom nodded in agreement. "We will just have to be satisfied with what we have accomplished…at least for now."

Summers are hot and dry in eastern Washington, with temperatures in the 90's and lower 100's. But winter is frightfully, unbearably cold with snowflakes constantly falling and snow piling up everywhere. Although it makes for a beautiful picture, it is painfully cold. Knife-sharp Icicles form outside and people warn each other to stay away from them. Dad would get up several times a night to fuel the fire in our little stove and check the electric heater in the extra room, yet it was still so cold inside that we could see our breath.

Despite the cold, the camp's tenants bundled up, and, along with the children, they played outside, building snowmen and sliding on the ice-packed paths they had cleared. With Mom and Dad's help, the family built the biggest snowman in the campo—indeed, our mono de nieve was bigger than any man. He was a unique work of art, and with everyone's help he was kept standing for quite some time. Mom and Dad had broken the ice, so to speak, and so other camp families followed suit—everyone had fun in the snow.

After living in the two-room shack for a long, hot summer and a brutally cold winter, we packed our belongings once again. This time we were moving to a bigger place just a stone's throw away from the row of shacks we had temporarily called home. We would still be in the camp, but our new home was more of a house than a shack.

This house also looked like it had been assembled from other labor camp shacks. But it was in better condition and much larger. It had wooden floors and cold running water. Still, despite the lack of hot water, it was quite an improvement. We had an old wood-burning stove for cooking and heating water. Unlike the small stoves in the shacks, this was a regular-size stove with four burners and an oven.

The house had three large rooms, including a big kitchen with cupboards and storage space. Just a few feet from the house stood a small shack. Mom, Dad, and the girls, would sleep in the house, and the boys would sleep in the adjacent shack.

Even before we moved in, my parents laid linoleum in the kitchen and main room. Mom was not going to have Baby Sally crawling and playing on a splintery wooden floor. The light-colored linoleum was clean and shiny. It gave the house a bright, happy look and made the rooms look bigger. Mom also liked the windows and the added natural light in the house, and the way the linoleum reflected the light, making the whole place brighter.

"Now, this is much better," she said as she inspected the new linoleum in the kitchen. With her hands on her hips, she looked around, then walked into the big main room, taking mental notes. She turned to Lydia, saying, "We have a lot of work to do, hija. There's a lot of cleaning to be done. I'll have to make curtains for the windows, but that I can do later."

"Mom, Dad put the cleaning supplies in the little shack—I mean, in the boys room," Lydia said, jumping up. "I'll get Viola and Elida and we can start cleaning."

The girls pitched in, cleaning and disinfecting until the place shined. It might not have been much, but it was quite an improvement. We were grateful for what we had, especially because we knew that many others had it much worse than we did.

One thing is strikingly clear—Mom and Dad commanded respect. They stood up for their rights and their family. We were able to improve our conditions only through their courage in facing the boss and insisting on more humane conditions. The patrón could have easily refused their petition, but he did the right thing instead. I know that the way my mother presented the case had everything to do with the patrón's decision to concede to my parents' request. It was also a safe bet that nobody had ever dared make such a request of the patrón before. Camp workers feared losing their jobs and accepted what they believed to be inevitable.

Mom and Dad did not know how the patrón would react to their petition, but they thought that anything that affected their family so strongly was worth standing up for—and, if necessary, fighting for. Their only weapons were courage, faith and determination. Armed with these, they repeatedly showed their family how much can be accomplished. As the great Mexican Revolutionary, Emiliano Zapata, once said, "Es Mejor morir de pie, que vivir de rodillas." (It is better to die on your feet, than to live on your knees).

People in the labor camp shared a common affliction. We were held in bondage by the poverty and oppression that dominated our lives; we were the undermined and demoralized, shunned by society, yet sought out to do the hard and dirty work that was beneath many. We had neither the acceptable social standing that money afforded, nor the right ethnicity to be accepted or even taken into account. But, in the labor camp, we were a community brought together through need and united by hope, dreams and plans of a better life.

Everyone was thankful to have work, and we all did the best we could with the meager means we were afforded. The migrant workers dared not dwell on their hardships and misery. Instead, they prayed and worked hard to acquire a better life through sacrifice and design. Parents expected that things would improve—either in their lifetime or thereafter. As long as their children had a better life, their own dreams could be deferred.

The patrón's big white house was nearby, close enough for him to keep an eye on the migrants, yet far enough to be somewhat isolated from the unsavory labor camp. With its huge, green, perfectly manicured lawn, the house loomed over the labor camp. It was landscaped with beautiful flowers, bushes, and trees—in stark contrast to the barren dust of the labor camp. To the north side of camp were hop fields, and on the south end was a gravel road. Only one small cluster of trees stood in the area, with many birds hopping and singing in the branches.

The great discrepancy between the patrón's house and the labor camp was like night and day. The shabby little wooden shacks were old and decrepit. They depicted the poverty of their inhabitants and surroundings. Yet even against these great odds, the camp workers stayed positive and enjoyed life.

Although it meant less money, my family never worked on Sunday. It was a holy day of obligation, as well as a day of rest. Sunday, inevitably, found the Cantú family dressed up and attending Blessed Sacrament Catholic Church.

People used to dress up in those days, which made Sunday all the more distinctive and special. Formality and respect prevailed, a sign of the times. Sunday was an extraordinary day, designated by God himself for worship and rest. So, on the day we gave thanks and honored the Almighty Creator, we presented ourselves before him in our best apparel and on our best behavior.

"Hurry! We can't be late for church. Quit wiggling so I can put your hat on," Lydia said sternly.

"Okay," I whined, but I don't like this thing," I said, pulling on the elastic string under my chin. "Do I need the string?"

"Leave it alone! It holds your hat on. You look so pretty! Now come on," she said. We ran out to the car.

Knowing that God was right there with me, I liked being in the beautiful church. But I didn't like the smell of incense when it was too strong. Even worse than the incense was having to sit still for so long. I knew I was wiggling too much, and Mom caught me holding my nose to avoid smelling the strong incense. "Sosiégate," she whispered sternly as she brushed my hand away from my face and signaled me to kneel.

I obeyed immediately, knowing that my mother did not forget an indiscretion, and misbehaving in church was a big one.

Every Easter Sunday, Mom and Lydia dressed us kids up in our new Easter outfits. For the girls, that included new hat, gloves, shoes and socks. Once we got home after mass, Lydia commanded, "Elida, keep the kids occupied while Viola and I go hide the Easter eggs. We'll come for you when we finish, okay? Oh, and don't let them get dirty—keep them inside the house."

"Yeah, okay. They're busy playing with their Easter baskets anyway. Don't take too long, though."

"We won't—we'll be quick."

After hiding the Easter eggs in the patrón's beautiful green yard, Lydia and Viola returned for the kids. We all marched over for the big hunt and Lydia commemorated our celebration by taking pictures. Year after year, Easter Sunday thus found us in the Patrón's yard, with our Easter baskets full of goodies. Our images are preserved in Lydia's photos of those bygone days.

Aside from her children, my mother was one of the very few people in the labor camp who spoke English. Grade school was the extent of her formal education, but she was articulate and could speak, read, and write fluently in both English and Spanish. I have no idea how she and her siblings were so educated without a formal education.

My mother was truly a woman of culture, dignity and class. She was a very proud woman. Like any mother she would fight tooth and nail to protect her family. She also firmly believed that a family should never air their dirty laundry in public. Any trouble or discord was attended to behind closed doors and only within the family.

Between pregnancies and babies, Mom now had to work in the fields alongside Dad. She had never worked outside the home before, but in Washington things were different than they were in Texas. It was the beginning of a long life of hardship, perseverance, and endurance for all of us. But the hard work promised to pay off in the long run. My mother never questioned what she needed to do for the family.

My Dad did not speak English and also had no formal education, but he was intelligent and wise. He believed that one needs not only book learning, but also that one must be honest, trustworthy and respectful. It was his conviction that good morals and dignity were as important as formal education. Mom and Dad insisted that all their children have good manners. They taught us to shake hands and formally greet company and family friends.

Reaching out my hand, I smiled with downcast eyes reluctantly saying, "Como está señor/a." I was embarrassed by my weak command of Spanish. I always hoped that the señor or señora I was addressing would not try to engage me in conversation. But I knew better than to try to avoid a formal greeting, for if we failed to do so, Dad would admonish us saying, "¿De qué sirve una educación sin modales?" (What good is an education without manners?) In my younger years I would think, Yeah, right, Dad, what does an education have to do with shaking hands? I didn't know then that, later, not only would I understand—I would also be very grateful for his keen insight.

My father's math skills amazed me, especially later when I struggled hopelessly with equations. I marveled at Dad's ease with numbers because they had always been my downfall. He never seemed to have trouble—he was such a whiz at figuring out just how much the family wages would be at the end of the week. I watched in awe as he scribbled equations and sped through calculations. I was always grateful that he didn't need my help. He kept meticulous records in his little pocket notebook, which he always carried in his shirt pocket along with his pen or pencil.

"Apá," I asked him once when I was struggling with fourth grade math. "¿Como aprendió a sacar cuentas?" (How did you learn to do equations?) He smiled as he explained that it was a survival skill. His father had handed it down to him, along with all the other things Dad needed to know, to earn a living.

"Oh, entiendo," I said, nodding my head as if I really did understand. But I still didn't get it. I thought if fathers taught sons, how did the first father learn? People didn't go to school in the old days. And look at me, I'm in school and I still don't get math. I decided I must just be really dumb. Maybe it was something that men just instinctively knew. But then I thought about all the boys I knew who were pretty dumb when it came to math. It was all so confusing.

What completely dispelled my idea that men were just instinctively good at math was my recollection of the story of Yoneh, who was working in the grapes with his family. For some reason, his dad was not around one day, so his mother, Doña Lola, asked Yoneh to figure out the daily wages.

"Aquí tienes, Yoneh," she said handing him a piece of paper and a pencil, "¿A ver, cuánto ganamos hoy? Saca la cuenta."

Yoneh was not too keen on the idea of having to do the math, but he didn't argue with his mother. Taking paper and pencil from her, he tried to calculate...

After a while Doña Lola called out, "¿Yoneh, qué pasó, ya tienes la cuenta?"

"Well, I don't know Ma," he replied scratching his head with the tip of the pencil. "I'm not sure it's right."

"Déjame ver, lemme see," his mother said reaching out her hand. "Come on—give me the paper, Yoneh."

Reluctantly, Yoneh handed his mother the scribbled calculations, as the rest of the family, relieved the workday was over, walked to the car. With Doña Lola in the passenger seat, Yoneh turned the key in the ignition…

"I'm very glad we all worked so hard today," Doña Lola said, tapping the pencil on her lap. "Porque según las cuentas de Yoneh, somos millonarios."

"Ah, come on Ma, I'm not very good with math," Yoneh replied as everyone laughed and teased him. "Gee Yoneh, if we'd known how easy it is to become millionaires, we would've put you in charge of figuring out our wages years ago," teased his sister, Connie.

"Oh shut up," Yoneh snapped. "Tú saca la cuenta, if you're so smart."

"Hey, Mom," Connie said with a serious demeanor, "let's have Yoneh take his calculations to the patrón and ask for our money."

"Ya, enough! Consuelo, stop teasing your brother y tú, Yoneh, just settle down," Doña Lola said sternly, "Let's just have a tranquil ride home. Your father will figure it out later."

# Chapter 5

Another house was located between the patrón's house and the row of labor camp shacks. This house was nowhere as elaborate as the patrón's. It was old, but it had a fenced green yard, an indoor toilet, bedrooms, a living room, and a kitchen. It was a real house, situated on the edge of the camp.

A family of three—mother, father, and their young daughter—lived there. The really striking thing was that this family was White, as in Caucasian. The daughter's name was Ada Belle, and she was Elida's age. They were best buddies. Ada Belle was tall and skinny, with red hair and freckles. I had never seen freckles before and I found them rather intriguing.

"Stop staring at her," Elida whispered to me. Embarrassed, I quickly turned away, but before I knew it, I was staring again.

"Why does she have all those little dots on her face?" I asked Elida. I never got an answer, but I loved to tag along with them whenever I could, which wasn't very often. They were teenagers, and I was, "just a kid."

"Sally, quit following me. Go back home," Elida scolded.

"But you're going to Ada Belle's," I whined, "I wanna go, too."

"Not today. We have something to do. Maybe tomorrow you can come."

"Okay," I said stomping my right foot. Even if I couldn't go all the time, I grabbed every opportunity to hang around with the big girls, especially when that meant being in Ada Belle's house. It never ceased to amaze me that this only child had a whole room to herself and that this house had an indoor toilet. Wow, I thought, this is all so much, I'd be happy with a room like this to share.

I wondered if it was just because they were White. None of the Mexicans I knew had a real house; we all lived in the labor camp. Out of all the people in the labor camp, why did it have to be a White family in this real house? Why was there always such a massive and unjust difference between Mexicans and Whites? I just didn't get it. I always wondered about these things, but it wasn't until I was about seven years old that I finally got the courage to inquire. Leaving Ada Belle's house, I asked, "Elida, how come Ada Belle gets to live in that house? Why can't we live there? Our family is way bigger."

"I told you not to tag along! What a dumb question," she replied.

"Why? What's so dumb about it? I really don't get it."

"Ay, Sally," she said putting her arm around my shoulder, "you know it's because Ada Belle's father is the patrón's foreman." Elida paused, looked away from me and added, "And they're White."

"Oh," I said, seriously processing what she had just said. "I knew it. I was right all along."

Elida shrugged her shoulders and rolled her eyes. Taking her arm off my shoulder, she gave me a little nudge as she grabbed my hand saying, "Come on—race ya home!"

Elida did a good job of distracting me, but I wasn't done with the subject just yet. Later, still bothered by what I had confirmed, I thought, Hmm, so Ada Belle's father is the Patrón's foreman. Elida had explained that being foreman meant that he was the boss over all the workers, especially when the real patrón wasn't around. I still wondered why the patrón didn't have a Mexican foreman. Who said it had to be a White guy? Oh, how I wished my Dad was foreman.

The vast difference between Mexican and White people was undeniably evident to me from the beginning. When I was very young, a preschooler, it became painfully clear to me that Mexicans were poor and White people were rich. I also sadly observed that White people fancied themselves superior. This false notion of theirs was the only license they needed to justify prejudicial and malicious maltreatment.

I remember an incident that occurred at Grandview City Park, where I loved to play on the green grass and playground equipment. It is one of my first memories of racism. I was around five years old, which would make Imelda ten at the time. On this beautiful sunny day, our older sister,

Elida, who was in charge of looking after us, begrudgingly watched as Imelda and I played. As a teenager, Elida wasn't exactly thrilled about being our babysitter. But we convinced her to push us on the swings. We were laughing and having fun when two little boys came our way. They were a few years older than I was, probably around eight. One of them grabbed a swing, but the other one hesitated. He stood there, staring at us, and then backed away.

The next thing I knew, the three of us sisters were off the swings and heading in another direction. It had all happened so fast. Elida stopped my swing, saying very sternly, "Vámonos de aquí." She grabbed my hand and I jumped off the swing. "Melda, come on!" she yelled, leading me away.

Imelda ran up next to Elida, saying, "What's going on? We're having fun. ¿Porqué nos vamos tan pronto?" Elida answered her in Spanish, obviously so I wouldn't understand.

Regrettably, I did understand—not only the Spanish words uttered, but the horrible message I would struggle with throughout my life. The boy who wouldn't get on the swing didn't want to be, "next to a Mexican."

Trailing along behind my older sisters, I couldn't believe what I was hearing, but there was no doubt in my mind about what Elida had said. I felt embarrassed and very insignificant. I glanced back at the swings that the two boys were now playing on. They were laughing and having fun.

I pretended not to understand what Elida had said. I didn't want to face or deal with it, so I feigned ignorance and hid my shame. It was such a crushing moment—one I have never been able to forget. The jolt of that upset was devastating. I felt that I could never measure up to my classmates when I started school and the majority of my classmates were Caucasian. Never able to forget the swing incident, I was extremely shy and quiet—I felt so inferior.

Living in the labor camp, seeing the hardships that Mexican people endured in contrast to the luxuries that White people enjoyed, being disliked and unaccepted by White children—all were factors that worked their way into the recesses of my mind to make me feel inadequate. Starting school and being in such a minority was the final straw. I had no self-confidence; I gave in to the belief that I was somehow beneath the dominant White people who surrounded me. The very few friends I had were those who persistently sought my friendship, for I was much too insecure.

As a child in the labor camp, I loved to listen to adult conversations, which were always in Spanish. The adults thought I didn't understand, but I managed to piece together some tasty morsels of chisme (gossip) and to get a vague idea of what was happening in the adult world.

Even so, I would be remiss if I failed to mention that I was always confused. I grew up speaking English, not Spanish, although Spanish was spoken all around me.

Furthermore, even if the conversation had been in English, I was much too young and innocent to understand adult matters. Adults spoke freely around me, confident that the child in their midst didn't understand a thing that was said.

"No te preocupes, comadre; la niña no habla español," the women assured each other. Thus, I continued to eavesdrop, acting as innocent as I could and pretending to be deep in my own thoughts, at play. I felt clever and self-righteous, and I never let on that I was picking up the Spanish they spoke.

I couldn't pull one over on my mother, though. Of course, I wasn't very smart about it. I'd often run home to Mom or Lydia and recount bits and pieces of the latest chisme.

"What are you talking about, Sally? That doesn't make sense," one of them would respond.

"It's true," I'd say, "I heard Mrs. Fulana tell Mrs. Sutana...." With that, they knew I'd been listening to the adults' conversations, but since my Spanish was limited I never had the facts straight. Still, the chisme I had badly recounted didn't take long to make the rounds. Everyone would know soon enough.

One day, when I was about seven years old, I was playing with one of my friends in the labor camp. Although Ana didn't speak much English and I didn't speak Spanish, we managed. We played together often and always had fun. For some reason, though, things were not running smoothly on this day and what started out as a minor disagreement had suddenly escalated into a major outburst on her part. Before I knew it, Ana was yelling at me. She was speaking so rapidly that I could barely understand what she was saying. I knew enough Spanish, however, to decipher some choice bad words. I stood in utter confusion as she shook her fist in my face.

Trying desperately to snap back at her with equal frenzy, my mind raced in an effort to shout something in Spanish at her. I straightened myself up and stood tall. With a stern grimace, I slapped her fist away from my face and glared at her defiantly, my chest puffed out, my head cocked. She stopped cold as we both stared, wide-eyed, at each other. I knew I had better blurt some hard words before she could regain her angry composure, so I stuttered, "Tú... tú... Y tú, la papá marrano!"

Yay, I did it! I thought as I turned around and ran home. Knowing that I wouldn't be able to hold a candle to Ana in a verbal debate in Spanish, I had quit while I was ahead. I wasn't about to give her a chance to continue her tirade against me. I had managed to get in the last word—in Spanish, no less. I was very pleased with myself. It had not been an easy feat, defending my position en Español. But I had done it, and I was beaming with pride. I had called Ana a papa pig because it was the only thing in Spanish that had popped into my mind. I thought it was a great comeback. I couldn't wait to tell Mom and Lydia how I had defended myself.

What I didn't know is that I had used "la" instead of "el", which is the correct article—"la" is feminine, whereas "el" is masculine. As I was calling her a papa swine, I should have said, "El papá marrano," or, better yet, "La mama marrana." But who cared? That was such a trivial matter. I was thrilled with my response.

Dad had been saving to buy a family car, and he still had some of the money saved from the sale of his car in Texas. It was 1956; we had been living in the labor camp for over three years, so a new car was Dad's top priority. Efrain set out with Dad and some of the other men to make the rounds of the local car dealerships. They had a list of dealers in the lower Yakima Valley, and, if necessary, they would make the trip to Yakima.

"This would be a great choice, Mr. Cantu," the salesman said, wiping the smudge on a shiny new car with his handkerchief.

"We're still shopping around, Mr. Harvey, but my dad would like to know how much the payments would be on this car if he put down $300.00 cash," Efrain asked.

"Well, let me see now," Mr. Harvey said pulling out his calculator, "The total price, including tax and license is $2,100.00—minus the special dealer discount of $50.00 and we can do a five year..."

"That's okay, Mr. Harvey," Efrain cut in, "The monthly payments would be $29.16 on a five year contract."

"Just a minute, son, let me calculate..."

"But sir, I already figured it out in my head."

"Yes, yes, $1,750 times..."

Efrain was a whiz at math. He didn't need a calculator, so he turned to dad and explained in Spanish what it would cost per month if they paid the car on a five-year contract and what it would cost on a four year contract.

"Thank you so much, Mr. Harvey," Efrain said holding out his hand, "Dad say's we'll be back tomorrow with the down payment." Dad also shook Mr. Harvey's hand. The salesman put his left hand over Dad's locking the handshake with both of his hands.

"But, Mr. Cantu," Mr. Harvey said anxiously, "We can take care of the paperwork today."

Dad smiled and said, "Tomorrow." Then he told Efrain to tell the salesman that they would return the next day, after work at 6:00 p.m., if that was acceptable.

The day Dad drove his new car into the labor camp was a day of pride and accomplishment for the Cantú family. Dad was beaming as he and Efrain pulled up in front of the house. "Honk the horn, Dad," Efrain smiled, "Let's see their faces when they see the car."

As Dad and Efrain were getting out of the car, Mom, Lydia and all the kids ran out to admire the new Chevy. Other labor camp residents came around to admire the car and congratulate Dad. It was a joyous occasion for all. Our new car was a shiny, red and white 1956 Chevy 210 Post. It was sensational.

As the years passed, our family continued to grow. Before I knew it, in addition to my six older siblings, I had two younger sisters and two younger brothers. After me, came Gloria Ana (1953), then Valentin Omar (Rudy) in 1955, Norma Linda in 1956 and finally—in 1958—came the baby, Alfredo Rogelio (Freddy). The adults and older siblings called us The Kids. And that's also how we referred to ourselves. If one of us was questioned about who did this or that, the standard response never changed: "It was The Kids!" My older brother Hector once commented, "Silly kids! They blame The Kids. Don't they know they are The Kids?"

My parents reveled in the knowledge that out of eleven children, not a one was lost to death or to la perdición (perdition). La Familia was their mission in life, and thank God we were all following the straight and narrow. Without a doubt, La Familia was Mom and Dad's greatest source of pride, joy and accomplishment.

# Chapter 6

When I was in the first grade, another little boy in my class was also Mexican. One day, the boys and the girls were separated and taken out of the classroom. The teacher ushered us down the hall into a room with no desks—just chairs. One long table with medical equipment on it stood up front by the blackboard. A man and a lady were in the room—I guessed they were a doctor and a nurse because they were both dressed in white. They examined us all, one at a time, while the rest of the group looked on. I was embarrassed, scared and humiliated. I didn't say a word, nor did I dare look when another girl was being examined.

I didn't understand what was happening—why were we being examined? But most of all—why were we being exposed in front of our classmates? Why were we not given privacy?

"All right, girls, please have a seat. As your name is called, step right over here," the nurse said, pointing to a chair next to the long table. We'll start with Jenny Anderson, please. Jenny?" As Jenny went up front, everyone sat quietly while the nurse poked at Jenny's head with two pencil-like sticks. Meanwhile, the doctor also used his instruments to check her.

I had begun to feel a bit more at ease when suddenly I was stupefied. "Oh, ikk!" cried one girl. Those of us watching and waiting our turn gasped and moaned. Shocked, I sat there with my mouth open, but I couldn't utter a sound. The doctor had looked under Jenny's underwear—front and then back.

No, no, no, I thought, oh God, No! I couldn't believe what was happening. I wanted to disappear!

"Quiet, everyone, the nurse said loudly. This is just a routine checkup."

Then the doctor raised both hands, palms out, saying, "Calm down, girls. There's nothing to get excited about. Just relax and let us get on with our jobs. We're not going to hurt you. We're just checking to make sure everyone is healthy."

I alternately closed my eyes or kept my gaze on my lap, but I was well aware that some girls were craning their necks to see everything they could. In a daze, I sank back into my chair, praying to be the last girl called. Then, although I didn't register it for a moment, the nurse called, "Mary Can-too. Mary? Where's Mary?" All eyes were on me. Oh, I forgot that I'm Mary. The nurse had called me by my first name, even though I wanted to be called Sally.

"I'm sorry, but we have another Sally. We'll have to call you Mary," the teacher had insisted.

Self-conscious, I quickly jerked my head up. The nurse was directing me to come forward. Dazed, I tried to disassociate myself from the spectacle unfolding in front of me. In my mind, I could see all the other girls gaping at me. Suddenly, the nurse's voice broke through. "Please stand up, Mary." I obeyed mechanically and held my breath. The doctor pulled open my panties, and he, the nurse, and the whole world looked at my bare nakedness. I wanted to die!

We were sent, one at a time, back to our classroom. Other kids were whispering and laughing, but I was so embarrassed that I wouldn't look or speak to anyone.

Then Fernando, my little Mexican classmate, returned with a big piece of paper folded in two and safety pinned to his shirt. His eyes downcast, Fernando slowly walked into the classroom. His fists were clenched tightly as he approached his desk and sat down, never once looking up. The other children murmured and whispered.

"He has lice on his head," Tommy whispered loudly to David.

"Ooh! Yuk!" David exclaimed standing up so suddenly that he knocked over his chair. "Fernando has lice! Don't get near him or they'll jump on you."

In an uproar, the whole class giggled and jeered.

"Move away from him," Debbie said with a frown, cringing as she moved her desk, which scraped the floor loudly.

As I began to understand what was happening, I felt a pang of anxiety and fear. Suddenly, my face was hot, and I felt sick in my tummy.

The pandemonium in our classroom soon brought the teacher rushing in. "Class, what's the meaning of this? Everybody," Miss Grant said clapping her hands, "back to your seats and settle down!"

"Uh, uh," Richie grunted, raising his hand and bouncing on his chair, "but, Miss Grant, Miss Grant—Fernando has lice!"

I rushed to the bathroom. I thought I would throw up, but instead all I did was spit and spit into the toilet. I peed and then washed my hands. As I looked in the mirror, I saw that my face was beet red, so I splashed water on it in an effort to cool down and compose myself. I didn't want to come out of the bathroom, so I stood with my ear pressed against the door, straining to hear what Miss Grant was saying.

"Everyone, please quiet down. I want all of you to settle down. Take out your crayons and draw in your tablets or practice you're ABC's. I want complete silence until everyone is back. Then we'll have our reading period."

All of a sudden—Oh, dear God!—someone was knocking on the bathroom door. Can't you read the sign? I thought. The teacher had made a point of telling us which way to turn the sign on the bathroom door to indicate if the stall was in use.

This sign business never made sense to me. On one side, the sign said IN, while the other side said OUT. I could never keep straight which side I was supposed to use. Did IN mean, "I'm in here? Don't come in?" or simply, "Come In?" Hoping that the person before me had turned the sign correctly, I always just turned the sign, not really knowing what it meant.

I hated being in the bathroom, and I would wait as long as I could before going. When I did go, I would hurry as fast as I could, always afraid that the door would open while I was still in there. It had happened once before. A boy had opened the door on me while I sat peeing! I was so startled that my body jerked, my pee stopped midstream, and a little yelp escaped from my throat. He immediately turned around, apologizing profusely. I sat motionless, my upper body stiff, as if at attention. I didn't want to come out of the bathroom. I wanted to disappear.

My classmate, Pete, tried to apologize when I finally came out, but I shrugged past him in a huff. I know he thought I was mad. I was just very ashamed.

Finally, I came out of the bathroom only to find Miss Grant standing before me.

"Are you alright, Mary?" she asked.

"Yes," I whispered, not looking at her as I walked to my seat. I glanced at Fernando. My heart ached for this helpless child, who had been publicly and cruelly humiliated. How could everyone be so insensitive? I knew that not only the teachers, but also the office lady and the principal were involved. I had seen them in the hall, directing teachers and their classes. I blamed all the adults.

Fernando was as shy as I was, and I could feel his pain and humiliation. Why had he been made to wear the huge safety pin? Why the big badge of shame? Worst of all, why did everybody have to know what was happening? I felt anger, disgust, and shame—the very things he must have been suffering. I wanted to cry.

I tried not to look at Fernando. All the kids were staring at him, and some were still whispering. I felt awful, but there was nothing I could do. We were helpless, he and I. Poor Fernando just hung his head. He wouldn't look up. I couldn't get that huge safety pin out of my mind, and for the longest time I couldn't look at a safety pin without reliving the shame and humiliation of that day—along with the pity and sorrow I felt for Fernando.

I wanted to be home. I wanted my mother or Lydia to make me feel safe and like I belonged. At home, I was free to interact with my parents or siblings, to play, to do anything and everything without a concern or second thought. At school, I was a prisoner of not only the rules and regulations, but of my own insecurities and the cruelty of others. I was a stranger among all the students and teachers. Almost everyone around me was White, and they made me feel so insignificant and inferior. I hated school. I couldn't relax. I felt out of place. I didn't belong. Always on guard and at the same time trying to be inconspicuous, I thought that if those kids didn't notice me, then maybe they'd leave me alone.

I never told anyone about Fernando or any of the shame and humiliation I suffered at school. These things were always a cross I bore alone.

One thing I did like about school was story time. Each day, the teacher would sit in a chair with the class gathered around her on the floor. As Miss Grant read to us, she would hold up the book so we could all see the pictures. Afterwards, she would ask us questions about the story. I always listened attentively because I loved stories, but I never took part in the discussion.

One day, Miss Grant read us a Christmas story. As she read, I was distracted by a classmate who was noisily rubbing his hands together. As he grunted, huffed, and wiggled around, I grew angrier because I was so interested in the story, and he was so distracting. I looked at him disapprovingly, and he sneered at me in return. I quickly looked away, but I was fully aware that he was still staring at me. He kept rubbing his hands together. Then he opened them, showing the black dirt that had balled up on his sweaty, dirty palms. He whispered, "Raisins."

I was thoroughly disgusted and embarrassed. The look on my hot, red face must have clearly reflected my feelings because completely satisfied, he grinned like the Grinch. His boyish prank had worked—he had really grossed me out. I slowly inched as far away from him as I could, determined that I would ignore him throughout the rest of the story.

Even with the rude disruption, I had enjoyed the story and taken comfort in its happy ending. As the teacher proceeded to the question-and-discussion part of story time, she asked a shocking and unthinkable question.

"Who believes in Santa Claus?" she said. "Raise your hand if you do." Looking around in shock, I realized that only about half the class had raised their hands. I quickly raised mine.

I thought, What's going on? I was confused. Who would even think to question the existence of Santa? For me, it was just a fact of life. Miss Grant might as well have asked, "Who believes in God? or "Who believes in parents?" It just didn't make sense. I was left to ponder this question for a long time—I couldn't shake the conflict it had caused within me. It felt wrong to question one of the basic truths I had lived with. Yet, here were a teacher and more than half of my classmates saying Santa Claus was not real.

I had so many questions, but I was afraid to ask them, afraid even to think them. I squirmed uncomfortably on the floor. I was angry. I needed to get away from the others, so I got up and went into the bathroom.

I didn't bother with the stupid IN/OUT sign on the doorknob—I just closed the door and leaned against it. When I finally came out of the bathroom, my classmates were back at their desks.

I still wonder how a first-grade teacher could have been so insensitive. I don't know what the other kids thought or felt, but Miss Grant had shattered my strong belief, a belief I simply wasn't yet ready to let go of. Sure, I would have found out the truth sooner or later, but this was a terrible and unexpected blow. In my young mind, a teacher was wise and intelligent, someone to look up to, learn from and respect. How could someone with such authority and importance be so tactless?

In the second grade, only one other student, a boy, could outrun me. I was proud of my title as second-fastest runner, but I also knew that I was number one—among the girls. Instead of being the second-fastest runner in class, I was the fastest girl, y punto.

In the third grade, during recess one day, a little boy came up to me and dangled an earthworm in my face. I screamed at the top of my lungs and sprang simultaneously into high gear, running at the speed of lightning. I was absolutely, positively, terrified.

He chased me, but he couldn't catch me, and he gave up. I don't know how long I ran, but by the time I stopped, I was sweating cold bullets and could hardly breathe. The little boy was nowhere in sight.

Amazingly, I didn't faint, although I was traumatized for life. To this day I am deathly afraid of worms—I have a true phobia when it comes to such creatures. I was the fastest runner in the entire school that day—faster than the fastest boy.

Because of our strict moral upbringing, I always felt terribly uncomfortable and sad when kids would gang up on, or make fun of, other schoolmates. Far worse, though, were the physical fights that would sometimes erupt after school.

The first time I witnessed two boys throwing punches and wrestling on the ground, I was in the third grade. One day after school, a crowd had gathered near the school busses. Kids were yelling and rooting the fighters on. As I approached the scene and realized what was happening, I felt a kind of panic. One kid had blood running down his nose and mouth. My stomach felt weird. I looked around nervously, wanting a bus driver or a teacher to run over and stop the fight.

There was no relief in sight. Fearing that someone might be hurt badly, I felt sick to my stomach. I thought about the boys' parents, and about how awful it would be if one of my brothers came home beaten and bloody.

My classmates, however, had transformed into bloodthirsty monsters, yelling for blood and encouraging the swings and blows. "Get him! Hit him! Kick 'm in the gut," they urged.

I ran to the bus, not wanting to see any more savagery. From then on, I would go out of my way to avoid such fights, but I always secretly rooted for the underdog's escape.

I stayed away from bullies. I hated them. I just didn't understand what drove them. Yet, when I was in the fifth grade, a small clique of snobbish, well-dressed girls sought me out at recess and gradually recruited me into their elite group. I never understood why they wanted me. Being part of their little clique caused feelings in me that I had not experienced before.

As I ran with those girls, I began to adopt a superior attitude, especially because we were the seniors of elementary school. Much to my later shame and regret, I had succumbed to peer pressure, without even knowing what it was. I was well aware that my so-called friends were often arrogant and condescending, and it did make me uncomfortable.

"Get outta my way, Verna. I'm in a hurry," Sharon said one day as she roughly shouldered her way past Verna.

"Yeah, outta our way, hillbilly," Kari laughed. Walking out of the girl's bathroom, I saw Sharon, Kari, and Cathy all mocking Verna. I cringed and tried to smile at Verna as I held the door open for her, but she didn't look up. I wanted to say something to make her feel better, but I didn't know what. Still, I continued to run with the group, enjoying the distinguished status it afforded.

One classmate named Patty got more than her fair share of teasing and bullying. She had frizzy blond hair that stuck out like a bush. To reinforce their false sense of superiority, other kids called her Fuzzy Wuzzy.

I did not join in this harassment, but I stood by and did nothing to stop it. I had always felt sorry for Patty, and I made it a point to smile or whisper hello to her whenever our paths crossed—It just felt right.

One day, our class was in the library when my friends started pushing me to go up to Patty and call her Fuzzy Wuzzy. I refused, "No way, man! I don't like those kinds of games; I don't like to be mean."

They continued to prod me, "Come on! Are ya chicken? Anyway, it's just for fun."

Reluctantly succumbing to their relentless coaxing, I finally gave in. As they giggled and rooted me on, I nervously went up to Patty, who was engrossed in a library book.

"Hello, Fuzzy Wuzzy," I said. The rest of the kids cracked up loudly behind me. Startled by their loud laughter, I jumped wide-eyed, looked back at the pranksters, and then quickly to Patty, who, red faced and confused, was peering up at me.

As she began to cry, Patty's face revealed shock, confusion, shame and—most of all—pain. Guiltily, I ran from the room, down the hallway to the girl's bathroom. I locked myself in a stall. I was mortified by what I had done.

I will never forget the weight of that sin on my shoulders. Guilt and shame haunted me. I wasn't able to look at Patty again, and I avoided her. I felt as if I had betrayed an intimate friendship.

I kept thinking that no amount of remorse could undo my horrible act. But I can apologize, I thought. I don't think she'll forgive me, but it's what I should do. I hate to admit that I was too cowardly to face Patty—I couldn't even face my own shame. What hit me hardest was the realization that I was capable of inhumanity and cruelty towards another human being. I was well aware of what it felt like to be on the receiving end of cruelty and ignorance. I did not deserve absolution. I had dishonored myself, and I now carried the burden of that guilt and shame.

But this awful experience taught me a valuable lesson. At home, alone in the upstairs bedroom, I locked myself in the closet, where I solemnly vowed never to act cruelly towards others. I told myself that I would never condone bullying—that I would never again even be a complicit bystander. "Please help me, God," I whispered. I swore that I would always follow the Golden Rule and put myself in the other person's shoes. Feeling a bit better, I closed my eyes and sighed heavily. Then I shuddered—Oh my God, I thought to myself, Confessions are this Friday.

I envisioned the darkened church and the line of people at the tiny confessional, the smell of incense and votive candles, the uneasy waiting in line while trying to recount my sins before going in to the dark, scary cubicle.

Oh well, I thought, the sooner the better—best get it over with. Although I had confessed to God and asked for his help, the thought of confessing to the priest was always frightening. No matter how much or how little I had sinned, I could never overcome that fear.

It didn't happen overnight, but in due time I learned to raise my voice to oppose bullying, and I finally came to accept that it didn't matter what others thought of me, as long as I knew I was doing the right thing.

Many years later, I adopted Shakespeare's words—"To Thine Own Self Be True"—as my motto, knowing that if I ever had a doubt about what was right or wrong, the answer would always lie within my own heart.

Later, as a young adult, I was deeply moved by Jerzy Kosinski's novel, The Painted Bird. Perhaps without even realizing it, I was drawn to the story because of how it portrays man's potential for evil, his capacity to treat other human beings so cruelly, and how the same thing is also found in nature. The story had a great impact on me, and I now realize that more than one childhood incident had everything to do with this theme.

They say we learn from our mistakes and that wisdom comes with age. También dicen, que no hay mal que por bien no venga (for every bad thing that comes our way, something good happens as a result). I have finally come to such an understanding in my own life. So often, as an adult, I have wished for the return of my childhood innocence, if only to ease an overwhelming dismay and hopelessness. Yet now I see that there is a purpose to all the stages of our lives. We need to experience them all to be fulfilled and wise as we grow old.

If Adam and Eve had not eaten the forbidden fruit from the tree of knowledge, we would not have found sin, and the world would be perfect. Yet I believe that we were meant to experience the world through knowledge—rather than to remain innocent and ignorant. Life is not meant to be perfect. Even in the Twilight Zone that kind of existence somehow never works out.

# Chapter 7

My dad did not speak English, so he and Mom went everywhere together. They were a team, and their main focus was the family. Second only to Mom and Dad, the two oldest siblings, Efrain and Lydia, were elders in the family hierarchy.

Because Mom and Dad worked constantly, the older siblings bore a large share of the responsibility for raising the children, although they too worked in the fields. Necessity forced my oldest siblings into adulthood before their time. The rest of us kids loved, respected, feared, and obeyed them, almost as much as we did Mom and Dad. The Kids required more discipline than most kids, and it took a whole command center to keep us in line.

I was a quiet child, and, compared to others, I didn't get into too much mischief. But my younger brother, Valentin, aka Rudy (after Rudolph Valentino) was a whirlwind. He was adorably cute, and he had inherited Lydia's big, beautiful dimples. But he was travieso (mischievous) as all get-out. He seemed to look for trouble—he certainly found it almost everywhere. His curiosity never failed to get the best of him.

When he was four, Rudy threw a kitty down the outhouse, an act that upset the whole labor camp. The upheaval that ensued was scandalous:

"¿Oiga, comadre, sabe qué hizo el travieso de Rudy esta vez?"

"No, dígame, comadre. Todo el mundo sabe que ese chiquillo es capaz de semejante travesura.

Everything and everybody was in an uproar:

"¡Ay… No puede ser… Eso sí que no…!"

The Patrón's son, Willard, had to come to the rescue, and somehow he managed to save the poor kitten. Everyone was upset, angry, appalled. People wanted to know: What on earth had gotten into Rudy? How could he do such a thing?

Trying hard to remain calm, Willard asked sternly, "Rudy, why did you do this? You could have killed that poor kitten. Is that what you were trying to do?"

Shaking in his little boots, Rudy replied, "No! I didn't wanna hurt him. We were just playing and having fun. I wanted to see what he would do. I thought he'd climb back out." This is one time when, instead of curiosity killing the cat, it very nearly killed our poor little Rudy.

Because of their many family obligations, Lydia and Efrain were forced to quit school. In spite of their intelligence, they both accepted their assigned roles without complaint or question. The care and advancement of the family was the most important priority. They gave selflessly and worked hard to that end.

Thanks to Lydia and Efrain, we were the first—in fact, the only—family in the labor camp to own a television set. I had more toys than any other child in the campo. Our beautiful red and white Chevy was my dad's pride and joy. Mom didn't drive, but Dad, Mom and Lydia would get dressed up for errands or business. They would set out in the Chevy, knowing that all the family's hard work was giving us things we needed, as well as luxuries we could enjoy and be proud of. Lydia and Efrain had a hand in all of this and more. They were always trying to improve our situation.

Like our mother, Lydia was outspoken and articulate—authoritative, yet warm and kind. She knew that life in the labor camp simply would not do, and she tried hard to find ways to improve and advance our lives. Perhaps because she and Efrain had been forced to quit school in order to work and help support the family, Lydia impressed upon Mom and Dad the importance of education. She was determined that The Kids would finish school and have the opportunities she and my older siblings had been denied.

"Mom," she said, "now that we're in Washington we need to make some changes. English is the main language here. Not like in Texas, where everyone speaks Spanish. The Kids have to grow up speaking English; we need to give them every advantage to insure they succeed, and we need to keep them in school. Sally and the younger kids are like a new generation—they need to have every opportunity." Her insistence that education was invaluable and that the younger siblings grow up speaking English paved the way for our futures.

Lydia also insisted that Viola, just below her in age, be allowed to finish high school. Viola was extremely smart, a straight "A" student, and she loved school. Lydia convinced Mom and Dad to let Viola complete her education.

"Besides, Viola will help with the kids, housework and meals," Lydia said. "There's no need for her to quit school. She'll help just as much as any of us, and she can work in the fields during summer breaks. Mom, she has to finish school. She's way too smart. It would be such a waste and…"

"Okay, Lydia, your dad and I agree. Viola will stay in school. "¿Verdad que si, Valentin?

Recognizing Viola's intelligence and common sense, Mom and Dad concurred with Lydia—they decided that so much potential could not go to waste. Viola later graduated from Grandview High School at the top of her class, in spite of the fact that at home she rarely had the time needed to open a book or do schoolwork. She earned her straight "A" report cards through sheer aptitude and motivation.

Mom and Dad had listened to Lydia and valued her opinion. They knew Lydia was smart and wise, and that her primary concern was for the advancement of the family.

Now it fell upon Viola to get up at 5:00 a.m. In the harsh Washington winters she would get the fire going in the wood stove, our main source of heat. We only had cold running water, so she would heat the water and then prepare breakfast. Mom always had a little one to care for, which made Lydia and Viola's help invaluable.

Next, Viola would get herself and the kids ready for school, fix breakfast, and make sure we all ate. Everyone would clear their dishes and help with the clean-up. Then Viola would rush off to the school bus. After school, Viola was back at her chores—dinner had to be prepared, kids changed out of school clothes, the house made spotless. It was never-ending work, yet she did it all without complaint. She was just relieved not to have to quit because she wanted to graduate more than anything, and she loved school.

I started first grade in 1958, at the age of six. Gloria was four, Rudy was three and Norma was two. Freddy was the new baby. My older siblings, Imelda, Hector and Viola were in school, but Elida had decided to quit. She wasn't interested in school and thought it was important to help the family work.

Life went on in the labor camp. My family worked hard, and we lived a decent life, never lacking necessities and even acquiring some luxuries. Family meetings were still essential as La Familia Cantú saved and planned for a better life.

The labor camp was my world. People knew and respected each other, and I felt safe and happy there. I was too young to question our poverty in such a place, although I definitely saw the discrepancy between the way Mexicans and Whites lived. Still, life went on.

I had a shiny red wagon that I absolutely loved being taken for rides in, but that didn't happen often. Sometimes, my older brother Hector would oblige, saying, "I'll pull you down to the labor camp, but you'll have to go back on your own. I don't have time to wait around."

"I know, I know. I'll be ready in a minute," I answered as I excitedly gathered my dolls and toys and threw them in the wagon. Then Hector rolled me down to the main part of the labor camp.

Parking me in the shade, Hector left me with a warning: "Be careful, and get back home before dinner."

"I know. I will," I answered with a smile as other kids came around to play.

Later, after what seemed like hours of play, I gathered my things and pulled the wagon home. I was dirty, dusty and happily tired.

Hop fields surrounded the labor camp. The fields and—La Kila, the huge cement building where the hops were harvested and processed—were mysterious and exciting places to play. We all knew well that those areas were prohibited, but forbidden fruit is always so tempting. And children are curious.

La Kila housed the kilns where the hops were cooked. It was a foreboding and fascinating place—it intrigued all the labor camp children. We were not allowed inside this room, where a huge fire burned. But sometimes Lupe, one of the men tending the kiln, allowed one of us to step briefly inside the door of the large room and watch for a few minutes. Lupe made sure we kept our distance from the fire.

Standing close to the door, he knelt on one knee and held out his left arm to make sure I stayed back. "No te pases de aqui", Lupe warned. As if drawn by the flames, I unwittingly took a half-step forward, only to be held firm by Lupe's big, strong arm.

The room was unbearably hot—the gigantic flames from the fire roared and snapped. I could see the twisting flames through big iron slats on the kiln, but when the other attendant, Pedro, opened the huge door to fuel the fire, it was a sight to behold. Whoosh! Thick gusts of hot air burst out from the fire, causing me to hold my breath. I stood mesmerized, my eyes big as saucers, as huge flames roared, flickered and danced like eerie spirits. Feeling the hot gusts of air hit my face, I imagined el mero demonio (the demon himself) was in the midst of those flames. It was astoundingly clear to me how easily Satan manipulated sinners and his disciples, hypnotizing them and then leading them astray—straight to the abyss, into the scalding flames of Hell, forever and ever.

To keep our imaginations fueled, the adults would threaten us children with the stark reality that, if we were bad, "Te va llevar el diablo." "The devil will take you" was their frequent threat, and it brought quick results. Everyone feared the devils power. It was also common knowledge that if one were bad, "Te va tragar la tierra" (the earth will open beneath your feet and devour you whole). This warning left no doubt whatsoever that the sinner's journey would end in the depths of hell. The eternal sizzling, molten fires of hell were a great deterrence. Many of us children were "scared straight" by threats of the devil and eternal damnation.

For as long as I remember, I have always feared El Diablo, The Devil. My childhood fears are instilled so deeply within that they will remain an intricate part of me forever. The devil and Hell scare me more than anything else, perhaps because, as a Catholic, I believe in both, and I fear for my mortal soul. I do not take eternal damnation lightly.

La Kila was a huge building with many different levels and rooms, each just waiting to be discovered by excited children. El Diablo couldn't keep me, or any child, from wandering and exploring. But of course, I would never attempt one of these explorations alone.

The huge main room of La Kila had a cement floor that could have served as a roller-skating rink. It's too bad nobody in the campo had a pair of roller skates. Adjacent was a large area equipped with gizmos that looked like miniature merry-go-rounds. They appeared to be made of wood and rose about three feet off the ground—too high for me to play on. I still don't know what they were for. We mostly avoided the rooms upstairs—they were off limits to all but the workers. But sometimes, when no one was around, we explored them, ignoring the warning signs written in both English and Spanish.

Following my two older sisters, Elida and Imelda, I climbed the wooden stairs. Elida warned, "Both of you do exactly what I say—stay close to me. They say it's too dangerous to play up here, and if anyone finds out, we'll be in big trouble. Got it?"

"Uh huh," I answered, scared, wide-eyed and excited.

"Yeah, we'll all stay close together. It's kinda spooky up here," Imelda said, looking around warily.

"Okay, shhh," Elida cautioned. "We need to be quiet so nobody hears us." As we reached the landing on the second floor, we passed through a big, open doorway and looked around.

"The stairs keep going up. There's another floor," Elida said. She seemed to want to climb higher.

"That's okay, this is far enough," Imelda replied nervously. We were in a huge, empty room with a cement floor. A few windows let in some sunshine, but it was still pretty dark. We noticed a big hole in the floor to the right side of the room. Holding hands, the three of us walked over to inspect it. Above the hole, a machine hung, suspended from the ceiling. It seemed that this was a machine that went down into the hole and then came up again.

"This hole is deep—it looks scary. Elida, what is that thing?" I asked.

"I guess it's some kind of machine they use for the hops. See? Look at all the little hop leaves way down there, at the bottom of the hole. And it's covered with that yellow dust the hops leave everywhere," Elida whispered. We were all peering into the hole when Imelda took a step forward. "Don't get too close!" Elida yelled, jerking us back suddenly.

Imelda and I both screamed at once.

I slapped my hand over my mouth, breathing hard as I whimpered, "Let's get outta here."

"Elida, you almost gave me a heart attack," Imelda said.

Suddenly, we heard a loud noise like thunder, only it sounded really close. We all froze. "What's that?" Imelda whispered. The sound grew fainter and fainter. Then we heard another loud, pounding noise. Elida took Imelda and me by the hands and started pulling us slowly towards the stairs. We were walking backwards, too scared to take our eyes off the door at the far end of the room.

"The sounds are coming from there," Elida said, pointing toward the door. "Somebody's in there."

"Get ready to run," Elida whispered. I started crying. "Now!" Elida whispered loudly as she pushed me and Imelda in front of her towards the stairs. "Run!" she yelled. We ran down the stairs and out of the building. Panting and trying to catch our breath, we stood, staring back at La Kila. Elida wiped my tears with the skirt of her dress. "Stop crying, Sally. We're in big trouble if any one finds out we were up there." We never found out what had made the noise—but that just added to the mystique.

On another of our many adventures in La Kila, Elida, Imelda and I found a baby bird that had fallen from his nest. The tiny, featherless creature looked half dead—helpless and hopeless. We searched for its nest or other birds, to no avail. All I wanted at that moment was to save him. I held him gently in my hand, but Elida protested.

"Sally, leave that thing alone. Don't touch it. It might have a disease," she told me. "Besides, the mother might be around, and she's gonna be mad. There's nothing we can do to help it anyway." Although I didn't understand, I reluctantly obeyed my older sister and set the bird on the floor.

"Do you think the mother bird will rescue her baby?" I asked.

"Yes, of course," she said reassuringly.

"But we need to get outta' here so the mother will come back," added Imelda. At that, Elida grabbed my hand and led us out.

"But I don't want to leave the baby bird alone. What if the mother doesn't come back?" I protested, trying to pry my hand from Elida's. "It's gonna die if we leave it," I cried.

The helpless, tiny creature had left its mark on the very sensitive, impressionable child that I was. I was sad and I longed for a pet bird. I thought about it all day, and one night I dreamed about it—I was alone in the big, main room of La Kila. I saw the bird fluttering in the corner. Approaching, I saw that it was hopping around, unable to fly. I scooped him up in both hands, saying, "What's wrong, baby bird? Where's your mommy?" The little bird answered, "Tweet, Tweet," and looked at me hopelessly. I knew he was asking me to save him, so I ran home with him and made a little nest in a shoe box.

Strangely, no adults inhabited my recurring dream. Baby bird and I were always alone. We were happy, but I always kept him hidden in the shoebox. I'd take him out to play and give him food and water, and he would sing happily. Then I would cover the box and put it under the bed, knowing that I wouldn't be allowed to keep him if anyone found out.

With my new obsession—I had to have a pet bird. I decided to try an old trick I had heard of. Someone had told me that if I put salt on a bird's tail feathers, I could catch it. I took the salt shaker to the only little forested area at the edge of the labor camp. I eagerly looked up at the sparrows in the trees. Now, as I look back, I know they were just plain and brown, but back then I thought they were beautiful and magical. I loved to hear their chirping, and they were in excellent voice that day.

I waited for a long time, but they refused to cooperate. I tried hiding, and then I stood in plain sight and tilted the salt shaker back and forth in my hand, hoping to entice them. I tried sprinkling salt on the ground, and

I even tossed some up in the air. Still, nothing happened—nada. It seemed to me that hours had passed—I was tired, dusty, dismayed, angry and upset. The "salt trick" was really the worse advice I'd ever heard. I resigned myself to not having a pet bird.

# Chapter 8

I don't recall the day of his arrival, or even how long he stayed, but El Viejito Thompson soon became a regular—if odd—resident of the labor camp. What set Thompson apart is that he was White. An elderly, frail-looking Gringo who seemed to have no family, he lived alone in his little labor camp shack.

Everyone in the camp liked Thompson. He worked hard, and he was gentle and kind to the children, who were drawn to his calm, good-natured disposition. He would sit in front of his shack, telling his stories, surrounded by interested listeners.

On one memorable occasion, Thompson performed a fascinating trick that had us all in disbelief. He was sitting in front of his shack after dinner one day, surrounded by kids. After telling us the story of the tortoise and the hare, he stood up and said, "You should all get home now before your parents start looking for you."

"Tell us one more story, Thompson, just one more." I pleaded.

"Si, una mas, señor Tomson," Manuel added.

"Tell ya what," Thompson replied, "I'll do one magic trick if you all promise to go home after that."

"Si, we promise, si, Tomson," everyone agreed with nodding heads.

Suddenly, Thompson clicked his tongue and his top teeth, every one of them, came half way out of his mouth then clicked back into place, as if nothing had happened. The scene was instantaneous, over in a flash, leaving all the children wide-eyed and doubting our senses.

Barraged by excited chatter, questions and requests for a rerun, Thompson did it again. His only explanation was, "It's magic."

I tried and tried to do the trick, clicking my tongue, pushing against the roof of my mouth and against my top front teeth—all to no avail. Thompson was the only one who held the secret to this magic.

One day, I happened upon the old Gringo outside his shack, where he was washing a faded denim shirt in a bucket of water. As I looked on, he invited me to sit, gesturing to the wooden box across from him. I watched as he wrung the water out of the shirt by twisting the material. My eyes focused on his task.

His old, weathered hands seemed to have no strength as they slowly and gently wrung out the water. Seeing that he was leaving so much water in the shirt, I wanted to wring it out for him. I know I can do a better job, I thought, He's leaving too much water in. I was positive that I had more strength.

I really wanted to offer my help, but I was too timid, and afraid of failure. What if I really didn't have the strength I thought I had? What if I tried and ended up making a fool of myself?

Anyway, I thought, He's an adult, I'm just a kid. I knew it would be disrespectful to insinuate that, just maybe, I could do a better job than he. No matter how I looked at it, my best course of action was to do nothing at all.

"Thompson, we saw a baby bird in the Kila. He fell out of his nest, I think, and he was hurt. I wanted to take him home, but Elida wouldn't let me," I said, excitedly.

"Well, I'm sorry," he replied, "but Elida was right, you know. Birds are wild creatures. They need to be free. Besides, you should never approach a baby animal. The mother could attack. Mothers can be mighty vicious when it comes to protecting their young."

"But the mother wasn't around, and the baby fell out of his nest and he might die and...." I rambled on, trying to make him see that the little bird needed to be saved. We talked until I had to get home for dinner. I said goodbye, but as I started to walk away, I turned back to Thompson and said, "I still wish I could've kept the baby bird." Then I ran on home.

On payday, the labor camp residents would go into town to cash their checks and buy supplies. One special day, El Viejito Thompson returned from his trip into town. I was playing outside with my younger sister, Gloria.

"Hello, girls," Thompson called to us.

"Hi, Thompson. Whatcha' doing?" I yelled back, as Gloria smiled and waved.

Thompson walked over to us. With both hands behind his back and a big smile on his face he said, "I have something for both of you. A surprise."

"A present?" Gloria asked.

Thompson beamed as he held out his closed fists towards us, "That's right, a surprise present," he winked.

Excited, we looked at his closed fists. "Pick one," he said.

Gloria and I giggled as we each pointed to a hand. Then Thompson turned over both hands and slowly opened his fists, revealing two beautiful golden rings—one glittering in each hand. We couldn't believe our eyes—each had an adjustable band and a brilliant precious stone. We squealed in delight. Wow! Our rings were gorgeous. We laughed and jumped up and down. "Look, Thompson—look how pretty," I said, holding Gloria's hand towards him. "And look at mine. Oh, thank you! Thank you!" I said.

"Thank you," Gloria smiled still holding out her hand.

"You're welcome, girls," Thompson smiled. "I'm so glad you like your rings."

"Oh, we love them," I said, admiring my ring.

I will be forever grateful to Thompson for his precious gift. Of all the gifts I've received in my life, that little ring gave me the most excitement and unexpected pleasure.

Gloria and I wore our precious rings proudly. I don't know how many times we sat at our window with our hands turned, showing off our beautiful rings to the world. We would stop intermittently to look at each other, giggle, admire our beautiful rings, and then turn back and continue waving out the window. It didn't matter to us that nobody ever passed in front of our window—we were deeply immersed in our fantasies, enjoying our precious gifts.

One day, Mom, Dad and Lydia got all dressed up and went into town. I thought nothing of it, because they often did this. They would buy groceries and tend to any other mandados that needed tending to. Every grocery trip meant a treat for The Kids, so we were always happy on grocery day. Our very favorite treat was Cracker Jacks, crunchy caramel-covered popcorn and nuts with a toy surprise inside every box. We loved them! And the toy surprises and trinkets kept us busy after we had eaten the treat.

But to the family's amazement and delight, this Saturday trip did not result in groceries. Mom and Dad returned with a huge, brand-new, television set. Everyone in the camp knew about TV's—the patrónes had one, but a new TV in the labor camp? Wow! It didn't take long for the news to spread. The whole camp was excited.

After dinner, the family would gather in front of the TV. We would shut off all the lights and watch Gunsmoke, Paladin, The Rifleman and other westerns. My dad had been a vaquero, a cowboy, in his youth. He had trained and worked with horses for his patrónes. Because of his small stature, agility and skill, he was known as the best of the horsemen and therefore the patrónes' preferred jockey. I love the fact that Dad had been a real cowboy.

Although my father did not speak English, he loved the TV westerns just as much as we did. Someone would often interpret for dad, but he seemed to understand pretty well on his own. Sometimes friends from the labor camp would join us, and we would all crowd around the television to enjoy the evenings. Life was good.

On Saturdays, The Kids watched Annie Oakley, Roy Rogers and The Lone Ranger. I loved the fact that Annie Oakley was a girl yet she was just as skilled as any of the guys. She was my hero, always doing good and making things right. I decided then and there that I would be a cowgirl when I grew up. Wearing my cowgirl outfit—guns, boots and hat—I would ride a beautiful stallion. Daydreaming, I saw myself ride into town from the horizon, bringing hope and relief to the underdog. I rescued the good people from the bad guys and the poor people from the rich, leaving a trail of justice, equality and civility throughout the land. In this fashion,

I ensured that good would triumph over evil and that harmony and peace would prevail. Life would thus be good for everyone—things would be fair.

One day, my friend Lisa and I were playing dolls in my older brothers' little shack. My brothers slept on two cots, one on each side of the room, with a chest of drawers between them. Lisa had her doll on one cot, and I sat on the other, so we had plenty of room to play. I noticed a bunch of magazines on the old wooden box that served as a little table at the foot of my bed. I jumped off the bed and grabbed the magazines.

"Look at what I found," I called happily, holding up the magazines.

"Wow, let's see," Lisa said, jumping off the cot and abandoning her doll.

We started flipping through the pages. I was in awe of the glamorous and beautiful movie stars—Marilyn Monroe, Lauren Bacall, and Elvis Presley, the greatest star of them all. Elida was in love with him, and she could dance better to his super-cool rock 'n' roll music than anybody I knew. She was always trying to teach us to dance. On Saturday afternoons, when the adults were out, she would gather The Kids in the living room and start the lesson. Armed with her precious forty-five-rpm Elvis records, which none of us dared touch, she would start the record player.

"Grab a partner and stand facing each other," she instructed. "Now, listen carefully to the beat of the music and just close your eyes and move your body to the beat. Like this." With her eyes closed, she was completely absorbed as she moved her head, her shoulders, arms, torso, and hips. "Now try it. Close your eyes. Listen. Move. Good. Now, open your eyes, hold your partner's hand, listen and move to the music—like this."

With everyone dancing, laughing, and having a great time, Elida demonstrated how to move our feet and how to twirl. "Okay, it's getting crowded in here," she said, "Let's take the party outside." Elida moved the record player to the open window at the back of the house and cranked up the volume. Outside, behind the house, where nobody could see us, we danced and kicked up a cloud of dust all around us.

"You all look like you're killing ants with your toes," Hector teased.

"Just 'cause you can't dance," Elida snapped back.

We were having a blast. Elida ran inside to change the record every time the music stopped. As instructed, we stomped our feet one at a time, hitting the ground, standing on tip toe, then grinding our toes into the dirt, shifting from one foot to the other while holding hands with our partners.

"Hold both hands! Get ready for the twirl!" Elida yelled over the music.

Oh no, I thought, clasping my partner's hands, this is the hard part.

We were supposed to hold our locked hands in the air, while one partner did a quick, light-footed twirl under the arched hands. At this point, most of us lost our grip, laughing as we did our awkward moves. But Elida was an expert who had every move down perfectly.

"Wow, look at this one," I told my playmate Lisa, pointing to Marilyn Monroe's picture. "She's the prettiest one. Look at her clothes and her jewelry. I want to look like that when I grow up." I was awed by her glamor, her glitter, her curvaceous body and red lipstick.

"You're crazy," Lisa said, rolling her eyes, "You'll never look like that. Anyway, she's a Gringa and she's blond."

"I don't care about that! Look at her jewels. Besides, what do you know? You don't know what I'm gonna look like when I grow up," I shouted back. We bickered back and forth for a bit, and Lisa ended up leaving. I was glad to be rid of her. Now I could look at the magazines in peace.

Lauren Bacall had a more natural beauty that I could appreciate: her eyes looked really pretty. But Marilyn was glamorous and almost magical; her shapely feminine figure was enchanting. "Oh, yeah—that's what I want to look like when I grow up," I said dreamily. My mind wandered off into a beautiful daydream of me wearing a shiny, tight-fitting gown like Marilyn's. As my long, flowing curls wafted in a cool breeze, my face was beautiful, with big eyes, long lashes and ruby red lips. Oh, how I loved red lipstick! I was so beautiful that I'd be able to enchant any suitor, any prince I fancied—only the most handsome need apply, of course. And we would live happily ever after in a beautiful kingdom surrounded by an enchanted forest, where all the creatures of the woods would be our friends.

"Wait a minute, what's this?" I said to myself as I grabbed a magazine with a picture of Frankenstein on the cover. "Oh, wow! Stupid Lisa doesn't know what she's missing out on. That's what she gets for getting mad."

The monster magazines were even better than the other ones. They featured all the Hammer Films' stars and characters—Vincent Price, Christopher Lee, Dracula, Frankenstein, and the Wolf Man. Scary, creepy and exciting! I was engrossed by it all.

I was particularly intrigued by Dracula, a living-dead immortal. What would it be like to live forever, to have his superpowers? Fascinated, I was certain that Dracula could easily hold me under his spell. He was dark and mysterious, and he captivated seemingly willing victims. Because of the iconic magazines I found that day in my brothers' room, I have been a classic horror movie fan ever since.

# Part II

# Chapter 1

As a young child, I was oblivious to my family's back-breaking work in the fields in 100-degree weather and my parents' many sacrifices. The labor camp was my playground and the only one I knew. Seen through my childhood eyes, life was good.

But for the adults in the family, life meant constant hard work while planning and saving for a better future. My elder siblings, Efrain and Lydia most felt and understood the hard life of the labor camp. Lydia held steadfast to the belief that the labor camp was only temporary. She never lost her faith that once the family saved enough we would purchase our own home. Dad was understandably reluctant to take the leap of faith necessary to become a property owner. He sat nervously in the Grandview Real Estate Office, saying, "Es un riesgo muy grande. Hay tantas cosas que podrían salir mal, hija. ¿Porque no nos esperamos un poco mas?"

"Apá, ya lo platicamos," Lydia replied. She turned to my mother and said, "Dad can't change his mind now. Everything will work out."

"Si hija," Mom reassured her, "your dad's just nervous."

"Valentin," Mom said patting Dad's arm, "no te preocupes, todo va a estar bien."

Dad knew he was out-numbered, and he knew Mom, Lydia, and Efrain, had been planning this move for some time. We have been saving for this, he thought. I just need to have faith that things will work out. But it's not easy, especially when I only have two dollars in my pocket. Dear Lord, what am I doing buying a house?

It was 1960. I was eight years old and in the third grade. Our new home was huge—two-stories, with a big front yard, on plenty of outlying property. The old house needed a lot of work, but it was ours.

We were thrilled! What a move up from the labor camp.

"Come on—this is the last load! Is everyone ready to go?" Mom said. She shooed us all out of our camp house for the last time. As we piled into the car, Mom and Lydia stopped to look back at what we were leaving. I couldn't hear what they said as they got into the car, but they laughed happily. Efrain drove the Chevy and Dad followed in the borrowed truck with our last load of belongings. We were on our way to a better life. And it was good.

Although we had heard a lot about the new place, none of The Kids had seen it yet. I was on the edge of my seat as we pulled into the driveway. Staring at the huge white house in front of us, I was stunned. I had a million questions, but all I managed to squeak out was, "WOW!" Climbing over me to get out of the car, Gloria and Rudy dashed to the house. When I finally composed myself, I ran to my mother.

"Mom...didn't you say that the girls get the upstairs room?" I asked.

"Si, hija, the girls get the big bedroom upstairs, and the boys get the smaller one. Vamos—let's go inside. Here's the key, Lydia—you open the door," Mom said. The rest of us stood anxiously, waiting to see the inside of the house.

"No, Mom, you and Dad. Everybody, let Dad through. Mom and Dad have to open the door together." Holding his own key, Dad stood next to Mom in front of the door. Smiling at Mom, he put the key in the lock and turned it slowly. Then, jiggling the door knob, he pulled the key out. I held my breath.

"Ahora si," he said, nodding at Mom.

Mom sighed, glanced at all of us, and threw open the door. "Our new home," she beamed. The front door opened into a huge dining room furnished with a big table and chairs. I was awed at the size of everything. Rudy dashed off to explore on his own, and the girls followed Mom and Dad on a tour of the place. Efrain and Hector began unloading the truck.

We walked from the dining room into the living room, which was just as big. A large chair and sofa furnished this room. I plopped down, first on the sofa, then on the big chair. They were both comfortable, but I loved the chair—it rocked back and forth!

"A rocking chair like Mrs. Mears has," I exulted.

Mrs. Mears, La Patróna in the labor camp, had a rocking chair in her living room. I sought out that chair whenever I had a reason to visit her. I loved gently rocking in it. Now we had our very own!

Just off the living room was one of the bedrooms. "This is Lydia and Viola's room," Mom said. A huge closet spread from one end of the wall to the other.

"And the other downstairs bedroom is for Mom and Dad," Lydia smiled. "It's over here," she said, pointing as we all followed her through the living room, through the dining room and into Mom and Dad's bedroom. The stairway leading to the second floor was right outside Mom and Dad's bedroom door.

"Ahhh, here are the stairs," I said excitedly. Just then, Rudy ran out of an upstairs room and stood at the top of the stairs.

"Come upstairs," he yelled. "It's so big up here!" Not waiting for a response, he disappeared as quickly as he had appeared. I was eager to see the upstairs, but not before I explored every inch of the first floor.

Mom and Dad's bedroom was also big, with a big closet, but not as large as the one in Lydia and Viola's room.

Next, we went into the kitchen. It was huge! A big sink, a white icebox, and a stove lined the kitchen walls, and a little table stood in one corner. "Everything's electric," Viola said running her hand over the large stove. "No more gathering and burning wood for cooking!"

"And no more heating water," Lydia added, holding her hand under the warm water flowing into the sink.

"Here's the bathroom," Mom added, opening a door off the kitchen. We had to walk around the left side of the stove to get to the bathroom. I was eager to see if it was a real bathroom, like the one Ada Belle and Mrs. Mears had. Like the one at school, with a white toilet that flushed.

In my haste, I brushed past Lydia. "Sally, watch where you're going!" she laughed.

"I didn't mean to hit you—I just didn't know we had a real bathroom," I said. "Ohh!" I exclaimed, slapping my hand over my mouth. "You didn't tell me...a real, bathroom!" I couldn't believe it. It was a big room, with a white toilet that flushed and a white bathtub that we could fill with water and then just pull the drain plug out when we were done.

"What's this?" Gloria asked. Her hand was on a big, cylinder white thing standing just inside the door.

"That's a water heater, it's what keeps the water hot so we can have hot water anytime we need it," Mom replied.

Gloria smiled at me. I whispered, "Can you believe it? We have everything now." I remembered that I had prayed for a real house with a real bathroom and that I had greatly envied Ada Belle for having one. Now we had a bathroom bigger and better than both Ada Belle's, and the Mears's!

We resumed our tour and inspected the big store room behind the bathroom. "Is this a bedroom?" Imelda asked. "It has shelves but no closet."

"No, it's too small for a bedroom; we'll use it as a storage room," Mom said. "And we also have the back porch as a kind of storage and laundry room."

"Yeah, one of the first things we need to save for is a washer," Lydia added, "It'll go in the back porch." The back porch was located behind the kitchen. It had been closed in and converted into a room.

Next, our tour led us to the two upstairs bedrooms. The smaller room was for the older boys, Efrain and Hector. The big room was for Elida, Imelda and The Kids.

"That door opens into your closet and storage room," Mom said, pointing to the door at the far end of the big bedroom. The storage room/closet ran the entire length of the bedroom, with a long bar inside for hanging clothes. Two big trunks stood at the right and left ends of the room, and a third trunk sat below the closet bar.

I was awed by our new house. It was a dream come true. "So many rooms," I said. "This is a big house. I love it here."

Finally, after seven very long and difficult years in the labor camp, the Cantú family had become homeowners, the first family in the Grandview labor camp to escape camp life and own property. Ours was a noteworthy and significant accomplishment. In my mind, this was front-page, headline news.

The family was ecstatic. Amazingly, Mom and Dad never let on how much they worried about keeping up on the mortgage and other expenses.

I had no concept of such things and enjoyed it all without a worry. Ah, blessed childhood innocence.

Mom and Dad, Lydia and Efrain carried that burden, along with the planning, budgeting, saving and endless work it all entailed. We used the large storage room behind the bathroom to store canned food, paper products and anything else we could store in bulk. We didn't run out of things because our storage room was always well stocked, especially during the peak work seasons, when my parents would buy in quantity—anything and everything to get us through the winter, when work was often not available.

I still do the same, although I know that it's no longer necessary. Something inside makes me buy in bulk and thereby have a surplus in store. This assuages my unwarranted fear of running out. It doesn't make sense that I should be this way, because we never ran out of things or did without. Still, especially for my parents, the fear of going without was ever-present.

Mom and Dad had bought the house from Fred Higgins, one of Grandview's leading landowners and farmers. Higgins owned the house and the vast acres of land that surrounded it—almost as far as the eye could see. The Higgins family had kids our age, and my sister Lydia would often babysit for them.

Now that they were homeowners, Mom and Dad's priority each month was to pay the mortgage, either early or on time, so they would drive over to the Higgins's to pay our monthly mortgage payment in person. My little brother Rudy loved to tag along. He was the same age as one of the Higgins children.

Desiree Higgins was a pretty little Anglo girl—blond and blue eyed. True to his Latin Lover namesake, Rudy was smitten by her beauty. Indeed, he started his romancing ways at a young age, and the little girls of Grandview were equally enchanted by his looks and charm.

1961 was our first Christmas without the whole family at home. Efrain had joined the army.

Mom and Dad sat at the dining table with Lydia and Viola, figuring out the December bills and expenses.

"Our biggest expense is the mortgage. It's due on the fifteenth," Lydia said, "but we can pay it on the tenth. Then we can buy The Kids Christmas presents."

On December tenth, Rudy tagged along with Mom and Dad to pay the mortgage. The Higgins home was elaborately decked out for the holidays. Colored lights festooned the house—inside and out—and the front yard was adorned with festive decorations. A huge, beautiful Christmas tree could be seen through their large living room window. Neighborhood kids were throwing snowballs in the yard, and Rudy glimpsed Desiree as she threw a snowball then ran around the side of the house. As soon as Mom and Dad were out of the car, Rudy jumped out and ran towards the front yard.

"Rudy, get over here!" Mom yelled. Reluctantly, Rudy obeyed.

Soon, Mom and Dad were sitting at the Higgins kitchen table, counting out the mortgage payment to Mrs. Higgins. Mom held Rudy's hand but she was preoccupied. She seemed not to notice when Rudy wiggled out of her grasp. He slowly inched his way towards the living room so he could look at the big Christmas tree. It was an amazing sight, surrounded by a plentiful abundance of colorful, shiny presents.

As the family got up to leave, Mom noticed that Rudy was acting strangely. He pulled away when she reached for his hand, and he insisted on sitting in the back seat on the ride home. "Qué tienes, Rudy?" Mom asked. You always sit in the front."

"I just want to sit in back this time," he replied nervously.

When they got home, Rudy was more than anxious to run off and play, but Mom knew something was amiss. His arms were stiff, and he was in a big hurry to get away. He ran into the house and tried to escape up the stairs, but Mom stopped him cold. No one could put one over on my mother. Mom, Dad and Rudy stood in the dining room, facing each other. Rudy was stiff, so Mom grabbed his arm.

"What is wrong with you? What are you hiding?" she asked. Rudy cringed and pulled away.

It turned out that Rudy had stolen a small Christmas gift from under the Higgins tree.

Mom and Dad were mortified. ¡Que verguenza!

"¿Rudy, como puede ser?" asked Dad.

Before little Rudy knew it, he was being hauled back to the Higgins home to face the consequences of his shameful theft. Mom was livid as she scolded Rudy and told him exactly what to say to Mr. and Mrs. Higgins. "You will confess what you did, Rudy. You will return the present and tell them how sorry you are and that it will never, ever, happen again. Do you understand what shame you've brought on our family? On me and your dad? Aren't you ashamed that you stole from that family?"

Rudy was cowering in shame. Through his tears, he kept saying he didn't mean to take the gift, but it was so beautiful and so shiny and he wanted it so badly. "I swear, Mom, I'll never, never, do it again. Please don't make me go back there."

"It's too late for that, Rudy. You should have thought before you took something that didn't belong to you. Now you have to face the consequences of your actions. That whole family is going to know what you did," Mom scolded.

Back at the Higgins house, Rudy was red-faced, shaking with fear and humiliation as he faced the Higgins family. He realized that nothing, not even his strong desire for that shiny gift, was worth this horrific consequence. He had never experienced such humiliation, and he had never seen Mom and Dad so upset and ashamed of him.

It was a very difficult way to learn a lesson, but learn he did. Stealing was not something he would ever again consider. Rudy found that he could not easily shake the intense humiliation and disgrace he felt.

Rudy never forgot the incident. When he recounts the story, he hails Mom and Dad for their wise choice of punishment. A spanking would have been easily forgotten. Being made to face his victims etched the lesson into his memory.

Even though we were happy with our four-bedroom house, it was still crowded for a family with eleven children. But we didn't mind. We were so much better off.

My second cousin, Sylvia, and I were only a few months apart in age, and we had been inseparable since we were babies in the labor camp. Because she was an only child, I would often stay overnight at her house. Sylvia lived with her grandparents, my Tía María y Tío Luis. María, Dad's sister, was the only family on my father's side that I knew, because Mom and Dad's families were all in Texas.

On many nights, if I didn't stay over at Sylvia's, she would stay at our house, which was always crowded with The Kids. For the first year in our new home, all five of us younger kids—including Rudy and Freddy—slept on one double bed in the girl's room upstairs. Two older sisters, Elida and Imelda, shared the other double bed. My two older brothers slept in twin beds, in the boys' room across the hall.

The five of us Kids slept crosswise on the bed, and when Sylvia stayed over, we were six. We never complained about the crowding or thought it strange. In fact, we liked it. We laughed and talked and Rudy never failed to crack us up. Mom and Dad's room was at the bottom of the stairs, and they would hear all our commotion.

Every night, when they sent us to bed, they would caution us to settle down. "Go right to sleep, no laughing and talking. ¿Entienden?" Mom admonished us. But we never took heed. Even if we wanted to behave, it was really quite impossible to expect five or six children in one bed to be still and quiet—especially with Rudy in the bunch.

So we would giggle and talk, until, suddenly, Mom or Dad would yell up at us from the bottom of the stairs. After a few warnings, Dad would shout, "Si no se callan voy a subir con la faja." If his threat of a whipping didn't do the trick, he would come up with his belt, say, "I told you so," and then hit us very lightly, over the covers, with the belt. It was more of a gesture than anything else. But it worked—after the spanking, we would settle down and fall asleep.

One night, Rudy was up to his usual antics, and we were almost to the point where Dad would come up with the belt. There was a bookcase next to our bed, and Rudy jumped up, grabbed a book, and said, "Everybody, quick! Grab a book and put it in the seat of your pajamas. Lie down on your front; you won't feel the belt." We all scrambled over each other. Poor little Freddy practically got trampled in our stampede.

"Here, Freddy," Gloria whispered, handing him a book. "Hurry, get under the covers."

We giggled so hard that when Dad came up with the belt we had to practically smother ourselves to stifle our laughter.

"¿Pues, que tienen?" Dad asked, telling us that we were acting worse than ever and he didn't want to come up again…or else he'd really have to spank us hard. Between muffled giggles, we got our spanking, and Dad went downstairs, wondering why we were being so weird.

After Dad left, we all wiggled around under the covers, pulling the books from our pajamas. "You and your big ideas, Rudy," Norma said. "A book on the butt didn't do any good."

"Yeah," I added. "Next time, don't forget to tell Dad just exactly where he can and cannot aim the belt. "Apá, nomas nos puede pegar aquí," I said, facetiously, pointing to my butt.

Our house was old and needed many repairs and upgrades, but Dad and Efrain, along with our lifelong family friend, Ponchito, did all the work. Even the driveway needed work, so huge truckloads of gravel were brought in. The men filled in the large hole in the middle of the driveway, and after much work, time, and expense, we had an attractive and functional driveway. Before long, Rudy and Freddy were being scolded for throwing rocks. In his very stern, scolding voice, Dad said, "¿Cuántas veces les tengo que decir? ¿No saben que esas pierdas cuestan dinero?" (How many times do I have to tell you? Don't you know these rocks cost money?)

Why those rocks cost money was beyond my grasp. I just didn't get it—gravel roads were everywhere, rocks were everywhere and there was no rule against picking them up if we wanted to. Our driveway rocks weren't any different, or any better, than any other rocks I had ever seen. No matter how much I thought about this, I simply did not understand it. ¡Que cosas! What things!

As we settled into our new house, it slowly began to take on the form of our home. We were still a large family for a four-bedroom house, but we were comfortable and content. Our home soon reflected our essence. Family pictures and religious effects lined walls. Tables were covered by beautiful embroidered and hand-starched linens and doilies. A large picture of the Last Supper hung in our dining room, next to the Sacred Heart of Christ, a crucifix, and a print of La Virgen de Guadalupe.

A standard fixture found in just about every Mexican home was a picture of our president, John F. Kennedy, and the First Lady, Jackie Kennedy. In seventh-grade art class, I baked and painted a pair of ceramic wall plaques. One was a silhouette of President Kennedy—the other, the First Lady. They were proudly displayed facing each other on our living room wall. Most of our friends and relatives greatly respected President Kennedy, a symbol of hope, democracy, equality, and better times to come for all people. The fact that he was a practicing Catholic didn't hurt, either.

# Chapter 2

Ponchito was a most interesting character. Tall and rail-thin, he was quiet and soft spoken. His wife, Guadalupe, was obese and almost a recluse, rarely leaving her home. But on occasion, she would accompany Ponchito on a visit. They seemed to me to be such an odd and dear couple. Their grandson Jesse lived like a son with them. So, there were Ponchito and his family: Lupe la de Poncho and Jesse el de Poncho—very close family friends throughout my childhood.

Adding "de Poncho" at the end of their names distinguished them, literally, as "belonging to" Poncho, which was a common way of referring to someone in those days. It wasn't meant in a sexist way, nor was it meant to have a negative connotation—quite the contrary, it was meant in an endearing way, especially with common names like Guadalupe and Jesse.

Jesse de Poncho was often part of the wild bunch of boys my brother Rudy led on notorious misadventures. Rudy and Jesse were both well known for their travesuras (mischievous antics). Jesse was constantly in trouble for one reason or another. Just like Rudy, he had a knack for bad luck and trouble.

Jesse could often be found playing at an intriguing old junk pile near his home. One time, a dirty, rusty, wreck of a car appeared at the junk pile. The front end was completely smashed, most of the windows were broken or missing, and the passenger door had been stolen. The upholstery was dirty and torn. The whole car was a smashed-up, dirty pile of junk, but it seemed to call out to Jesse invitingly, promising adventure. Ponchito forbade Jesse from going near it.

"Ni te acérques," his grandfather warned. "¿Entiendes, Jesse?"

"Sí, abuelito," Jesse assured his grandfather. He claimed that he wasn't interested in it anyway, "It's just a pile of junk," he said, dismissing it with a gesture of his hand and running off to play.

But as the days passed, Jesse's curiosity grew until he could no longer stay away. Today's the day, he thought. I'll just play there for a while and they'll never know. He figured that if he hid in the old car, nobody would be the wiser, and he could have some real, uninterrupted fun. Grabbing the wooden matches he kept hidden under his bed, Jesse stuffed them in his pocket and ran out the door.

Glancing back at his grandparents' house, he saw that nobody was at the window, so he slowly headed toward the junk heap, kicking an old ball in that direction. Aiming the ball toward the car, he gave it a good kick. The ball came to a stop near the door-less passenger side of the old car. He glanced around furtively. "Yes! The coast is clear." He dove onto the dirty front seat. Coughing and choking, he fanned the air with his hand until the dust settled.

Jesse crouched so he wouldn't be seen. He wiped away spider webs and dust from the dashboard and began pulling levers and twiddling knobs. "It smells in here," he said. "Oh, I know…" Stretching his legs forward, he lifted his butt and reached into his pocket for the matches. Lighting a match, he watched the flame burn down almost to his fingers and then blew it out at the last second. "Ay, that was close," he smirked, throwing the burnt matchstick to the floor. He sniffed the air, enjoying the smell of burnt sulfur.

Having a great time, Jesse started planning for the future. This would be his secret hiding place. He laid the remaining matches on the seat, counting them. "Only twelve left. I need to sneak a few everyday so 'buelita won't notice. I'll hide them in the car," he said, lighting another match. Closing his eyes and leaning back comfortably, he imagined all the fun he would have. Suddenly, he felt the burning heat of the match on his fingers. "Ay!" he yelled as he flicked the match away. "OW!" The matches on the seat burst into flames, but instead of trying to extinguish them, Jesse panicked. He managed to jump out of the car and save his hide, but rather than run and scream for help, he stood, mesmerized, watching in trepidation as the fire quickly spread. The flames were hypnotic.

Seeing the flames from the kitchen window, Ponchito's first thought was for the safety of his grandson. His heart raced. "Ay Jesse, ¿Que hiciste?"

he yelled. Pulling out the bandana from his back pocket, he wiped his sweating face and forehead. Although dripping sweat, he felt the icy chill of La Muerte run down his spine. ¡Que susto!

Ponchito ran towards the flames, yelling, "¡Jesse, Jesse! ¿Donde estas? Diosito Santo…"

Almost as quickly as it had come on, his fear was replaced by the blessed relief of seeing Jesse a safe distance from the burning car. Ponchito stopped momentarily to cross himself. "En el nombre del Padre, del Hijo y del Espíritu Santo. ¡Gracias, Dios, Gracias!" He thanked God for his mercy as he rushed toward the old hose attached to the faucet at the edge of the junk heap. Turning the water on full blast, he sprayed the flames. The fabric and stuffing of the front seat fueled the wild fire. "Cálmate," Ponchito told himself. "It's not as bad as it looks."

"Jesse, espérame en la casa," he shouted. "Ya me encargaré de ti."

Ponchito had never been one for corporal punishment; he was such a gentle soul. It truly hurt him more than Jesse when Ponchito had to resort to spanking Jesse to keep him in line. For all his mishaps, Jesse almost always managed to get away with just a firm scolding. This situation, though, called for a firmer hand. The fact that Jesse could have killed himself could not be dismissed.

"Oh geez," Jesse mumbled under his breath, "No getting out of this one."

Finally, Ponchito managed to extinguish the fire. He stared at the smoldering ashes, dreading what he had to do next. "No way around it," he whispered shaking his head. "I can't be easy on him this time." He looked toward the house. Jesse stood meekly in front of the door, waiting for his punishment.

As he slowly approached his grandson, Ponchito noticed that Jesse held a single match in his left hand. Caray, he thought, El tontito doesn't even bother to hide the incriminating evidence.

Ponchito knew he needed to find out how all this had come about and patiently but firmly confront Jesse about playing with matches. He would not let himself rush to judgment.

Breathing heavily, Ponchito tried to remain calm. "Bueno, ahora si Jesse, esplícate. ¿Dime lo que pasó, y porqué estabas jugando con mechas?" Jesse was not accustomed to seeing his grandfather so upset.

"Think fast," he told himself. His mind raced, as he tried to come up with a good excuse, something that would appease his abuelito.

"¡Las ratas!" he exclaimed. That's right—it was the rats! Everyone knew that the junk pile was infested with them, so Jesse stuck with his explanation. "Si, fueron las ratas, se metierón y..." Yeah, this is good, he thought, it's a logical story. Jesse told Ponchito how the rats had managed to crawl inside the old car. He said they had chewed at the matches, thereby igniting a small fire, which had quickly turned into an uncontrollable blaze.

Ponchito sternly told Jesse that it was highly unlikely that rats could light matches. "Quiero la verdad, Jesse," he insisted, reminding Jesse that a lie, on top of everything else, was going to make matters worse... and things as they stood were already pretty bad.

"Si, abuelito," Jesse insisted. "Fueron las ratas—it had to be the ratas. How else could the fire start?" Jesse couldn't stop fidgeting, nor could he look at his grandfather. Tottering back and forth, Jesse avoided Ponchito's stern gaze.

"¿Bueno pues qué te pasa, Jesse? Estas más nervioso que la tiznada, y ni me puedes mirar. Aver, mirame a los ojos. Me estas mintiendo," Ponchito replied. Ponchito insisted that he just wanted to know why Jesse had set the fire. "¿Pero porque lo hiciste, Jesse? What got into your head? What were you thinking?"

Jesse stared straight ahead, at a loss for words. Ponchito repeated his question, adding, "¿Que pasó? Did the ratas get your tongue as well?"

Burdened with fear, guilt and trauma, Jesse looked up hopelessly. He shrugged his shoulders, and with a huge sigh, he answered, "Se me metió el Diablo." (The Devil got into me.)

Jesse hung his head. He was afraid to raise his downcast eyes. He shuffled his feet. Silent for a long moment, Ponchito sighed in resignation and slowly unbuckled his belt.

At the clinking sound of the buckle, Jesse's eyes glanced upward. Oh no, he thought hopelessly.

Slipping off the belt, Ponchito said, "Well, let's see if this will take the Devil out of you."

I can attest to the fact that the whipping exorcised the Devil right out of Jesse. Perhaps it was a combination of the unexpected whipping and

Jesse's fierce crying and carrying on, but that old Devil was sure enough expelled.

The bad news is that the Devil repeatedly found his way back. Much too often it would turn out that what had started innocently for Jesse somehow made a sharp turn and ended up being mischievous and sinful. It wasn't his fault—he certainly didn't want to be bad, but what's a child to do against el mero demonio? (the Devil himself)

Ponchito was a jack-of-all-trades. He intrigued me with his vast skill and knowledge. Ponchito could even make a chalkboard—not buy one, mind you. He could actually make one. That was rocket scientist stuff!

The day I saw him working on the electrical wiring of our newly purchased house, I stopped my play to watch. He installed a light fixture in the dining room, and when I saw him make it work with the switch he had also installed, I was mystified. "Wow!" I exclaimed. How did you do that?" Ponchito went into a confusing and lengthy explanation that baffled me.

I stood, dumbstruck, not understanding a thing he said, but nodding as if I did. All the while, I was thinking, He is a genius! Yes, Ponchito can do anything. Amazingly, he had no formal education. He was living proof that school is often overrated.

We had been in our new home for about a year when my oldest brother, Efrain, joined the army in 1961. During his absence, he sent Mom and Dad a tape recorder with a microphone. The family gathered around the dining table as Lydia read Efrain's letter to us. He said he was doing well and enjoying Army life. He missed everyone and wanted to hear our voices, so he asked us to make a recording and send the tape to him. The Army base had a recorder he could use to listen to our tape.

"How exciting!" Lydia exclaimed, "This is great!"

We decided that Hector, Lydia and Viola would learn to set up the tape recorder within the next few days so we could all talk into the machine. Everyone was excited. We Kids were chattering and giggling. We wanted to touch the machine.

"You Kids get off the table," Mom scolded, "Now, everybody settle down."

Saturday evening finally rolled around and we were all ready for our recording session. "Efrain wants The Kids to sing a song for him. We'll do that first so they can get to bed," Lydia instructed.

"Ay, hija, estoy muy nerviosa," Mom said.

"No te preocupes, Vieja," Dad replied, but he looked a bit nervous himself.

Lydia tried to reassure Mom and Dad. "I'll put the microphone here in front of you. Just talk as if Efrain was right here with us. We'll let The Kids go first."

"Kids, are you ready? Come stand over here in front of the mic," Viola said. We scramble noisily to our designated spot as Viola continued, "Okay now, one at a time, you're going to say hi and say who you are. Then you'll sing. Ready?"

"Yeah. Got it. We know," we all answered at once.

"We're ready. We all have copies of our song," Rudy yelled. We had picked "America the Beautiful" because it was, indeed, a beautiful song, and we had often sung it in school.

Lydia and Viola, acting as masters of ceremonies, introduced each presentation and directed us. We Kids all said our hellos into the microphone, and then we started to sing.

"Wait!" I said disgustedly. "Everybody needs to start at the same time and stay in tune! Geez, you guys! Can we start over again?"

With a bit of difficulty, Hector managed to erase our first take. "This is it," he exclaimed grouchily, "You don't get another try, so do it right this time." We did our second take, and it was a wrap. We were so hyped up and giggly we didn't want to go to bed.

"Mom, can't we just stay up and watch for a while?" I pleaded.

"Yeah, we'll be quiet," Gloria added.

After several protests and Mom and Dad's repeated insistence, Elida and Imelda ushered us upstairs. "You guys be quiet now. No laughing and talking, or you'll be in big trouble," Elida warned. "Mom and Dad need to do their recording tonight so they can mail it to Efrain on Monday."

"Yeah, and all the rest of us need to take our turn. This is serious, so please be quiet and go to sleep," Imelda added.

We were extra careful to be quiet that night, but we wanted to know what was happening downstairs. We snuck out of bed and tiptoed to the landing at the top of the stairs. It didn't do any good, though; we couldn't make out what was being said. "Shh," I whispered with my finger to my lip. We all got up from our huddled positions, and looking at Norma and Gloria, I pointed toward our room. I led Freddy to bed and tucked him in. Along with Rudy, he now slept in Efrain's twin bed. Gloria, Norma and I climbed into our own bed and soon we were asleep. Without the boys to contend with anymore, our nighttime scoldings and spankings had lessened.

Downstairs, the adults continued with their project. Mom and Dad apprehensively talked into the contraption, but not without a few complaints.

"Ay, Efrain," Mom said to Dad, "Como se le ocurre… bueno pues."

"Here Mom—you have to talk into this microphone," Hector explained, handing her the mic. "Apá, hable en el micrófono como si estuviera Efrain aquí."

After Mom and Dad finished their recording, Lydia, Viola, Elida, Imelda and Hector each got their turn. It was incredible that we could all send our greetings and messages to Efrain through that recording machine. What excitement!

A few years later, Efrain ordered us a set of Encyclopedias. Thumbing through one of the books, I said, "Wow, look at this Lizard. Look, it says here that if his tail gets cut off it'll re-gen-erate. That means it'll grow back. That's crazy."

"Lemme see," Rudy rushed over to see the unbelievable lizard. There were so many amazing things in those books.

We had also received a big dictionary and several extra books. They were so very cool, so full of information I never knew anything about.

Whenever I had to do a school report, I rushed to the encyclopedias. I was in the seventh grade when I wrote a report for my social studies class.

"What are you going to do your report on?" my friend Rosie asked as we walked out of class.

"Mine's on the Nez Perce Indians," I said excitedly. "I love the way Indian tribes live in harmony with nature. I've already read a little about this tribe."

"Really? Where did you read about them?" Rosie asked.

"In our encyclopedias. We have a really neat set that my older brother sent us. He's in the army."

"Wow, you're so lucky. You have them at home?"

"Yeah. You can come over and use them if you want."

"That would be so cool, but my mom and dad won't let me," she said. "I'll have to use the school library."

"Well, if you ever can come over..." I shrugged. "See you at lunch," I said over my shoulder as I rushed on to my next class. I felt bad for Rosie. She was very smart, but I knew her family was really poor, and she never got to go anyplace.

Our house was in the country, and it sat on a sizeable piece of property. We had a very large front yard. A gravel road ran in front. To the sides and the back of the house were huge fields owned by the farmer, Fred Higgins, who had sold us our house. The fields were sometimes used for growing corn or wheat, and other times, Higgins used that land to keep livestock.

We didn't mind either way. For us Kids, country living provided a million ways to play, discover, and get into mischief. We had some excellent climbing trees at the edge of our front yard, and a small irrigation ditch ran just in front of the trees—perfect for wading. Everything around us held the promising potential for fun and adventure.

On a very hot day in the summer of 1962, I was ten years old. All of us Kids were wading in the irrigation ditch.

"Ooh, squish the mud between your toes! It feels good," Rudy called out.

"Yuk! It feels weird," I said, "but it's so cool."

"Mom," Norma yelled, "can I get all wet? Can we sit in the water?"

"First, go in and get some old towels," Mom answered, I don't want you all dripping and making a mess in the house when you're done."

"I'll get the towels. I haven't gotten wet yet," Gloria said running towards the house. Right about then, I decided to get out of the water, thinking, If The Kids are going to get all wet, they'll be splashing all over the place.

"I'm getting out," I said. "You guys take care of Freddy."

"No, don't get out so soon," Norma pleaded. "Come on! Don't be a party pooper."

"Naw," I answered, "See you guys later."

Balancing myself on the edge of the ditch, I raised one foot out of the water. Stepping down onto the grass I noticed that something was wrapped around my middle toe, so I bent down for a closer look. My heart practically jumped out of my throat as I realized that it was an earthworm! "Ahhh!" I screamed at the top of my lungs. I leaped out of the ditch. "Ahhh!" I kept screaming as I ran around in circles, trying to shake the slimy, horrid creature off of my foot. Terrorized, I caused such a commotion that everybody was concerned.

Mom dropped the hose she was watering the flowers with and ran towards me. "¿Que pasa? What's wrong? Help her!"

"But, she won't stop! I can't catch her," Rudy yelled chasing me.

"Sally! Is it a bee? Stop running! What is it? Mom! What's wrong with her?" Gloria and Norma were yelling and holding on to Mom while little Freddy, still in the water, stood with his eyes closed and his hands over his ears. Gloria ran to get Freddy and wrap him in a towel.

Finally, they managed to subdue me. Still gasping as I sat on the grass, I yelled, "It's on my toe! Get it off! Get it off!"

"Hold still, Sally! What's on your toe? Let us see," Mom said, kneeling next to me and holding me down. "Rudy, grab her feet."

Rudy was finally able to hold down both of my ankles. "There's nothing on your toes! What are you yelling about?"

"Look, Sally," Mom said, sweeping the hair out of my face with her hands, "No tienes nada, hija. You're okay. Fue sólo un susto, ya pasó."

My heart racing, I was out of breath, shaking and crying. Standing up, I screamed, "It was a worm! An earthworm!" I ran into the house, crying so hard that I couldn't catch my breath. I felt like such a fool. As I stood, leaning on the dining room table, Mom came into the house. The Kids followed closely behind. I quickly realized that they weren't laughing at me, as I had expected them to. I dreaded their ridicule.

"Que susto," Mom said leading me to the couch. "Lie down here. Calmate y relajate."

"Gloria," she yelled, "bring me a wet towel, y tú, Rudy, bring a glass of water." As she rubbed my face and forehead ever so gently, I began to get ahold of myself. But I never, ever, stepped into that ditch again.

# Chapter 3

My little sister, Norma, was in the kitchen, up to her elbows in flour and who knows what other ingredients as she attempted to make a pie. To poor Normita's dismay, the results of her pie-making attempt looked like anything but a pie. As she struggled with the dry, crumbly dough, the boys ran into the kitchen to get a drink of water. After gulping down his water, Rudy slipped into the bathroom.

"What are you making?" Freddy asked, looking into her bowl with a smirk.

"It's supposed to be a pie, but I can't get the dough to stick together. It's just all crummy and dry," Norma answered, throwing a hunk of dough back into the bowl in disgust.

"Yeah, it is dry. Put more water in, that'll make it stick, like when you make glue," Freddy suggested.

"Oh, Freddy, I'm not making glue! You're no help. Get out of the kitchen."

Sitting in the dining room, I slammed my book shut, rolled my eyes, and shook my head. Trying to ignore their comments, I stood up, thinking I had better find Mom and warn her. Mom was in the living room, on the phone with one of her comadres. "Mom," I frowned, pointing towards the kitchen with my thumb. Mom nodded as she said goodbye to her friend. "Okay, comadre, mañana nos vemos. Adios."

"What is it? What's going on?" Mom asked.

"I think you're needed in the kitchen," I told her.

Norma's attempt to make a pie turned out to be a disaster in every respect. The Kids knew that Norma's so-called pies never passed the taste test—and they looked awful and lacked the proper texture.

Mom tried to comfort Norma, telling her not to worry.

"But Mom," Norma replied fighting back tears, "what am I going to do with it?"

Mom assured her she could try it again another time. "But for now, let's just throw this one out."

Rudy and Freddy looked at each other and said, "No! Don't throw it away! Give it to Clutcher!" What a great idea. We all ran out, eager to give Clutcher, our pig, his treat. Desgraciadamente, to my poor sister's dismay, even Clutcher wouldn't eat poor Norma's pie. The boys started in with their usual banter, and soon we were all cracking up. Norma was not amused; being the youngest girl in the family always meant she got picked on.

"Shut up!" she screamed. "I'd like to see you guys make a pie. I'm telling Mom."

"Yeah, tell her even Clutcher doesn't like your pie. It's not our fault," Rudy yelled after her.

This failed endeavor and its accompanying humiliation continued to haunt Norma for many years to come. As far as I know, my little sister never tried to make another pie. Now, she doesn't bake at all. This is not to say, however, that her children are denied the wonderful smell and taste of fresh baked goods. We can thank Grandma, Betty Crocker, and Pillsbury for that. This also doesn't mean that she can't be assigned the task of bringing desert or pastry for potlucks and fiestas. After all, what are bakeries for?

Mom grew beautiful roses and flowers. She also had a snowball bush in the front yard, which over the years, transformed itself into a beautiful tree, covered with huge snowball blossoms.

Dad planted his garden at the edge of our property, between the corn field and our lawn. He loved tending the vegetables and strawberries, jalapeños and other chiles, onions, zucchini, tomatoes. Every year, he had a thriving crop.

We also had chickens and fresh eggs daily. At the rear of our property stood a huge chicken house, built with separate little units for the hens to lay their eggs, opposite their roosting area. Another room held other animals, and the property also featured an outside corral.

Feeding the chickens and gathering eggs was a daily chore. Mom or one of The Kids scattered the grain for the chickens: Here, chick, chick, chicka, chick! Come on, come and get it! Clucking and fluttering their wings, they ran right over to eat.

"Mom, why are chickens so dumb?" I asked. "Just look at 'em, running and clucking, and fighting over the same grain of food when there's plenty all around them!"

"Ay, MiCeli, dejalas, son animalitos de Dios. Just finish feeding them, y te metes, Mom responded shaking her head and smiling.

"Hey, let's play Pica, Pica," Freddy called out to Rudy.

"Okay, I'm first," Rudy answered. "Go get a sheet from the house."

Running into the house, Freddy snuck a clean sheet out to the yard. Taking the sheet from Freddy, Rudy handed him a bowl of corn, commanding, "Don't throw the corn until I say."

"I know. Hurry and cover up," Freddy said as Rudy lay face down on the grass. "Here, lemme cover you. Ready?"

"I'm ready," Rudy responded lying perfectly still.

Freddy threw a handful of corn over the sheet, covering Rudy, and the chickens came running to eat the corn.

"Ow!" Rudy shouted. "Keep throwing corn…Ahha, ow! Both boys laughed uncontrollably. Freddy kept throwing corn until Rudy yelled, "Stop! I can't take it anymore!"

We often had a calf or a pig, which would be butchered for food. To Mom and Dad's dismay, The Kids invariably made a pet out of these beasts. Clutcher, the pig, once had us scared to death after he swallowed a bone that stuck in his throat. "Get Dad! Clutcher's choking! He's going to die!" Freddy yelled busting through the back door. "Apá! Apá! Clutcher… está muriendo!"

"What's wrong Freddy?" Mom grabbed him by the shoulders.

"Clutcher's dying!"

Dad ran out to the corral with Mom and Norma at his heels. When I saw Clutcher gagging and choking, I panicked. I didn't know what to do. Dad yelled at Mom to keep The Kids from watching, and Mom pushed Norma away. I grabbed Norma and lead her to the house. With all the commotion and Norma crying, I was shaken up, but I tried to act calm.

"Where's Gloria?" I asked. "Have you noticed that she's never around when we play with Clutcher?" Taking Norma to the kitchen, I poured her a glass of water."

"I don't want any water," she protested.

"It's good for you. Just take a sip," I said, holding back her long bangs. "Okay, that's good. Let's go to the sofa and wait for Dad. He'll take care of Clutcher. Come on—let's watch TV."

After a long wait, Mom, Dad, and the boys came through the front door. Norma and I jumped out of our seats.

"What happened?" Norma yelled running to Mom.

"Todo está bien," Dad assured us. "Ya está bien.

"¿Pero, qué pasó?" I asked.

Dad explained, "Se le atoró un hueso, pero ya se le salió. Está bien."

"See?" I told Norma, "Clutcher's fine and dandy. Dad took care of him." We were all happy and relieved that Clutcher was now safe. He had swallowed a bone that stuck in his throat, but Dad took care of the problem and Clutcher was fine. For a while, anyway.

Dad bought a special grain mixture to feed the hogs, and he had an arrangement with the local grocery store. Every day, Dad picked up the produce that wasn't fresh enough to sell. He mixed it with grain for feed. Rudy and Freddy loved to watch the pigs stick their snouts in the pig trough and inhale their mushy food mixture.

Sitting on the fence, they got a big kick out of the entire scene. "Look at 'em eat," Freddy laughed, inching away from Rudy as he spoke. When he was a safe distance, Freddy continued, "They look like you when you're eating. Ha! Dirty face and all." Freddy was off and running before Rudy even had a chance to smack him.

"You can run, but you can't hide," Rudy warned.

One day, while watching the pigs eat, Freddy said to Rudy: "Hey, how much you wanna bet I can ride Clutcher or one of the pigs?"

"You're crazy. He won't let you ride him. He won't even let you get on him," Rudy laughed. "But, hmm," he said clicking his tongue, "maybe if we get on while they're distracted, like now, when they're eating."

"I told you," Freddy giggled excitedly. "But we can't do it now. Dad's here."

"We'll do it as soon as we get the chance, when Mom and Dad aren't around."

It wasn't long before Rudy and Freddy got their chance, and the Wild Hog Ride became a regular attraction. Of course, the adults never found out, and the boys developed a full routine of bad behavior with the poor, unsuspecting pigs. First, they pilfered the choice pig grain that Dad kept in the garage. Then they snuck fruits and vegetables from the kitchen. They mixed the pig meal like Dad did. It had to be scrumptious, so the pigs would be completely caught off guard.

Finally, they were ready.

"Step right up, ladies and gentlemen," Rudy commenced. Any kid within hearing distance rushed to the corral as Rudy continued, "See it to believe it! See the Wild Hog Ride! Try it if you dare. Our spectacular show will start in two minutes. Come one, come all!"

Neighborhood kids came running. Perched on the fence, everyone anxiously awaited the show.

At the fence, Rudy sat on the "Riders' Spot."

"Okay, Freddy, the food!" he yelled. Freddy was ready, and the hogs grunted and snorted as they began to gorge on the feed.

"Hiyah!" Rudy yelled, jumping onto Clutcher. Rider and pig went for a wild, but very short ride, while the rest of us cheered and clapped for joy.

Unfortunately, despite the fun and games, Clutcher's sole purpose was to provide meat for our family's scarce winter. It was a harsh fact we Kids just couldn't get into our heads, no matter how many times we were told. Thus, when Clutcher's time came, we were in an uproar, crying and making a scene—all of us except for Gloria. We were so upset that we refused to eat meat for some time—until we could be sure that it was not our beloved Clutcher.

Getting ready for another day of school, I ran down the stairs and burst into the dining room on my way towards the bathroom. I stopped in my tracks, staring at Gloria, who was sitting prettily, eating her breakfast.

"Gloria! What are you doing?" I exclaimed in horror and disgust, "You're eating bacon. Do you know what that means?"

Mom quickly intervened, "Sally, leave your sister alone. You all should be eating."

"But, Mom!" I said in shock, "She's eating Clutcher!"

Gloria dropped her fork, looking sternly at me with a smirk and a roll of her eyes. "It's only bacon," she said, her brow furrowed. "Man! Why do you think I didn't make friends with Clutcher? I'm not about to pass up bacon. Geez, it's a pig…for eating."

Mom went over to Gloria and patted her on the shoulder.

"Termina de comer, hija," she said gently. Then, shaking her head, she looked at me. I knew that look only too well. It stopped me cold.

I closed my gaping mouth as Mom continued, "That's enough, Sally. If you're not going to eat, just leave." Mom paused for a moment, then added, "And leave Gloria alone. I don't want to hear another word about this. ¿Entiendes? Not from you or any of The Kids."

"Yes, okay," I answered, hanging my head and turning away in defeat. Walking away, I glanced back, only to see my kid sister chewing a big piece of bacon. As Mom turned toward the kitchen, I glared at Gloria and mouthed the words, "You're The Pig!"

The Kids often played Indians, and Rudy never failed to designate himself as Chief. I loved playing as though I was one of the Indians from Peter Pan, so I didn't care if Rudy was Chief; I had my own coveted role. Being the oldest of The Kids, I always hogged the role of Tiger Lily, the beautiful Indian princess. My poor little sisters never got a chance at that role. Lydia had discarded an old black dress, which I claimed to make my Indian outfit. It was a sleeveless, fitted dress, with silver trim around the neck and a "V" back.

My alterations included cutting fringe around the bottom and painting colorful Indian stripes on the front. I was twelve and starting to develop a feminine figure. With my small waist and shapely hips, I filled out the dress well. My long braided hair and leather headband completed the look.

I was getting too old for such games, but I was not ready to give up my starring role. I reveled in being the beautiful Indian princess. My fantasies were wonderful fairytale stories in which I, the damsel in distress, never failed to be rescued by a Prince or Knight in shining armor, the good-guy cowboy, or the handsome Indian brave.

My mind housed an array of rescuers, always bringing me safety, security, justice, love and a happy-ever-after existence of joy and peace.

Because we always had chickens, they were commonplace to us. But we loved it when Mom and Dad came home with a fresh clutch of baby chicks.

Hearing the sound of a car pull into the gravel driveway, all of us Kids ran to look out the windows.

"They're here!" Freddy yelled, running towards the back porch.

"Yeah, they're bringing the baby chicks. Run and open the back door," I said, elbowing Rudy.

Dad walked up the back steps, yelling, "Abrenme la puerta." He was carrying two crates full of tweeting baby chicks. How exciting! Freddy held the back door open.

"Careful!" Mom cautioned. "Don't get in your dad's way." I stood in the doorway, holding Norma and Gloria back. "We can play with them later," I whispered.

Dad put the crates down on the old ringer washer and shooed us out with a warning to leave the pollitos alone. Light bulbs warmed the chicks in their crates, and Mom and Dad fed and cared for them until they were ready to go outside on their own. Then they would be introduced into the chicken coop and become part of our pollo community.

But until that time we Kids would sneak into the back porch to hold the soft, chirping baby chicks every chance we got.

Sneaking in with the chicks, I stuck my finger into the crate and rubbed a little chick on the head. "Hi little tweety. Ooh, you're so pretty," I cooed. I looked around before closing the door. "Okay, tweety, come on," I said, picking up the chick and nestling it against my cheek.

"Leave those chicks alone!" Mom scolded, "They're not pets. You know what happens when you get attached to them."

"Ahh! Mom! You scared me. I didn't even hear the door," I said reluctantly putting the chick back in the crate. "But Mom, you don't have to worry about us getting attached to the baby chicks. They're only cute when they're babies. Once they grow up they're just chickens."

"Well, you know it's for your own good that your dad and I don't want you kids making pets out of our animals, Mom replied, "Besides, it's not good for them to be handled so much."

We never gave up on sneaking into the back porch. Holding and playing with the chicks was well worth the scolding.

We were accustomed to Mom's expertise in killing chickens by wringing their necks. This was a necessary skill, and we never disputed it. My mother was quick and precise, so the poor animal didn't suffer. Some of us were squeamish about the grisly routine, but it was a familiar occurrence.

The boys loved to play with the chicken feet, running after one of us girls and threatening to touch us with the ugly, disembodied claws. The chase went one of two ways. If we are lucky, Mom or Dad would rescue us, and the boys would be forced to stop the torture with a good scolding. On the other hand, if luck was not on our side, they would chase us until we gave up, promising to be their slaves and do whatever was demanded of us. "Just get that horrid thing away from me!" we would shriek.

The whole chicken slaughter scene disgusted and sickened me, and I was too smart to be caught in a vulnerable position. Somehow, I managed to absent myself on these occasions.

One sad inevitable day, Mom killed our adored pet, Henny Penny, a beautiful grey chicken we had nursed and raised into adulthood. She was very pretty—with a unique grey and reddish brown coloring that made her different from all the other chickens. We had never made a pet out of a chicken before, but Henny Penny was special.

We cried and carried on when we realized her time had come. "No, Mom! Not Henny Penny!" I shrieked when I saw what Mom was up to. "Gloria!" I yelled, "Call the boys! Call The Kids! Mom's going to kill Henny Penny!" Soon, all of The Kids were in an uproar.

"Stop! Mom! What are you doing?" Rudy screamed, running towards Mom, followed by the rest of The Kids. We pleaded and begged, but Mom was firm. She scolded us for the umpteenth time about making pets out of our animals. Not about to be swayed, she had no time for our nonsense.

Upset and frustrated, Mom sent us all upstairs to our rooms. "And I don't want to hear any more from any of you! Now leave me alone so I can make dinner."

"But, she can't kill Henny Penny. Sally, don't let her." Norma cried.

"Come on—we're in enough trouble, and there's nothing we can do about it." I said solemnly. Norma and Freddy were taking it the hardest as they huddled together, crying. For weeks, all of us grieved, even Gloria. Of course, we wouldn't eat meat, even when we were told it wasn't chicken. We knew that with Mom's cooking skills she could fool us without even trying. We weren't about to take any chances!

I never saw another hen as beautiful as Henny Penny, and none of us ever made another pet out of any of the hens.

We also had a huge white rooster that Mom and Dad referred to as El Gallo Viejo. Old Gallo was meaner than mean. He had the nasty habit of chasing, attacking and pecking at people, especially vulnerable children. We all kept our distance and were always on guard when he was around.

Freddy, the youngest, often had to be rescued from Old Gallo's attacks. One time, I was out in the back, hanging clothes, when I heard Old Gallo in an uproar and little Freddy screaming and crying. I dropped the shirt in my hand and ran. Freddy had come out the back door but was only half way down the stairs when Old Gallo started his rampage. The old rooster ran toward Freddy repeatedly, his outstretched wings flapping. Squawking threateningly, he jumped in the air and batted his feet.

"Hey! Get away!" I yelled, but mean Old Gallo kept right on. I picked up a long, dead branch and ran quickly toward Old Gallo. The stubborn old thing turned on me. "Ahh!" I yelled. "Freddy, run inside, hurry!" Having dropped my stick, I started throwing rocks, and finally Old Gallo backed off. I ran in the back door and there stood Freddy, scared to death. I was shaking as I grabbed Freddy, dried his tears, and tried to comfort him. "I've had it with that mean old thing," I huffed. "Just wait till Mom and Dad hear about this."

Shortly after, the day finally arrived when Mom announced that Gallo's time was up. Dad would butcher Gallo as soon as he got home from work. Mom usually killed the chickens, but she was not about to tangle with Old Gallo. He was just too mean. Mom would leave this chore to Dad.

The Kids were happy. That afternoon, we played on our swing set, singing and chanting a little tune that Rudy composed on the spot.

THE WHITE ROOSTER CHANT / DEDICATED TO OLD GALLO

Heidi, Heidi ho, time for you to go.

Just so you know, 'cause Mom said so.

Your days are numbered...

But you'll always be remembered,

For providing such a tasty meal.

That's what you get for pecking at our heels.

And with that happy and perhaps slightly vengeful sendoff, Old Gallo paid for all his meanness and provided a tasty caldo (soup), to boot.

Rudy and Freddy went on to have other pets, like Homer and Gomer, the jumping race frogs, but they were too creepy and slimy for me.

"Keep those awful things out of my sight," I warned when the boys first brought Homer and Gomer home. "Don't even get near me with them! Where did you get them, anyway?"

"We caught them by the big canal over by the Aguilars'," Rudy said.

"Well, you can take them right back there," I snapped.

"No, they're going to be our pets," Freddy said, holding one of the frogs behind his back.

Rudy looked at me with a smirk, saying, "Ah, come on, Freddy." At that, both boys ran outside.

"Humph," I grunted, going back to my work.

Who would have guessed that over time the little frogs would grow on me? I developed a kind of affection for them after all. What can I say? They turned out to be quite entertaining.

Rudy and Freddy drew a line on the ground to mark the beginning of the race course. Sportscaster Rudy yelled, "Ladies and Gentlemen, you are about to witness an amazing feat. Hold on to your seats, boys and girls. Today and today only, straight from Looney Tune land, we have the amazing racing frogs, Homer and Gomerrr. Make your bets, and take your seats. The race is about to start."

With Homer in one hand and Gomer in the other, Freddy was ready at the starting line. Norma stood at the finish line, the starter's whistle hanging from her neck. Rudy dropped his hand like a race flag. Norma blew the whistle. Freddy set Homer and Gomer down on the starting line, and andale! The race was on! Everyone was jumping, clapping, and cheering.

With so much commotion, the poor little frogs didn't stand a chance. They didn't seem to get the idea of the race. But who can blame them? They were probably scared out of their wits. They hopped around aimlessly, every which way, dazed and confused. After a while, Freddy announced, "Okay everybody, the frog who went the farthest distance is the winner. As soon as the judges figure it out, we'll announce the winner."

Rudy, Norma and Freddy scrambled about with the measuring tape, and although it was ridiculously hard to determine, they declared a winner.

"And the winner is...," Rudy paused for dramatic effect, "Gomer!" he yelled.

"No it isn't," said Joe Aguilar, shaking his head. "Homer was ahead."

"But, he didn't win," Rudy said.

Freddy cut in, "Gomer won. It was close, but..."

"Yeah," Norma agreed. "We measured, and the decision is final. Anyway, Joe, it's not like you had real money on the bet."

When a Homer and Gomer race was underway, I was drawn to the mounting excitement. Anytime I thought I was too adult and too mature to retain my position as one of The Kids, something like the frog races drew me back in.

In keeping with the cycle of life and the rules of nature, Homer and Gomer meet their demise one sad day. Ironically, they both died together. It got us to thinking that perhaps they had been husband and wife—perhaps one refused to go on living without the other. We had always assumed both were male. Or maybe they were brothers—we all agreed they were very close. Whatever they were, we'll never know.

Rudy and Freddy decided that Homer and Gomer should be buried together so they wouldn't enter the Great Beyond alone. "We need a little coffin," Rudy said. "Freddy, let's get them ready for their funeral."

"Funeral? We're going to have a funeral?"

With a sad sigh, Rudy responded, "Of course, what else can we do? We need to give them a decent burial. Come on—we need a coffin."

Mom always kept a big box of wooden matches in the kitchen cupboard. With Freddy trailing behind, Rudy ran into the kitchen and headed straight for the cupboard. Reaching towards the back and groping around, he finally gasped, "Here it is! This matchbox is perfect. Come on." As he dumped the matches on the counter, Rudy told Norma to announce that the funeral procession would soon commence.

Elida and Imelda were the adults left in charge of The Kids that day. Norma, acting as town crier, solemnly entered the living room to announce the upcoming funeral. All of us girls rushed around, looking for veils so we could respectfully cover our heads. We invaded Mom's room, searching for veils, shawls, anything appropriately black and funeral-like.

I rushed upstairs and threw on my beautiful black Indian princess dress. Perfecto! Soon, all of us, including the older sisters, were outside, in our funeral attire. A sad, low moaning could be heard as the little procession, led by Rudy, marched toward the back of our property. Freddy held the coffin and marched alongside Rudy, who wielded a garden hoe. The rest of us followed. Our histrionic wailing grew louder as the march continued to the back of the chicken house, where an old camper top had been abandoned.

The camper top was just big enough for The Kids to sit in. It would serve as the burial spot. Rudy dug a hole with his hoe, and the boys knelt. Freddy carefully placed the little coffin in the hole, and Rudy covered it with dirt. The girls wailing increased. We said overdramatic words of farewell and waved our hankies. "Ahh! Ay, no!" Raising his hands, Rudy asked for silence as he placed a little cross—made from the palms handed out at church every Palm Sunday—on the grave.

"Remember, frogs, that thou art dust and unto dust thou shalt return." Rudy cleared his throat and whispered, "Who's the patron saint of animals?"

"Saint Francis," I whispered. I knew because I had picked Francis as my confirmation name.

"Okay." Rudy continued, "Saint Francis, please take Homer and Gomer into your heavenly animal kingdom. They were good little frogs and good little pets. May they rest in peace. Amen."

In that instant, our little play area was transformed from playground to holy ground. We never played in the camper again.

Although the wailing had ceased, a few sniffles could still be heard as the funeral procession silently departed. We girls returned to the house to remove our veils. We left them on the dining table, but Imelda warned, "Put the veils back where you found them. Fold them neatly. Otherwise, we'll all be running around Sunday morning, looking for veils."

"Okay," we answered in unison.

Gloria leaned across the table and grabbed the veil she had worn. "Poor Homer and Gomer," she said sadly. "I wonder why they both died at the same time."

"They're in heaven now," Norma replied, "so, they're happy."

We all folded our veils, and I said, "Gloria, will you put these back in Mom's room?"

"Okay," she answered, gathering up the veils.

"Norma's right," I added. "They probably weren't too happy being pets. They're wild creatures, and they're happy now in heaven. Anyway, I'm going upstairs to change."

After what must have been the shortest period of grief and loss ever, life returned to business as usual for the Cantú family. Rudy and Freddy felt bad for a bit, but they continued with their outdoor adventures and soon forgot all about the little frogs.

# Chapter 4

My childhood began to deteriorate at the age of eleven. I was in the sixth grade when my teacher, Mrs. Gran, addressed the class. "Quiet down, everyone," she admonished, "Take your seat. We're going to see a health film today, so I need the girls to line up here and the boys to line up over there," she said directing us.

Just then, Mr. Baker stuck his head in the doorway. "Oh, hello, Mr. Baker," said Mrs. Gran, nodding and pointing to the boys' line. "Girls," Mrs. Gran continued, "you'll be following me to the auditorium… and boys, you will go with Mr. Baker. Okay, girls, let's go."

Everybody started chattering and asking questions. As the girls followed Mrs. Gran down the hall, Kathy raised her hand. "Mrs. Gran, I have a question. Why are we being separated? Are we going to see different films? All my classmates had been asking the same questions among themselves only to be hushed by the teachers.

The film explained that the female body was different from the male body. It explained reproduction and other very confusing things. The only thing that stuck with me was how the inside of my body, supposedly, looked like some kind of sci-fi creature with weird horns.

After the film, the whispers began. There was so much speculation among the students, and some of my friends vowed they would find out more by asking older sisters or friends, but I had no intention of discussing these things with my family. I just wanted to forget about that ugly film, so I pushed it into the recesses of my mind. It worked for a while, but by the time I was twelve, that film came back to me with a vengeance.

The start of my period was a life-impacting moment, another loss-of-innocence-welcome-to-the-real world incident. I had seen menstruation referred to in the school film, and my older sisters had explained it to me, but the actual reality was more than I could bear. To put it mildly, the sight of blood made me uncomfortable and queasy.

Less than a year before, Lydia and Viola had taken on the task of explaining this fact of life to me. As I walked into Lydia and Viola's big-girl room, Lydia smiled and told me, "Close the door. We need to talk to you."

Caught off guard, I simply raised my eyebrows and grunted, "Huh?" I couldn't imagine what they wanted. Lydia was smiling, so I figured it was nothing bad.

"Here, sit down," Viola said, patting the bed.

"What's going on?" I asked apprehensively.

"We just need to explain something to you," Lydia smiled. "It's just a fact of life, something that happens to all girls. You're eleven now, which means you're growing up, and your body is going through some changes."

Oh God, I thought. Squirming and feeling nervous, I halfheartedly said, "Okay, so I'm going to get boobs and stuff. I know. What else is there?"

They proceeded to explain how I would soon be starting my period. I was disgusted. "But why?" I asked. "I don't want that to happen, I don't want to have babies, ever! How can I stop that from happening?" I wanted to cry, but I held back the tears as my older sisters continued to explain.

Kicking off my shoes, I inched my way back on the bed until my back was against the wall. Wishing I were invisible, I brought my knees up to my chest and hugged them closely. Viola, who was leaning on the chest of drawers, turned around and grabbed something from the top of the chest. She handed the stuff to Lydia, who sat on the bed next to me. Lydia placed the stuff between us, saying, "This is a sanitary pad, sometimes called a sanitary napkin, and this is the belt you'll need to wear." She explained and demonstrated how these things were to be used.

I was repulsed. Dear God, how can this be?

Lydia held out the pad and belt. "Here," she said, "Try hooking the pad to the belt."

"No way!" I said, turning away, "I don't want to touch it." Tightening my grip around my legs I pulled them closer to my chest and buried my face. I didn't want to look up. I just wanted out of there.

After an awkward pause, Lydia said gently, "Well, don't worry. Just let us know when you start your period, and if you have questions or want to talk about anything, just ask us, okay?"

"Okay," I said, getting up from the bed with downcast eyes. Dejected and deep in thought, I walked out of the room. The whole thing was just too much for me. I kept turning the facts over in my mind, but there was simply no making sense of it. It was all so messy and scary, and I didn't want any part of it.

On the day I started my period, I was appalled and devastated. Lydia and Viola had explained that the things I needed would always be in the big storeroom behind the bathroom. I rushed into the bathroom and locked the door. Breathing hard, I entered the storeroom. Sure enough, the box of pads and the belt were there on the shelf, as promised, as though the horrid things had been waiting for me.

I grabbed a pad, but for the life of me I couldn't remember how to hook the pad to the belt. After several failed attempts, I knew I needed to ask for help. I wrapped the items in a towel and marched myself over to my big sisters' room.

"How do you use this stuff?" I asked Viola, handing her the towel. "I don't remember how to hook the stupid thing to the belt."

"Oh," she smiled. "It goes on like this," she said. "Here, you try it."

On my second try, I got it right. "Okay, thanks. I got it," I sighed.

Back in the bathroom, I wondered why all women had to go through this horrendous ordeal every month of their lives. Every single girl, every woman in the world, I thought. It was very difficult for me to comprehend. Even Elizabeth Taylor, even all those movie stars, my teachers, every single woman and girl? Yet, they all act so normal, like nothing this awful could ever happen to them. "I just don't get it," I said, shaking my head.

I felt hopelessness, a despair that I would soon internalize. It would surface with a vengeance as I experienced the beginning of what would become a lifelong struggle with chronic depression. I couldn't shake the horrible feeling of sadness and dread that had enveloped me.

Outside, I sat on the grass, just staring into space. I felt so lost in my hopelessness. My oldest brother, Efrain, appeared. He tapped me on the shoulder, arousing me from my bleak reverie. "Come on, esquincla," he said, motioning towards his motorcycle, "Let's go for a ride."

As I looked up at him, I sighed. "Okay," I said unenthusiastically, rising slowly to my feet.

He didn't ask me what was wrong, but he knew something was up. Usually, The Kids had to beg for a motorcycle ride. This was the first time Efrain had ever offered any of us a ride. Does he know something? Oh, God, I hope not!

How I loved the feeling of riding behind my big brother on the motorcycle! We would speed down the highway, the wind blowing back our hair and the scenery flashing by. Such a feeling of freedom, control and exhilaration!

But on that day, I just didn't feel any of my usual joy. I had changed irrevocably, and nothing felt the same. Would things ever be simple again?

As life would have it, the next thing on the real-world agenda was discovering S-E-X. It was another fact of life I was just not ready for. And my know-it-all peers used every dramatic trick they could muster to make it all the more eerie and creepy.

Rumors and speculation about S-E-X spread like wild fire among my schoolmates, who whispered about it in dark hallways, the lunchroom and empty classrooms—anywhere, really, where adults were absent or out of earshot. The self-proclaimed experts among us wove their tales with such drama that they could have been contenders for an Actor's Guild award. And so we learned, "What Married People Do."

A group of us girls were outside at lunchtime, sitting on the grass, when Elena excitingly announced, "Come on. Let's sit in a circle. I have something really secret to tell you guys." She lowered her voice and whispered, "It's about sex."

"Whoa, I don't know," I said, looking at my cousin Sylvia. Sylvia made a skeptical face and shrugged her shoulders.

"What do you know?" asked Diana.

"A lot. Shh, listen. Come on over here by the big tree. Everybody, sit. Hurry." We inched our way into a tight circle. Elena waited for all of us to sit before she began.

"This is how it happens."

"How what happens?" one of the girls asked.

"Sex, I said sex, didn't I?" Elena said excitedly. "Anyway, the man and the lady get naked and they roll around in bed, kissing and touching and stuff."

"Elena, how do you know?" Diana asked again, "Have you done that?"

"No way, man! I know cause my older sister told me. She's married. But there's more, you guys. Wanna know more?"

"Yeah, tell us, what else?" Irene implored.

"Okay, you asked for it, but don't blame me if..."

"Come on we don't have all day, you know," Josephine cut in, "So tell us before the bell rings."

I wasn't so sure I wanted to know. Cousin Sylvia and I exchanged a concerned glance but remained quiet.

"Well," Elena continued, "The man," she paused and looked around at all of us, "takes his thingie. You know." She pointed to the spot below her waist.

"His what?!" Irene yelled. We were all wide-eyed in shock and suspense.

"Shhhh! Quiet, you guys," I whispered.

"Well, the man takes his pee pee," Elena continued, "and puts it in the girls pee pee, and..."

"Oh Elena!" I jumped up. "You're so disgusting! You're lying!"

"I'm not lying, I swear!" Elena said. "How could I know this stuff? I'm telling you, my married sister told me and she wouldn't lie."

Everyone started talking at once.

Sylvia spoke first. "Well, why did she tell you this stuff, Elena? I mean, I don't know."

Suddenly, the bell rang, and everyone started. I ran ahead of the group, not wanting to hear more lies. Sylvia caught up with me. "I don't know, Sally. We need to find out if Elena's telling the truth."

"But, how?" I asked, "Who are we going to ask? All I know is I'm never getting married. I'm not taking any chances. No ifs, ands, or buts about it!"

"Me too," Sylvia yelled back at me as she rushed ahead to her classroom.

There is no denying that my twelfth year was a turning point. I started working in the fields and left my innocent, ignorance-is-bliss childhood behind for the darker, real world. Now I knew that my family was poor, that we had to work in the fields and tolerate indignities, injustice and low pay for the difficult work that we did. I became aware of so many things that my childhood innocence had shielded me from. And now that physiology and sex had entered the picture, I slowly succumbed to a chronic depression that I would fight for the rest of my life. Once I entered Junior high school, reality stripped away my innocence piece by piece.

I never indulged in the boys' rugged play—running through the wheat fields or making hideouts by the big canal farther up the road, near the Aguilar house. Chisme (gossip) had it that my younger brothers, Rudy and Freddy, the three Aguilar boys, and my little sister, Norma, had fried and eaten grasshoppers at their waterside sanctuary. I didn't care—I knew only too well what the boys were capable of doing, especially under Rudy's command.

Of all The Kids, Rudy was the one who stood out most. He was a natural born leader—fearless, daring, perceptive, mischievous, outgoing, and likeable. With his big dimples and natural smile, people immediately warmed to him. His sense of humor endeared him to even the most skeptical and stand-offish.

Even so, the baby of the family, Freddy, was adorable. Cute and sweet, he was the most beloved.

Gloria was only one year and nine months younger than I. As little ones in the labor camp, we had played a lot, but as we grew, I pushed her away, thinking she was just a kid. Much later, I sorely regretted this.

Like a wild thing, Norma was constantly running with the boys. As fast as the wind, she could keep up with—and even outrun—any of them, including Jesse de Poncho, the Aguilar boys, and the neighbor kids down the road. She was Juana Gallo*—not to be underestimated.

On the day Rudy realized that his little sister Norma was even faster than he was, he chased her at top speed but couldn't catch up. Determined, he shifted into his fastest gear, but the harder he tried the faster she flew.

As they both whizzed by, Rudy yelled, "Catch that Neemie Bug!" They ran out of the yard and onto the gravel road in front of the house. Realizing that his efforts were in vain, Rudy conceded that there was just no catching her. Trying to save face, he came to a sliding halt on the gravel, feigning disinterest in the chase. "Yeah, you better run," he yelled. "You better be glad I'm tired of this game." If the guys find out she can beat me, he thought, I'll never hear the end of it. This would remain his secret. He would never admit that she was the faster runner.

Norma's athletic prowess would later win her the President's Award for Physical Fitness. An award she truly had coming, for she was a natural athlete. All those years of climbing trees and running with the wild boys had paid off. Norma was also the most outgoing of The Kids—never timid, quiet, or shy, like me and Gloria. She regularly stayed with friends overnight or had friends over to our house—something that Gloria and I never did, except with our Cousin Sylvia.

Gloria was little goody-two-shoes. She was Dad's favorite because she combed his hair while he relaxed in his chair after work and gave him manicures and pedicures—stuff like that. Dad sat in his recliner, freshly bathed, and Gloria catered to him. He looked so relaxed and content, with his eyes closed and a satisfied little grin on his face. Gloria ran the comb through his hair and followed each section combed with a gentle pat. Then she whispered, "¿Se siente bien, Apá?"

Dad took a contented breath and answered in a gentle voice, "Si, hija, muy bien." This special little bonding ritual between them continued for many, years.

Gloria was prim and proper, so sweet and cute with her angelic smile and dimples. Dad even helped Gloria wash the dishes. She stood on the little step stool, scrubbing and rinsing, and Dad stood right next to her, drying them. Nobody helped me when it was my turn.

Rudy always called her fragile because of her bone-thin, petite stature, and because she was such a "girly girl." Gloria was also the smart Kid.

---

* "Juana Gallo" was often used to describe a female who didn't submit to the stereotypical woman's role. It referred to any girl or woman who was strong, brave, steadfast, valiant, and athletic, and who scoffed at perceived female weakness.

Wearing her cute cat-eye glasses, she could usually be found sitting poised in a secluded corner, engrossed in a book.

I was different. Even as a pre-teen, I was often deep in thought, contemplating tough issues such as racism, injustice, and war. At the age of twelve, I began writing poetry as a release for my pent-up frustration over such issues. I had no other way to sublimate all of my deep, intense feelings. Still shy, quiet, and introverted, I had finally found my outlet. Through my writing, I could say anything I wanted in whatever manner I chose. I could be anybody; I could bear my soul without fear of reprisal or shame. Finally, I had discovered an outlet for my tortured soul, a safe haven for all my teenage angst. It was as if my discovery of writing were a lifesaver, for I am certain I wouldn't have survived without some kind of expressive outlet.

Bob Dylan became my idol, and I thought he was the only person in the entire world who could understand me. A crucial influence in my life, Bob Dylan represented hope, freedom, acceptance, equality and all things good in a dark and ugly world. He was a beacon of hope—a positive force in my tortured, insignificant life. He was somebody, a real person who actually thought and felt as I did:

Yes, how many years can some people exist
Before they're allowed to be free?
Yes, how many times can a man turn his head
Pretending he just doesn't see?
The answer, my friend, is blowin' in the wind
The answer is blowin' in the wind.

I was grateful to have Bob Dylan to look up to. I wondered if celebrities like Dylan, whose fame was colossal, realized that they influenced ordinary lives. I wished I could tell him that he was an essential and positive force to my young and tormented twelve-year-old soul, and that he never lost that special and positive influence on me. In my dark world, he sang of justice and equality. He invoked a sense of sunshine and hope, a reason for being, something to believe in and something to strive for.

I always loved music, and I played the radio while I did my household chores. Soon, I was off in my own little world, singing with Bob Dylan and fighting for social justice alongside my idol.

Throughout my teenage years, and after, I was amazed that White people idolized Black celebrities and singers, yet when White people encountered a Black person in "real life," that Black person could become invisible, patronized, or hated. Discrimination was rampant, and I just didn't get it. I fervently hoped that Dylan could get the world's attention through his songwriting.

Another thing that amazed and astonished me was how White people were always trying to darken their skin, yet they couldn't tolerate non-whites. None of it made sense. I wondered if White people ever saw the contradictions and the irony in their actions and beliefs. I concluded that not being able to see one's own faults was part of the human condition, not just a racial thing. I guessed we all shared in that guilt. But still, there was no excuse for racism, discrimination, injustice, and all such worldly evils.

I didn't like to dwell on such things because, no matter how I looked at it, I never got an answer. Racism raged out of control—it was a huge issue, much too big for me to understand or resolve. I wondered if there would ever come a time when mankind would be free of prejudice and racism. As unlikely as it seemed in this crazy world, I still had my dreams, and, as people often said, hope springs eternal.

The adults were always working, and so we, The Kids, learned very early how to do our share. All the Cantú girls learned how to make homemade tortillas, cook, do laundry, iron, and clean the house from top to bottom—mopping, waxing and vacuuming floors. I didn't know much about the boy's chores—I was too busy with my own. What I did know is that I was an excellent housekeeper and I loved to sit back and admire my finished tasks.

"Gloria," I said, "which do you want to do—mop and wax the floors, or iron the clothes? Whichever one you choose, we need to get going on it now 'cause we both have to make dinner at 5:00."

"I'll do the ironing this time," Gloria answered, "Can we put the radio on?"

"Here," I said grabbing the radio, "I'll plug it in, so we can both hear it while we work. Norma can do the dusting."

"Rudy, Freddy," I yelled up the stairs, "I hope you guys are cleaning your room. Mom wants that done today, and you know she'll check, so do a good job."

"Okay, okay, we are!" Rudy yelled back.

"And don't forget—you have to change your beds today, too. Throw your dirty sheets and towels down," I reminded the boys."

I loved a spotlessly clean house and enjoyed decorating, arranging and rearranging. I took great care and pride in my work, and I had a real feeling of accomplishment and pride once I finished. "You know, I think I'll be an interior decorator when I grow up," I told Gloria. "What a fun job that would be!"

I was good at all but one thing—cooking. Gloria, on the other hand, was little Miss Betty Crocker. She could plan and make a meal from soup to nuts, and finish with a fresh baked dessert with a cherry on top! My greatest problem was that I never knew what to cook. Unlike Gloria, I could never plan an entire meal, so whenever possible, I traded chores with her. Gloria wasn't always willing to trade, so when I had to cook, I always made the same thing.

It turned out that I could make a halfway decent sarten de fidello. Fidello is the thin angel hair pasta that comes twisted up and tightly packed. Mom taught me how to break it up into the skillet with diced onion and then lightly brown it, adding several Mexican spices. Next, I added tomato sauce and water with caldo de pollo. Then I let simmer. It was delicious, and variations could be made by adding diced vegetables, and browned pork, beef, or chicken.

Because I had mastered this dish, I made it over and over when it was my turn to cook. I just didn't have any other meals in my repertoire. It became my routine, and after a while, on my night to cook, The Kids would invariably sing out, "Sally's turn to cook... fidello again!" Oh, well,

I couldn't be a master at everything. I figured when I grew up, I would be rich. Then I would have a maid and a cook, and a huge, beautiful house.

On the day we got the great news that my mother's younger sister Alice and her husband, Leo, were coming for a visit from Texas, Mom was ecstatic. It had been nine years since Aunt Alice and Uncle Leo had seen our family—since 1953, when we left Texas for a new life in Washington State. Now that we were out of the labor camp and owned our own home, we were able to host family. Everyone was excited, and my mother wanted everything to be perfect for her sister's visit.

Aunt Alice looked like mom—meticulously put together, with attention to every detail, she was beautiful and petite, with dark hair. I loved her signature red lips. Uncle Leo was a handsome man, and he had a wonderful way with kids. Tall, dark, and handsome—he cut a masculine profile. We all loved him from the start, and we fought for his attention.

Mom hadn't seen her sister in a long time, and they had much catching up to do. Meanwhile, Uncle Leo spent time attentively playing with The Kids. After dinner, he made it a ritual to take a walk with the five of us, leading us up the gravel road that ran in front of our house.

"Okay, who's ready for a little exercise and fun?" he asked.

"Me! Me!" we sang out in unison. We all wanted to hold his hand, so we ended up having to take turns.

On our first walk, we chattered like playful chipmunks. We had a rock throwing contest that Uncle Leo initiated, saying, "Now, everybody, pick up three or four good throwing rocks." We scrambled around gathering ammunition.

"Ready?"

"Ready," we replied. Rudy assumed a throwing stance. I looked at him, smirked, and rolled my eyes.

"Turn toward that field," Uncle Leo indicated, pointing to the right. "We'll throw our rocks in that direction so nobody gets hurt."

"But then we can't see where they land and we won't know who won," Norma protested.

"I'll win anyway," Rudy responded, "You guys can't throw worth beans."

Norma fired back, "Who says, Rudy? I can throw as far as you…."

"Hold on," Uncle Leo laughed, "That's the whole point—we'll throw the rocks into the field, and who cares where they land? You're all winners in my book. You're my special nieces and nephews."

Everyone was satisfied with that response. Our dear uncle knew how to keep us happy.

We threw rocks for a while and then continued our walk to the corner by the Aguilar house, where we turned around and headed for home. Uncle Leo started humming and asked, "Who knows this song?"

"I do! I do!" Rudy replied tugging on Uncle Leo's shirt.

"Fats Domino," Gloria and Norma yelled simultaneously.

I cut in, "I Wanna Walk You Home."

"It's Fats Domino," Norma yelled again.

Uncle Leo began singing:

"I wanna walk you home. Please let me walk you home.
You look so good to me, ooo-ooo-wee.
I love the way you walk. I love the way you talk…"

He had a great voice. We hushed, giving him our full attention. We were enthralled, and we looked forward to more daily walks, complete with serenatas.

During the evenings, after The Kids were in bed and not climbing all over Uncle Leo, the adults sat around and reminisced about the "good old days" back in Texas.

After that first visit, Aunt Alice made it a point to visit every few years, but Uncle Leo, always busy working, never got a chance to return. It was great for Aunt Alice and Mom to spend time together—and for us to be able to bond with our far-away Texas aunt. We never forgot Uncle Leo.

❦

Of my older siblings, Viola was the one who stayed with the family the longest. When Viola was fresh out of high school, Lydia's insistence, guidance and perseverance helped her secure a job with a prominent attorney, William D. Aikin, in Sunnyside, the next town over from Grandview.

"Viola, look, there's a job announcement in the newspaper. It's for a secretarial job in Sunnyside."

"What? Let's see," Viola said sitting next to Lydia at the dining room table.

Lydia pushed the paper towards her. Pointing at the job announcement she said, "This is perfect."

"Lydia, it says, 'Legal Secretary and experience is required'. I'll never get this job."

"Don't you want a good office job? Isn't that what you stayed in school for? You don't need to work in the fields anymore. Here's your chance."

"Let's go to our room," Viola said looking around, "Don't let Mom and Dad hear us." She grabbed the paper, and Lydia followed her into the bedroom.

Viola closed the door and then sat on the bed opposite Lydia. "Look, Lil," she said nervously, "They want legal experience. I don't have that."

"You're smart, you'll learn," Lydia reassured her. "Anyway, they want Spanish fluency. You have that. You have the diploma, you…."

"They also ask for office experience. I don't even have that. I'll never get the job, Lil!"

"You do have office experience. You worked in the school office every year in high school. I think you'll get the job. But even if you don't, you'll still have the experience of applying and interviewing. Either way, you'll come out ahead. You lose absolutely nothing. So come on! Let's figure out what you'll wear."

Reluctantly, Viola gave in to Lydia's insistence. Jumping off the bed, she rushed over to the closet and pulled open the curtain. "What should I wear?" Together, they decided on the appropriate attire for the interview.

Then they rushed out to tell Mom and Dad that they needed the car to go to Sunnyside. Dad ended up driving them to Mr. Aiken's office, and while Dad and Viola waited in the car, Lydia went in for the application form.

Within a week, Viola was called in for an interview. She had not wanted to go, but Lydia had insisted. Viola amazed Mr. Aikin with her intelligence, professionalism, and her typing and shorthand speed. The fact that she was fluent in Spanish was an added bonus. After the interview, Mr. Aikin promptly hired Viola as his legal secretary, a position she would keep for many years.

Mr. Aikin purchased a technical contraption—a dictation/typing machine that was designed to be of essential use in a busy office. It soon became evident that Viola typed faster than the machine. Mr. Aikin returned the gizmo straightaway, saving a lot of money, and again demonstrating Viola's exceptional competence, aptitude and skill.

Thanks to Lydia's persistence, Viola secured the job, embarking upon what would be a lifelong career. Even after marrying and moving out of town, Viola continued working in the legal profession, in a job she loved and excelled in.

Viola helped the family financially, and she also took on the all-consuming role of guardian to all of The Kids. In the late fall and early winter, Mom and Dad had to follow the work. Viola stepped in as guardian, taking charge of our home and The Kids.

Mom and Dad packed up and moved to Othello—and then Quincy—to work in the potatoes. They were getting older, but necessity required them to continue weathering the ice-cold Eastern Washington winters, as well as the long, unbearably hot summers.

One year, as luck would have it, we went through a traumatic experience in their absence. Rudy, Freddy and Norma were out running wild after school, as usual. As dinner time approached, they ran home from play, little Freddy trailing behind.

Gloria was reading in the living room and I was seated in front of the big oil heater in the dining room, engrossed in Edgar Allan Poe's, The Black Cat.

Rudy ran in, followed by Norma. I heard the ruckus but paid them no heed. All of a sudden, my story was interrupted by a knock at the door. I begrudgingly set down my book to see who was there. My baby brother, Freddy, stood in front of me. His face and white T-shirt were drenched in blood, and the flap of his eyelid hung over his eye. Consumed with fear, I stared at him. I had never seen so much blood!

What followed was something of a blur, but I remember rushing out to the car, holding a towel to Freddy's face. Viola took the driver's seat, and I sat with Freddy in the back seat. We headed straight to Dr. Spratt's house—Spratt had been the family physician since we arrived in Grandview.

Little Freddy was in shock—he didn't utter a word for the entire drive. I was terrified that my baby brother would lose his eye and be disfigured for life, if he even survived.

"Dear God," I prayed silently, "please help us. Please heal my baby brother… let him be okay. Please, don't let him lose his eye. Lord God Almighty, have mercy. Please do not forsake us!"

Finally, we were at Dr. Spratt's house. I followed Viola, Freddy, and the doctor down the hallway, and into a sterile-looking room. Dr. Spratt put his hand on my shoulder saying, "Sally, you make yourself comfortable… and, don't worry, your brother will be fine."

I did as he instructed, without question. I was still in shock and I was terrified for my little brother. I kept praying, repeatedly imploring God for mercy. As I tried to review what had happened, it dawned on me that none of us had said a word during the drive to the doctor's house. I knew I hadn't stopped my silent prayers. If Viola had said anything, I didn't hear it.

Sitting in an overstuffed chair in the hall, I realized I was shaking, and my heart was racing like never before. I slipped off my shoes and curled up my legs. For the first time in my life, I feared losing a loved one. I just didn't know how to handle this new fear. All I could do was pray, as I had often seen Mom do. I had faith—both in God and in the doctor's skill—yet the fear that enveloped me was staggering. I felt weak.

I wished I had a rosary, something to touch and make me feel closer to God. "Please hear my prayer, God. Please heal my little brother. He's so innocent, please help him." Oh, how I long for my mother! I wished she were here with us. I knew God heard Mom's prayers—always—she had an open line, a special connection. But perhaps I wasn't worthy. Maybe God wouldn't or couldn't hear my pleas. Surely God wouldn't punish Freddy for my sinfulness. He was an innocent child. I agonized over my baby brother's fate.

After what seemed like forever, the door Dr. Spratt had taken Freddy through, opened. Viola walked out leading Freddy. Dr. Spratt followed, saying, "Now, then, I'll see you in a few days to take a look at your stitches, Freddy."

"Yes, doctor, I'll make the appointment," Viola replied.

"Don't worry, Freddy. Everything is going to be fine," the doctor said, nodding at Viola. "You're going to be good as new."

I vaguely heard Viola thank Dr. Spratt. I sighed deeply, realizing that God had heard my pleas and answered my prayers. Dr. Spratt was a hero.

On the ride home, Viola said, "Freddy, thank God the cut is above your eye. Things could have been a lot worse. We need to thank God that you're going to be okay. We'll go to the six o'clock mass tomorrow."

Freddy nodded his head as I whispered, "Yeah, we should."

We later learned that Freddy had fallen into the end of the irrigation ditch that ran past our house. Because he had been trailing Rudy and Norma, nobody was aware that he had fallen. The end of the ditch was a dangerous spot. It was where water was either released and allowed to flow, or shut off when the area farmers wanted to stop the flow.

When Freddy fell in, he hit his head on the ragged edge of a sawed-off pipe. I shuddered to think what might have happened if he hadn't closed his eyes. My two little brothers kept their guardian angels working overtime! That day, we were all thankful for the divine intervention that saved Freddy and his eye.

Dr. Spratt had put fifteen stitches inside and fifteen on the outside of his eyelid. Today, the scar is hardly noticeable, but Freddy says that he will never forget the incident. He says he remembers it every time he looks in the mirror.

We will always be eternally grateful to our good doctor for saving little Freddy. Knowing that Dr. Spratt was Catholic only deepened our faith in him.

As a child, going to Dr. Spratt's office—on Grandview's main street—was a scary experience. Mom held my hand tightly as I entrusted myself to her motherly warmth and security.

Entering the door off the street, I faced a wide, steep and dark stairway. The lighting was dim, and the stairs were dark, which only intensified the ominous aura. I always had a pang of fear in the pit of my stomach as we entered the dark hallway and climbed slowly up the stairs. The floor was shiny and spotless, and the smell of alcohol and disinfectant became stronger as we neared the top. Dr. Spratt's office was sterile and immaculately clean.

Inside, I faced a large waiting room that looked much like the stairway. The dark floor was spotless. Chairs were lined up against the wall, and patients sat and waited in solemn silence. Small tables held dated magazines and other reading material. Behind her counter, the receptionist typed away and quietly answered the telephone.

A large portrait hung on the wall. It showed a silver-haired, majestic-looking man with a big silver moustache dressed in a white doctor's shirt (like Dr. Ben Casey on T.V.). He was impeccable, with a look of authority that commanded respect. Every hair—on his head and his moustache—was in place. His nails were clean and perfectly manicured. His creased white outfit looked like it came straight from the dry cleaners. This was Dr. Spratt, our doctorcito who had often come to our aid. He delivered the four youngest in the family—Gloria, Rudy, Norma and Freddy, who were all born in Washington after our move from Texas.

Dr. Spratt was a very tall man with perfect posture. He was such a looming figure—I always had to take refuge behind my mother. As we sat in the waiting room, I nervously but quietly swung my feet. Mom thumbed through a magazine as I fidgeted. When Mom's name was called, I swallowed hard, jumped off my chair, and reached for Mom's hand. We walked together down the hallway and then into Dr. Spratt's office. There he sat, behind his big desk, in all his regal splendor.

He stood politely, his hand outstretched to greet my mother. "Good afternoon, Mrs. Cantu. I hope all is well today."

"I'm fine, doctor, how are you?"

While they chatted, I shivered, knowing my fate. I never let go of my mother's hand, my link to safety. When Mom and Dr. Spratt simultaneously rose, my stomach fell. Swallowing hard and licking my dry lips, I followed them into the doctor's torture chamber.

Mom helped me up onto the examining table. The thin, white sanitary paper only intensified my fear. As I whimpered and squeezed my mother's hand, she looked at me sternly, "Sally, don't make a fuss, pórtate bien hija," she said, rubbing my arm gently. Then, it was time to turn over and lie face down on the table. I dreaded what was inevitably next. I closed my eyes and tensed my entire body while Mom pulled my undies down on one side, saying, "Relajate, o te va doler más." (Relax, or it will hurt more).

Neither the doctor's words nor my mother's reassuring touch could ease my great fear or my anticipation of the impending pain. Dr. Spratt had developed a tried and true technique: First a firm, little slap on my butt, which I was never prepared for, accompanied by his telling me gently to relax. Then came the rough, abrupt shot of penicillin, administered to my little quivering butt.

"Owww!" That awful sting never failed to bring on a torrent of tears, no matter how hard I tried to hold them back.

Viola was so smart that her teachers repeatedly held her up as an example to the rest of The Kids who followed her. All her teachers loved her—what was not to love? She was a straight "A" student, well-mannered, and respectful. A pretty, petite girl, who always had the right answer and excelled at everything.

I recall my high school history teacher, Mr. Freel, admonishing me: "Why can't you be like your sister, Viola?" I shrugged it off and walked away, determined not to dignify his insensitive question with an answer. He didn't have to be so mean.

Although I was just a teenager, I accepted my reality; trying to be like Viola was simply not within my grasp. I didn't realize it at the time, but she was my role model. She was so smart, successful and good. Many people in the area—kids and adults—admired and respected her. Family friends, neighbors, co-workers and clients, all had good things to say about her. They sought her out and valued her opinion and advice. I looked up to her as well, but I didn't think I could ever be as smart or as good as she was.

Maybe when I grow up I'll be at least a little bit like her, I thought. She just always does everything right. Maybe that's what happens when you become an adult. Yeah, right, as if I'm going to magically change into an intelligent person when I grow up. I shouldn't be so stupid. Viola was just born with the gift of intelligence. I was not.

And, of course, Viola was a great guardian when Mom and Dad were gone. In fact, she was too good—too strict, always correcting our errors, insisting on manners at the dinner table, making us do our schoolwork, and chores. Worst of all, she did not allow me to go out, unless I was with her.

Viola's guidance mitigated my low self-esteem. When I learned that my Jr. High Home Economics class was focused on sewing, I thought I was lost. As our final exam, we were expected to show our sewing projects to the entire class and explain how we had made them. That's it! I'm sunk, I thought. No getting out of this one. My only saving grace is that we were allowed to work on our projects at home.

Sitting at the dining room table after dinner, I looked hopelessly at the pattern. It was like a foreign language to me, and the sewing machine and all its intricacies were impenetrable.

Just when I was ready to give up in complete desperation, Viola came to my rescue. "What's wrong, Sally?" she said as I stared hopelessly at the pattern. "What are you having trouble with? Maybe I can help."

"Oh geez," I shrugged, "I just keep looking at this and reading the stupid pattern, but none of it makes sense to me. I don't even know where to start."

"Okay, she said sitting next to me. "Don't worry. It's really easy once you get the hang of it, and you will. I'll show you. I'm surprised your teacher didn't... Oh, that's okay. Never mind. Here," she said, turning the pattern on the table. "You have to start at the beginning of the pattern, see this?"

I nodded.

"This marks the beginning of the pattern, and you follow each step, one at a time. Don't skip a step or go on until you complete each step. So, let's start. First, lay out your material. I did as instructed, and she showed me how to find the grain of the fabric. She read the pattern aloud and we began—laying down each pattern piece, pinning, and cutting.

She taught me how to read and follow the pattern and how to handle the sewing machine like a pro. With her help and guidance, I soon realized that sewing was easy and fun. Initially, I had let myself get overwhelmed, but it was simply a matter of following instructions, step by step.

I worked on my sewing project every spare moment I had, staying up way past my bedtime, never wanting to stop. I loved sewing! To everyone's amazement, I ended up making a five-piece outfit that consisted of a double-breasted jacket with matching skinny pencil pants, an A-line skirt, knickers, and a mod cap. I had attended to every detail, and, at the final hour, the home economics teacher recognized my outstanding work and asked me to model my outfit for the class and some of the teachers. Looking like a model straight out of a fashion magazine, I was proud and very chic! Indeed, I was suddenly the coolest chick in school.

Now a master of design and fashion, I was always one of the first in school to wear the latest craze. When barbarian sandals become the rage, they were nowhere to be found in the entire Yakima Valley. Determined to have them, I bought a pair of sandals and cleverly laced them up to my knees. What a coup! Word got around school, and fellow students went out of their way to peek into my classroom or find me in the hall—they had to have a look at my latest fashion statement.

I loved the attention and the compliments: "Wow, I love your outfit! Where do you get all your cool clothes?" I always smiled and said proudly that I made a lot of my own clothes.

I was very creative, and I seriously considered being a fashion designer when I grew up—either that, or an interior decorator. I couldn't decide which.

If I had only had the proper guidance and assistance, I might have pursued one of those professions. I had the passion and some of the necessary creative skills. But, of course, career counseling wasn't for us Mexican kids. Even Viola, as smart and as perfect as she was, never received career or guidance counseling. That sent a clear message to the rest of the Mexican kids. Thank God Viola had Lydia to encourage and support her, and I, in turn, had Viola.

In contrast to my junior high success in sewing class, my high school success with cooking and becoming the perfect little homemaker was less than stellar. I was simply not interested in becoming a little Miss, nor did I aspire to grow up to be Mrs. June Cleaver, prancing around the kitchen in my high heels, pearls and fancy apron.

The art of cooking was never my forte, although I had learned the art of spices, sauces, and homemade tortillas from my mother. In spite of this, my efforts at cooking were rarely a hit—in fact, they left much to be desired.

When I was a senior in high school, my home economics teacher, Mrs. Rice, informed the class that our final exam would require the preparation of a dish in front of the class while we explained, step by step, what was involved in its preparation. My first priority was to pick a simple recipe.

"Well," I told my cousin Sylvia, "It's not going to be fidello—that's for sure, even if it is one of the few things I can cook."

"Oh, I know, Sal, that's too…, um, you know."

"Spit it out, Syl! It's too Mexican, right?"

"Well, yeah, but too simple, you know? Like too… poor people's food."

"Aha, I know! How about pollo en crema? That's perfect—delicious and it's kind of Mexican and kind of Gringo."

We both agreed pollo en crema—a mouth-watering chicken dish smothered in a rich cream sauce served over cheesy biscuits—was the perfect choice.

I had pre-measured everything, and I had pre-cooked and shredded the chicken pieces. I was very well prepared as I explained the recipe to the class: 1 cup of this, ¼ cup of that, teaspoon, tablespoon, mix and knead, etc.

My presentation was going smoothly. I prepared the biscuits in a jiffy, spooning them onto the baking sheet and placing them safely in the oven. I moved to the next step, preparing the deliciously rich chicken sauce. When I had all ingredients in the pan, I suddenly realized that something was terribly wrong. This isn't right! Why is my sauce so thick and lumpy? In a matter of seconds, I found myself panicking, sweat beading on my forehead. I felt warm and flushed. My heart raced as I wiped my sweaty hands on my apron. I glanced quickly at the recipe and realized what I had done. Instead of a quarter cup of flour, I had used a whole cup. No! Aye, Dios Santo! What now? I hemmed and hawed, opening and shutting drawers until I finally found a hand beater.

"Uh, there's a little problem," I said, looking up at the teacher. "Uh, just one minute, okay?"

I scanned the class and gave my cousin/best friend Sylvia, a wide-eyed frantic look. Sylvia could see I was panicked. She jumped up from her seat and rushed to my side as I desperately tried to work the hand beater.

Syl and I stood, facing the counter, our backs to the class. "Oh, my God!" I whispered between clenched teeth. "Syl, this beater won't budge…."

The mixture was much too thick for a simple hand beater. I was getting hotter by the second. I could feel my face redden. In desperation, I tried with all my might to make the damn beater work, but I lost my grip.

"Eee!" I squeaked loudly. I slapped my hand over my open mouth as the beater went flying. It hit the counter, bounced against the wall, landed back on the counter, and finally rolled off the counter onto the floor. There was pasty gunk everywhere. I looked down at my feet. The beater had splattered me, the floor, and anything else within reach, with thick, sticky particles of dough.

Before I could even look up, Sylvia was on her knees before me, wet paper towels in hand, wiping off my shoes and legs.

"It's Okay, Sal," she whispered, grabbing the doughy beater and throwing it in the sink. My vision blurred as I stood helpless. Embarrassed, I looked up at the class.

Finally, Mrs. Rice said, "Everything is all right, class. We just have a little mishap. Sally, we'll move on to the next person to give you a chance to clean up, and then we'll come back to you."

"Yes, Mrs. Rice…um, thank you. I just need a few minutes. Sorry." I smiled lamely.

In a frenzy, Sylvia and I began throwing away lumps of dough and quickly cleaning up the mess. Luckily, it was an easy recipe, so I just started over, and by the time the class returned its attention to me, everything was fine—I was no longer in shock.

Despite the mishap, I managed to complete my final project successfully. Thanks to Cousin Sylvia's quick intervention and Mrs. Rice's sympathy, I passed the class, producing a beautiful, delicious dish. If this presentation had only been videotaped, we simply would have cut the horror scene.

My cousin Sylvia and I were inseparable. Syl and Sal—together through good times and bad, we triumphed over many challenges and difficulties, and we shared all of our teenage dreams, schemes, agonies and glories.

Even during the seasons when we didn't work, we Kids never had time for sports and after-school activities. Spring and fall, we worked in the fields after school. Along with Mom and Dad, we picked grapes and current berries, worked in the hops—whatever work there was, we did. When we weren't working, we were needed at home. Our chores and responsibilities were never-ending. Dad didn't have time to drive us to and from school for activities, nor could we afford such luxuries. It was the same with all of our Mexican friends. Regardless of how much initiative or talent we had, we realized, sadly, that sports and other extracurricular activities were for the White students.

The entire family was good at sports, especially the boys. My older brothers, Efrain and Hector, excelled in the Army—both physically and intellectually. Because they had worked in the fields, they were in excellent physical condition as they were used to the hard farm worker life. But they also performed very well on intelligence tests, amazing their superiors because neither of them had earned a high school diploma.

The younger Kids—Rudy, Freddy and Norma—also excelled at sports, but they couldn't realize their full potential. Most teachers and coaches simply weren't willing to work with or help the Mexican kids.

One year, the four boys on Rudy's track team broke the school record for the 440-yard relay. To acknowledge their great achievement, the coach and principal posted their names on the board in the main hallway of the school. A few years later, Freddy and his three track teammates broke the earlier school record. Rudy's name came down, replaced by his little brother's. Freddy beamed with pride—to take Rudy's place was a major accomplishment.

When Freddy's track team was scheduled to compete against other schools, they proudly held on to their first-place standing. Unfortunately, Freddy had to miss some practices and couldn't afford to pay the towel fee that the school had recently imposed. Mom and Dad didn't understand having to pay for the use of towels. "Hijo, we have plenty of towels," said Mom. "We don't need to spend money on things we already have. Just take some towels to school."

"But, Mom, I can't. They won't let us take our own towels. It's a rule. We have to pay the towel fee. I already asked the coach."

"Well, tell the man to talk to me. It's ridiculous. No tenemos dinero." Mom was firm. She had already spoken to Dad about it, and the decision was final. They were not about to pay for something we already had. Money was tight.

Freddy tried to explain his dilemma to Coach Ryan, imploring him to understand. The coach refused to listen, saying, "Rules are rules, and there will be no exceptions. You either bring in that towel fee tomorrow, or you're off the team."

Without Freddy on the team, they were beaten by another school. Grandview High School lost its first-place standing. Freddy knew his team would have won if only the coach hadn't been so heartless and cruel by denying him the chance to participate. It was a devastating blow, but it was a typical example of Coach Ryan's backward thinking.

Later, Freddy went to pick up his sports letter from the coach. "You don't have a letter coming, Fred. You quit the team," Mr. Ryan admonished.

"No, I didn't. Mr. Ryan," Freddy replied, "you know I didn't quit and I won every race I ran—and my team won."

"Freddy, you're dismissed. It's no use arguing. My decision is final," Mr. Ryan responded callously. Fighting back anger and tears, Freddy left the coach's office. He knew he had earned his letter through hard work and exemplary performance.

Rushing down the empty hall, he said, "And now I'm late for history." He punched the wall with his fist. "I earned that letter. He can't deny it to me." Freddy was crushed, but he was also very angry.

As he sat in history class, Freddy fumed over this great injustice. I earned my letter, he thought, how can he get away with this? Other guys missed events. They didn't get kicked off the team, and they still got their letters. Freddy slammed his fist on his desk.

"Mr. Cantú! I'll thank you to join the rest of us and stop disrupting the class," said Mr. Freel.

"Yes, I'm sorry, Mr. Freel. I was just trying to swat a fly on my desk." Everyone laughed. Freddy just smiled. Alright, he thought, for now I need to let this go. I'll think of something... but I will get my letter.

The very next day, Mr. Ryan was not in the school office. Freddy calmly walked up to the counter. Cool and collected, he greeted the school secretary, "Hi, Mrs. Jones. I'm here to pick up my sports letter."

Mrs. Jones smiled and walked over to the files. Freddy held his breath while he waited. As she sorted through the letters, Mrs. Jones mumbled to herself.

"Oh, here it is," she smiled, pulling out his letter. Freddy sighed deeply as he put both hands on the counter, quietly drumming his fingers in anticipation.

Just then, the telephone rang.

No! Freddy thought, Give me my letter first, before Mr. Ryan shows up.

"Good afternoon—Grandview High School. Can you please hold? Thank you."

Whew, thought Freddy, biting his lip. He relaxed his clenched fists as Mrs. Jones handed him his letter.

"There you are, Freddy, and congratulations," she smiled.

Freddy politely thanked her and walked out into the hallway. "Yes!" he beamed, raising his clenched fist in the air.

Mom sewed the letter on his jacket that evening, and Freddy wore it proudly.

Freddy also excelled in wrestling, but because of work, he missed too many practices, and, once again, he lacked money for equipment and towels. Mom and Dad simply did not understand the importance of sports and extracurricular activities. There was no time. They were always working, and The Kids' work after school provided much-needed additional income. Their utmost priority was providing for the family. The family's survival meant everything. They expected all of us to make sacrifices. Still, it was hard for The Kids to understand this—we were just trying to fit in at school, despite our difficult circumstances.

Because he was older than Freddy, Rudy always had the upper hand. He was suave and debonair, the Latin lover lady's man. He was good at sports, a cool and trendy dresser, and a joker who always had the other kids in stitches. When Freddy reached high school, he felt he was destined to be in Rudy's shadow. Because of his haircut and his resemblance to the beloved and handsome Vulcan in the very popular Star Trek series, Rudy was known as Mr. Spock by all his peers. Kids often approached Freddy asking, "Hey, where's Mr. Spock?"

It didn't take long for Freddy to tire of this nonsense. He decided to put an end to it, once and for all. The next time someone approached asking for Spock, Freddy pulled out his wallet, flipped it open with a quick turn of the wrist, and spoke into it, "Kirk to enterprise; come in, Spock." He flipped the wallet shut again, put it back in his pocket, and walked away, without so much as a sideways glance at the inquiring bystander left behind in his dust. Freddy was done with bowing down to Rudy and scrambling to do his bidding. Winning his sports letter just put the icing on the cake. No longer the baby brother, Freddy was now his own man.

Although all of The Kids graduated from high school and went on to the University of Washington, we had all begun working in the fields at the age of twelve. Unlike our older siblings, who had quit school in order to work full-time, The Kids only worked after school in the spring and fall, and full-time in the summer.

Thanks to our oldest sister, Lydia's, insight and influence on our parents, we stayed in school. But in the summer, there was no such thing as summer break or vacation. For us, summer meant back-breaking work in the fields alongside Mom and Dad. It was a rude awakening and an abrupt, early end to childhood.

It was the summer of 1964 when Mom, Dad and all of us Kids first packed up and moved to Quincy, Washington, for the sizzling-hot months. We didn't know it then, but Quincy would be our summer home for many years to come.

Viola was the only older sibling still living at home. The others had married or joined the military. Viola was also the only older sibling who had, upon Lydia's insistence, graduated from high school. Consequently, she did not go to Quincy with the rest of us. During our summer absence, she worked at her job as a legal secretary and she took care of everything at home.

Working in the fields was a sudden and abrupt change from our daily routine as school children. It had lasting consequences—the hot, hard labor was traumatic, and it imprinted itself on our collective psyche. I didn't see it coming. Leaving our comfortable home was difficult for all of us, but this was The Kids' induction into the real world, a world where we could no longer be shielded from injustice, hardship, sorrow and indignity.

My childhood world seemed but a dream and oh-so-far away. Try as I might to hold onto the innocence, joy and comfort of childhood, it was no longer possible. I had embarked upon a whole new journey in life. That shift was a cruel, harsh point of no return. Leaving childhood and its innocence behind, I felt as though the good part of life was over and only hopelessness and hardship lay ahead.

It was as though every grueling summer brought the wrath of the cruel and jealous ancient Gods upon us. I struggled to understand why we were being punished—why I was being punished. How I cringed every time I heard kids in school talking about their summer vacation plans!

"We're going to Disneyland this summer. What are you doing for vacation?" Someone would ask.

"Oh, I can't wait!" someone else would respond. "We're going to visit my grandparents in California. They have a big ranch, with horses and everything."

I detested these excited exchanges:

"We're going here."

"Well, we're going there. And we get to do this, and we get to do that..."

It was always the White kids who got to take vacations and the Mexican kids who had to work. That just made the whole ordeal more agonizing. "Why?" I asked myself, knowing that the simple truth was that we were poor. There was no sense dwelling on the injustice of it all—yet I couldn't let go of it either.

When we arrived in Quincy, Mom and Dad always rented a house from one of the farmers we worked for. The details had been worked out by mail and telephone before our arrival. In the summer of 1967, however, the house we had arranged to rent was not ready when we arrived. It was determined that we would stay in a cheap motel for a few days until the farmer had our house ready. It would be a short stay, so we were told only to unpack the few things we really needed. By the time we arrived at the motel, it was late, and we were all tired and in bad spirits.

I was fifteen years old and thus accustomed to our hard summers—I had a few of them behind me already. I might have been used to the hard, hot farm work, but I hated and resented it nonetheless.

I loathed moving to Quincy. I loathed leaving the comforts of our home and living the migrant life for those long, unbearable months. I thought we were past that when we moved out of the labor camp. But, more than anything, I dreaded the actual work in the fields. Still, I had to acknowledge that we were very lucky we didn't have to work full-time during the rest of the year. I knew kids who had to quit school to work, just as my older brothers and sisters had done.

In that ugly motel room, as I wallowed in self-pity, I disdainfully opened the kitchen cupboard. Something scurried by in a flash and I quickly jumped back.

"Oh, my God!" I screamed, jumping back and banging against the wall behind me. "Help!" Before I could even finish my thought, another huge thing—a bug, I thought—scurried out and froze in its steps as I screamed again. It ran out of sight as I cautiously leaned forward and slammed the door shut.

Rudy and Freddy rushed in, followed by Norma and Gloria. Choking on my words, I struggled for breath.

"A huge bug or some kind of animal!" I cried. "Animals…in there!" I shouted, pointing at the cupboard as I backed away. Mom and Dad rushed in to see what the borlote was about.

"¿Qué está pasando?" Dad asked.

"¿Qué tienes, hija?" Mom echoed.

I continued sobbing and carrying on. Mom was doing her best to calm me down. She sent me and the rest of The Kids out of the kitchen so she and Dad could investigate. Por su puesto, Rudy stayed in the kitchen with Mom and Dad.

"I'll help," he said, shooing the rest of us out.

It didn't take my parents long to determine that the place was infested with cucarachas!

"What?" we all gasped, looking at each other and then at Mom and Dad. I saw that my mother was upset, but she tried to make light of the situation while Dad assured us everything would be fine and that we would leave first thing in the morning.

I felt faint. I simply wanted to die! I was completely self-absorbed in my anguish and devastation. All I could think of is how incredibly miserable and unfortunate I was. In my selfish teenage angst, I didn't even think of how my poor parents must be suffering. I didn't give the rest of The Kids a second thought.

We had no choice but to spend the night there, though I doubted anybody would get much sleep. I kept hearing noises, but the rest of The Kids said I was imagining things. I had dark and scary dreams in which the cucarachas rallied against me. They had turned into big monsters, and they laughed at my helplessness against them as I ran and tried to hide. My efforts to scream were futile—I couldn't find my voice. I woke up gasping for air.

Early the next morning, my mother called the health department, which promptly closed the entire place down. I didn't know where all the residents would go, but at least they wouldn't continue living in those infested, disease-ridden conditions. Thanks to Mom and Dad, who would not tolerate such indignities, we were all saved from such inhumane conditions.

We suffered many injustices throughout our lives. Many situations were beyond our control, but for my parents there was a limit. Fully aware that the law afforded us at least a modicum of protection, they did not hesitate to do what was necessary to stand up for themselves and the family. It was a blessed relief, and it afforded us a very satisfying sense of justice.

My Mom and Dad were something else, absolutely incredible. I'm sorry to say that it took me quite some time to realize, much less appreciate, what remarkable people my parents were.

Every morning, my mother woke us at the last minute in an effort to let us get a little extra sleep.

"¡Levantense! Get up! It's almost time to go. ¡Niños! Come and eat."

She and Dad had been up for some time, preparing for the work day. Mom dressed quickly and rushed to the kitchen to prepare breakfast and lunch for the day. She prepared a hot, fresh breakfast—including homemade tortillas—every morning. Frozen, packaged or canned food was not an option. Whatever Mom cooked would be rolled into soft tacos for lunch. Regular staples for breakfast and lunch included papitas, huevos, ham or bacon, beans, tortillas and picadillo or chicken taquitos.

Mom moved through the kitchen so quickly that I often thought she could navigate it blindfolded. She left the breakfast dishes soaking in the sink for quick clean up before dinner.

While Mom was working in the kitchen, Dad was busy filling insulated gallon jugs with water. He packed the cooler with ice and sodas and anything else that needed to be kept cold—Mexican cheese, salsa, whatever. Mom prepared café de olla and Dad poured it into the thermos.

When it was time to go Dad yelled out, "Vámonos ya, apúrense."

We responded by running out to the station wagon, yelling, "Okay! Coming!"

By the time we Kids ran out, everything was already packed: food, drinks, hoes, blade sharpener, sombreros, gloves, extra scarves. Each and every workday throughout the summer, it never occurred to any of us Kids that all the preparation and packing entailed so much extra work, all done by Mom and Dad, although Rudy often helped Dad with the water jugs. Rudy didn't take as long as us girls to get dressed.

Dressing for work in the fields was an act of survival. As hot as it was, we had to be completely covered to avoid sunburn and sunstroke. We covered ourselves in long sleeves and gloves and tied up our long hair in a farmworker scarf—red, navy or black bandanas. A huge Mexican straw sombrero was the final touch to cover our heads and shade our faces from the blazing rays of the sun. Comfortable shoes, usually boots or tennis shoes, were a must for walking miles over the uneven, dusty terrain.

As soon as the car was loaded, off we went, as early as possible, to take full advantage of the cool morning hours before the sun's full force blazed down upon us in the 100-degree-plus weather.

The first time I worked in the fields, I dressed appropriately, but when Mom handed me the big straw sombrero, I protested. "I'm not wearing that ridiculous thing!" I said defiantly.

Mom and Dad looked at each other knowingly and Dad told Mom, "Dejala, más tarde se lo pone." He was right. After a while in the fields, I asked for the ridiculous sombrero to shield me from the blinding, blazing, sun. Promptly, I learned that being a farmworker was serious business. I had to leave my vanity by the wayside. Besides, ridiculous or not, who would see me out here? More to the point, who cared?

I would learn very soon that a ridiculous sombrero and my general appearance were the least of my worries. I was in the big leagues now, yet at this stage in the game I was still totally unprepared for all that lay ahead.

In Quincy, we usually worked in the beets, but on occasion we worked in the bean fields. Using a long-handled hoe, we carefully dug out all the weeds from our rows, making sure we did not damage the plant in the process. Dad cautioned us to be very careful not to pull up a beet or bean plant and to be sure to remove all the weeds.

The bean fields were harder to hoe because of the difficulty distinguishing the tiny bean plants from the smaller weeds. It was easy to destroy the bean plant along with the weed. Those darned bean plants were very delicate. During lunch and after work, I would discretely empty my bulging pockets of the little bean plants I had accidently cut with my hoe. Since I wore a big, loose shirt, my bulging pockets didn't show.

"I'm going to the bathroom," I sang out when we broke for lunch or at the end of our workday. Off I ran with my hoe to find a discreet spot, dig a little hole, and bury the evidence of my many mistakes. "Hurry!" I whispered to myself, emptying my pockets as fast as I could. This became my daily ritual in every bean field we worked.

I doubt that I fooled Mom and Dad, but I proceeded cautiously with my supposedly secret little ceremony. They probably pitied me and laughed it off. We had to make light of our suffering or go crazy, I suppose.

Our summer days were an endless march up and down the rows of whichever field we were weeding. Covered from head to toe, we walked with bowed heads intent on our work. Up and down, in and out, row after never ending row.

Glancing up, I saw the heat waves slithering like snakes up and off the ground then dissolving into the suffocating, hot air. Suddenly, a popular song popped into my head and I began singing softly to myself as a veil of sadness came over me:

"To everything, turn, turn, turn/There is a season, turn, turn, turn/ And a time to every purpose under heaven...."*

Every "turn, turn, turn" seemed like the endless row before me, which I would finally finish, only to turn around into the next, and then the next, and the next. "Forever and never-ending," I muttered. "World without end. Amen."

---

* From the book of Ecclesiastes in the Bible; in 1965, the Pete Seeger song became an international hit song for The Byrds.

What was the purpose? What was my purpose, our purpose? To work like beasts of burden for minimal pay? Where was the justice? "Dear God, why have you abandoned us?" I wondered. "Why?" I prayed for God to release us from our hardships. "God, it's too hot. I'm so tired… there's no end."

I wiped my sweaty forehead and face with my shirt sleeve then slowly pulled off my right glove. My cracked, dry lips stung, yet I licked them repeatedly, knowing full well that licking only made them worse. Reaching into my pocket with my sweaty, dirty hand, I pulled out my melted chap stick. I saw Dad in front of me, up ahead, followed by Mom and Rudy, in the rows next to me. I was falling too far behind.

"Oh, God, give us strength," I whispered looking up helplessly at the sky. "Lord, are you there? Do you see our suffering? Why don't you help us?" I closed my eyes in everlasting hopelessness.

Then, I hurried to catch up, knowing that if I fell behind, poor Dad would have to help me out of my row. I hurried, trying to ignore what I had just said to God. I had been disrespectful. I had even dared to question his very existence. I felt like Cain, fleeing God in the garden after his great sin. I pushed it all down into the recesses of my mind.

"Just hurry, you fool," I admonished myself while at the same time trying to occupy my mind with other thoughts. It was important we all work at a steady pace. Besides, the end of the row meant a cool sip of water.

I preferred working in the newer fields, where the beets were small. By the time the beets had grown high and leafy, it was harder to maneuver between the rows. The bigger the beets, the more difficult it was to see the smaller weeds underneath, and there were always creepy crawlers under those huge beet leaves—bugs, spiders, mice, worms, and even snakes. I had a phobia of snakes, worms, and caterpillars. The beet plants often become infested with caterpillars, so much so that the whole plant was covered with the horrible, wiggling creatures. It was like a horrible nightmare!

I thought that it was only by the grace of God that I had not died of fright! More than once, I asked God to release me from the horror of my phobias and the burden of my life. My silent nightly prayers implored God to be merciful: "Please, Lord, don't let me encounter any creepy crawlers tomorrow. Please. Amen."

Mom and Dad never forgot that I was terrified. They never failed me. As if by instinct, Dad would come to my rescue, sending me way ahead as he and Rudy worked a large segment of my row, insuring that I could circle widely around the infested area. I was accustomed to their warnings; one of them would yell out, "Go around this part." With my heart pounding wildly, I promptly heeded their instruction. They afforded Gloria the same courtesy.

Por lo contrario, Rudy never needed rescuing; he was always muy macho, and he bragged dramatically, "I fear not these harmless critters!" Holding the hoe in his right hand as though it were his mighty sword, he stood valiantly, with his left fist in the air. Little brother Rudy, always such a character, trying to make light of difficult situations with humor. He always proudly assumed the role of protector.

Rudy got many of his humorous cues from the Looney Tunes Cartoon series we watched on Saturday mornings, during the school year. But our summers didn't allow for Saturday morning cartoons or anything much, other than work.

Rudy was always a sight to behold. More often than not, he wore one of Dad's big shirts. He might not have even been conscious of the fact that was trying to fill Dad's shoes. After all, as a macho with so many sisters, he had a reputation to uphold. Next to Dad, he was the man—and, thus, the protector—of the family.

He was still so very young, yet he carried a huge responsibility on his small shoulders. But to him it was not a burden—it was an honorable duty. It just went without saying. That's the way it was, y punto.

I felt sorry for Gloria. At least I could tolerate bugs and even the little bucktooth/yellow-toothed field mice, as long as they didn't touch my skin. I even held and petted the little mice with my gloved hands. They were kind of pathetic looking, and I almost felt sorry for them, but they seemed happy and relieved when we let them go. We never harmed them. I'm sure they were a nuisance to Mom and Dad, but to me they were a welcome distraction. We were always careful to keep them away from Gloria. She didn't share our enthusiasm, and we didn't want to upset her. I could relate to her fear only too well.

Fear was the biggest part of my agony in the big beet fields. Sure, I didn't care about the mice, bugs or even spiders, but dear God! I was scared to death of those other crawling, abhorrent, vile things! The fact that we were practically dying of heat stroke, thirst and fatigue—if not hopelessness—paled in comparison to my horror of those repulsive, wiggly creatures.

Of course, we had water, but it wasn't going to magically appear in the middle of a long row. Mom and Dad never complained. Instead they tried to distract us with talk or funny stories.

Mom looked up at the sky on those dreadfully hot, dry, days and called upon San Antonio's mercy. Her little ritual was always the same: Looking up at the sky, she would take off her right glove, cup her right hand to the side of her mouth, and sing out, "Sopla, San Antonio, Sopla." Sure enough, San Antonio answered her plea, and a slight breeze would blow against our cheeks.

I was always ready for San Antonio's response. With my head raised and eyes closed, I waited for the little breeze. Then I smiled, saying softly, "Umm...gracias, San Antonio."

We constantly bothered my poor mother: "Mom, call San Antonio."

She always obliged us. It was a funny thing though, San Antonio answered my mother's plea almost every time, but he didn't seem to hear any of the rest of us very often. My mother had a special, ready audience with God and the members of La Corte Celestial, because she had seriously earned it. I guessed the rest of us had not yet earned that special privilege.

As meticulous as Dad was about keeping records in his little pocket notebook, he was even more meticulous when it came to our work in the fields—indeed, any field worked by his family had to reflect good work. The Cantús were widely known as good, dependable, and hard workers. Dad made sure that we started and finished our workday on schedule, taking time for lunch and appropriate breaks. We were all conscientious about our work, just as Dad had taught us. Work was a serious matter, and none of us Kids ever messed around with anything work-related.

Many people worked in big crews, but Mom and Dad were adamant about the fact that often a crew would get a bad reputation due to one or two careless people. They explained that in a crew if one person did a bad job it reflected badly on the entire crew.

I hoped we would work with a crew, thinking it would be a great distraction to have other kids my own age to talk to, but my parent's explanation made sense. We would never jeopardize our family's reputation in that way.

Dad said, "No podemos correr el riesgo. Nuestra reputación está en juego y nuestra reputación es precisamente la garantía de un trabajo estable cada año."

I understood perfectly and couldn't argue against Dad's logic. I never touched upon that subject, nor did any of The Kids. Work was not something to be taken lightly, it was our very means of survival. We all understood that only too well.

On an incredibly hot day, as I sat in the backseat on the drive home from work, I took off my farmworker scarf, untied my ponytail and shook my long hair loose. The cooler sat next to me on the seat. Hot, tired and sleepy, I was thankful that the work day was over. I closed my eyes, slumped down into the seat, and lay my head back. My breathing slowed to a steady pace as I started to drift off. The drive was quiet until, suddenly, I heard Mom and Dad talking.

Slowly opening my eyes, I saw what they were talking about. Several teenagers with hoes were out in a field, as if they are working. They were laughing and playing and inappropriately dressed for field work. Mom said it was, no doubt, the patrón's daughter and her friends earning extra money.

I found myself wide awake, staring fixedly at the teenagers. They were dressed in shorts and sleeveless t-shirts, their blond hair flying loose. The sight jolted me out of my peaceful, dreamy state. I sat straight up on the seat, feeling a penetrating inner heat envelop me. My hands were sweating and shaking, and I could hear my heart pounding as I turned my head, staring intently out the back window. Rage, anger and hatred boiled inside me. They were making a mockery out of what we did out of necessity, for our very survival.

"Idiots," I said, shaking my head and clenching my jaw. They're out there having fun, laughing, playing. They're not seriously working. To them, it's all a game, I thought angrily.

Soon, the nauseating scene receded from view as we drove on, but the sight of them was etched in my mind. Thankful that I was in the back seat, where Mom and Dad couldn't see my reaction, I took a deep, enraged breath in an effort to contain myself. Closing my eyes tightly and rubbing my forehead, I struggled to hold back tears. With my elbows on my knees, I held my palms tightly against my tired, stinging eyes. I cleared my constricted throat, unclenched my jaw and slumped back in my seat.

The profound and inexplicable sadness that rushed over me was more than I could bear. Without an outlet for my anger, I caved in on myself. I closed my eyes again, pushed the cooler sideways and lay down on the seat in a fetal position, feeling completely drained of strength as an overwhelming sense of hopelessness swept over me. Crazy, mixed-up thoughts raced through my head as I finally resigned myself to the fact that no amount of anger, hatred or sadness was going to change this cruel reality. Right or wrong, this is the way it was and there was nothing I could do to change it. I was so incredibly tired, tired to the depth of my bones.

Arriving home, I rushed from the car and tried my best to compose myself, but I didn't even have the strength to take off my shoes and shake the dirt out of them. I didn't care. Feeling powerless and desperate, I wanted to cry. It took every fiber of my being to hold back the tears.

I couldn't let Mom, Dad, or any of The Kids know anything was wrong. I couldn't answer any questions or explain anything to anyone. I felt all mixed up inside and didn't even understand the extreme feelings I was experiencing. I just felt a deep, empty sadness. I wanted to escape. Why, dear God, why? I kept thinking. I just wanted to sleep and—though I knew it was mortally sinful—I did not want to wake up again.

Going straight to the bedroom, I dropped face down on the mattress I shared with my sisters on the floor. Burying my face into the pillow, I finally let my tears flow. The next thing I knew, Mom was calling me to get up for work. I had slept hard, through dinner until morning. I woke up in the same position where I had fallen the day before, lying on my stomach with my feet (my shoes still full of dirt) hanging off of the mattress.

# Chapter 5

Summer, 1968, was like any other, with sizzling-hot days. Heat waves rising from the dirt in blurry, writhing motions through the harsh brightness of the sun, while we trudged—sweaty, dusty, thirsty and fatigued—up and down the rows of yet another torturously long beet field.

As the sun burned down upon us, no one mentioned the heat, except for Mom, whose occasional pleas beseeched San Antonio: "San Antonio, sopla." Calling upon San Antonio often brought a very slight breeze across our cheeks, just enough to be grateful for. We didn't talk about how hot it was or how tired or dusty we were. I knew—we all did—that talking about the obvious and being powerless to change it would only make things worse. So, we trudged onward, occasionally wiping our brows or sighing deeply, but rarely did we complain aloud. Our best defense was distraction. We talked and laughed as much as possible—without compromising the quality of our work.

Estimating how much distance we might cover before our next break, Dad had parked the car accordingly. Rudy would proudly drive the car farther up as we progressed, always thrilled with any chance to practice his driving. I wanted to drive too, but I was not as ambitious as my little brother.

Day in and day out, we endured the same hopeless routine. Tending two rows at a time, we began hoeing out the weeds, stooping to pull them out when we had to. The weeds that grew too close to the beet plant had to be pulled out by hand. We could not risk damaging the plant. Finishing the ends of our rows at the far end of the field brought no respite, no relief. It was simply our cue to turn around and take the next two rows, heading back down the field, again, to where we had started—up and down, repeatedly, throughout the interminably long, hot day.

We tried to make a complete round before drinking any water, but when we couldn't hold out that long, we yelled at little Freddy to bring the water jug.

Rudy or Norma whistled. "Fred! Water!" Poor little Freddy, still too young to work, came trudging through the beet rows, struggling to carry the heavy jug.

"Come on! Move it! We're dying here," Rudy yelled impatiently.

Finally, it was time for an afternoon break. We took a brief rest while Dad sharpened our hoes. Then, almost as soon as we had sat down, it was time to return to the field. Again immersed in our work, we tried not to think about the 103-degree heat and the sun's blinding, burning rays. I was sixteen. Today, Dad and I worked side by side.

I listened intently to my father's soft voice, feeling a special connection between us, as he told me stories he had heard as a child about Pancho Villa, Emiliano Zapata and the Mexican Revolution. Dad had never spoken to me about the Mexican Revolution. I certainly hadn't learned about it in school. I found it fascinating. Completely engrossed in the story, I imagined the impoverished Mexican villages and the revoluciónarios riding for justice, freedom, and the dignity of los campesinos—working people just like us.

Suddenly, a chilling scream shattered my beautiful dream. "¡Apá! ¿Que pasa?" I shouted, jerking my body around as the big weed I had just pulled sprayed dirt everywhere and the hoe slipped out of my grasp. The ruckus was coming from behind us. Something was happening over by Rudy and Norma. As Mom rushed towards them, Gloria stood, motionless. Dad ran towards the commotion. Mom yelled a warning and grabbed Dad's arm. I stared, openmouthed, still holding the big weed in my gloved hand. My heart pounded, and I swallowed hard, trying to clear the choking sensation in my dry throat. I struggled to catch my breath and to comprehend. Something was terribly wrong.

Norma had been working in her row next to Rudy when she suddenly screamed and froze in terror. Rudy immediately saw the huge rattlesnake. Faster than the speed of lightening and fearless as any storybook hero, he ran to the rescue, yelling and swinging his hoe like a sickle, left to right, distracting the snake and turning its attention towards him.

Dad wanted to take Rudy's place but could not get the snake's attention, nor Rudy's, for that matter. Was it that the creature sensed something about Rudy's indomitable intent? Upon realizing that he might do more harm than good by interfering, Dad resigned himself, saying, "Almighty God, our fate is in your hands. Have mercy. Please, take me instead."

The snake raised its head toward Rudy. We could hear the dry rattling sound it made. Rudy stood, motionless, his eyes locked with the snakes. Neither the snake nor Rudy was backing down.

Staring straight into the snake's beady eyes, Rudy swung his hoe wildly and moved toward the snake. The snake slithered backwards over the rows in a swift, almost graceful sidewinding motion. Never taking its eyes off Rudy, the snake lunged repeatedly at him, even as it moved backward, leaving its fang marks on the wooden hoe handle with practically each strike.

In the blink of an eye, the snake suddenly stopped. Its tongue flickered, its eyes still locked on Rudy. The snake now took the offensive and moved toward Rudy, striking again at the hoe. Now the tables had turned. Rudy was forced to back up—momentarily tottering over the uneven, dusty rows.

We all watched in horror, knowing that it would take a miracle to keep Rudy from falling. We were unnerved by the near silence and the intensity of the scene before us. Everyone was still, except Rudy and the snake, as they moved in slow, precise movements. Horrified and white as a ghost, Mom whispered prayers:

"Padre Nuestro que estás en los cielos, santificado sea tu nombre.... Santa María, madre de Dios...."

The demon serpent now moved quickly, determined to eliminate its pursuer, but el Diablo didn't know who he was dealing with. Suddenly, Rudy and snake again stopped abruptly. Everyone frozen in surreal time. The only sound was the rattle: Tssss, Tssss, tssss....

Again, Rudy took the offensive. The snake slithered backward. Rudy's aggressive display showed it that he was not about to lose this life-or-death struggle. Rudy lunged forward, violently swinging the razor-sharp hoe back and forth. As it retreated, the snake lunged repeatedly, biting at the wooden hoe handle. In a flash, Rudy saw his chance. He quickly lifted his hoe high above his head and brought it down swiftly, the sharp blade glinting in the hot sun. The blow was sharp—a powerful, clean cut. The snake, now in two pieces, lay motionless.

Standing the length of his hoe handle from the snake, Rudy cautiously poked at it with the blade. The venomous reptile lay dead. But just for good measure, Rudy gave it one final blow, beheading the creature. Quickly, he swung once again, slicing off its rattle. Then he buried the snake's angry-looking head. "Good riddance," he said triumphantly, snatching up his trophy against Mom and Dad's protests. "Sorry," he replied, determined not to leave without a relic of his heroic victory.

Rudy had earned the bragging rights to a fantastic story, and he was not about to leave his only tangible proof behind. Like a proud and valiant warrior, he pocketed the rattle as his trophy. At the tender age of thirteen, my little brother was now a man, valiente and muy macho.

Mom and Dad quickly rounded up The Kids, ushering us to the car. Dad told us we were going home early—that the dead snake's mate might still be lurking nearby. Rudy beamed with pride, Norma was pale and faint, Gloria and I were still dazed and little Freddy just wanted to know, "What happened? What's going on?"

Mom never stopped praying as she hugged Rudy and then nudged him towards the car. Next, she hugged and reassured Norma. After a quick drink of water, we all climbed into the car. Rudy sat up front between Mom and Dad. On the ride home, Mom cupped Rudy's chin in her hand. Making the sign of the cross on his forehead and chest, she gave him la bendición.

Mom turned to the rest of us in the back seat, saying, "Aver hijos. En el nombre del Padre, el Hijo, y el Espíritu Santo. Que Dios los bendiga y los guarde en su cuidado siempre. Amén." Then she pulled her rosary from the glove compartment and continued her prayers. Rudy rested his head on Mom's arm, reposing in the safety of her motherly warmth. We rode home in silence. The only sounds were the gentle hum of the car's engine and my mother's soft murmur as she prayed. "Creo en Dios, Padre todopoderoso, Creador del cielo y de la tierra. Creo en Jesucristo, su único Hijo, nuestro Señor, que fue concebido por obra y gracia del Espíritu Santo..."

That evening, as I washed dinner dishes, Gloria stepped into the kitchen. "Sally," she said excitedly, "Mom and Dad are lighting a bunch of holy candles, and Mom's going to curar Rudy and Norma de susto."

This was serious business. Mom was going to perform the prayer ritual that entailed passing an egg over Rudy and Norma as they lay face up. I was not surprised, but I was still stunned by what had happened in the beet field. Rudy had slain a rattlesnake.

"Come on! They're waiting for us."

We both rushed to join the rest of the family in the living room. The Kids all look scared and confused. They had never seen Mom do this before, but I had seen it done a couple of times. I didn't really understand it, but I certainly believed in it.

"Mom, what are you doing?" I whispered.

"Shh, silencio," Dad said. "Y rezen."

"Pray," Mom repeated.

We stood around Rudy and Norma as they lay face up, Norma on the couch and Rudy on the army cot. We encircled them as best we could, with bowed heads, quietly reciting Our Father's and Hail Mary's in English, while Mom and Dad prayed in Spanish.

"Our Father who art in heaven, hallowed be thy name..."

"Padre Nuestro que estás en los cielos, santificado sea tu nobre..."

"Hail Mary, full of grace, the Lord is with thee... Holy Mary Mother of God..."

"Dios te salve María, llena eres de gracia... Santa María, Madre de Dios..."

I knew Mom and some of the older ladies she knew had performed this prayer ritual with the egg before. And I knew it was done only in serious situations, but we Kids had never been involved in the ritual. I glanced up at my mother several times, careful to keep my head bowed. I stopped praying for an instant as I focused on her movements and closely listened to her prayers. She held the egg in her right hand and waved it, in a sweeping motion, back and forth, head to toe, over Norma and Rudy. In an unexpected moment, I saw her not as just my mother, but as a holy person. It was the strangest sensation watching her perform this ritual in the soft glow of candlelight. I shivered, but I felt safe.

After the ritual, Mom and Dad told us to turn in early. It had been a hard day, and everyone was visibly tired. Mom and Dad were solemn as they blew out candles. "Don't forget your prayers and thank God for his mercy today," Mom called out. Norma and Rudy seemed okay.

I returned to the kitchen to finish the dishes. I could still hear Mom mumbling prayers as she blew out the last burning candles in the living room. My head was filled with thoughts of what had happened in the beet field, as well as during my mother's prayer ritual. What a crazy, incredible day. I shuddered as I thought about how things could have gone terribly wrong, but I thanked God that all was well. How could Rudy have been so brave? My little brother really was a hero. Incredible!

"A real hero," I whispered to myself. "Si, señor," as Mom always said, "Dios es grande!" There was no doubt in my mind—God was indeed great.

The next morning, we arrived at the field early, as usual. Dad unloaded the water jugs from the trunk of the car, along with the hoes and sombreros. Rudy placed the water jugs under the car, where they would stay cool in the shade, and Dad began sharpening the hoes—after what had happened the day before, Rudy insisted on an extra sharp hoe. Promptly at 6:00 a.m., we set upon our work, pretty confident that the snake's mate had abandoned the field.

Again, I worked next to Dad, anxious to hear more stories about the Mexican Revolution. Norma quickly paired up with her big brother, knowing he would protect her from all evil.

Rudy was determined to be the scout, and he surveyed the surrounding ground before beginning his row. On full alert, he worked carefully—and faster than usual. He had put Norma strategically in the rows to his right, and Mom was working to his left.

We had only been at work a short while when Rudy saw that ahead, in Mom's row, a huge, coiled rattlesnake was sleeping—as if it was waiting to avenge the death of its mate. He realized that this was the male—it was much bigger than the one Rudy had killed the day before.

Rudy waved silently at Norma and Mom, warning them to be quiet and back away slowly. He turned back toward the sleeping serpent and stared intently. The snake was in a deep sleep—it hadn't budged an inch. Relieved, Rudy thought, Oh yeah—you're mine sucker! Knowing his hoe was razor sharp, he slowly raised it above his head. Gripping the handle, Rudy aimed precisely and brought the hoe down with all his might upon the sleeping serpent. From the moment he had laid eyes on the snake,

Rudy knew that he had to deliver two slicing blows to be extra sure it was dead. Without hesitation, he again raised his hoe to deliver the final blow.

Suddenly, Rudy saw that his first strike had not made a clean cut through the snake—the hideous creature had stuck to the blade of his hoe! It dangled, suspended in front of his face, its tongue flickering in and out.

Horror stricken, Rudy screamed and hurled the hoe away, just as the reptile lunged menacingly at him, its fangs bared. Thank God, the rattler had missed its intended mark.

As the demon lay dying on the ground, the sound of his rattle slowly faded. "Tsss! Tsss, tsss...." Then silence. Once it was dead, Dad and Rudy examined the remains, discovering that the last venomous lunge the snake made had been inadvertently suicidal. Miraculously, the creature had a self-inflicted wound—one fang had punctured its own flesh.

Again, Mom and Dad herded The Kids into the car. Dad wet a hanky and wiped Rudy's head and face. Rudy gulped a cup of water voraciously, asked for more, and splashed it on his face.

Mom exclaimed, "Ay, mi Rudy, estas pálido, (You're pale). Vámonos ya, Valentin... Lo sábia, lo sábia..."

Rudy was almost limp, as Dad helped him toward the car. But, Rudy had still managed to inspect the dead snake and scoop up its rattle.

Sometimes after dinner we got permission to run across the railroad tracks to Tortilla Flats and see our friends. Rudy couldn't wait to tell his tale, and the rest of us were just as eager to hear it. Wolfing down his dinner, Rudy was off and running before we knew it.

"Freddy must have gone with Rudy," I said, not seeing either of them.

"Yeah, they're both gone already," Gloria answered. "They couldn't wait to get to Tortilla Flats."

"Norma, are you ready to go? We're waiting. Come on! Let's go," I yelled.

Norma rushed out of the bedroom as Mom cautioned, "Don't be late!"

"Y le dicen a los muchachos tambien, que no se tarden," Dad yelled after us.

As the three of us girls approached Tortilla Flats, we noticed a crowd of kids standing around. "That's gotta be Rudy," I said. "I can't see him, but what do you want to bet Rudy's in the middle of that borlote?" Norma ran off ahead of us to join the crowd.

"Look, there's Rudy," Gloria said, pointing. "He's basking in his glory, when all I want to do is forget I ever saw those snakes."

"I know, but can you believe that he was so brave?" I responded. "Come on! Let's see what's going on." We quickened our pace, and as we got closer, we saw that, sure enough, Rudy was talking and the whole crowd was listening attentively.

"Oh, my God!" I said, nudging Gloria with my elbow and pointing to Rudy's feet. "Do you see that?"

Rudy was standing on a wooden crate, addressing the crowd. Gloria and I snickered.

"He's encantado de la vida...Loving every minute. And he's got a prop!" Rudy had a long stick in his left hand. Every now and then, when he needed both hands, he handed the stick to one of the guys standing next to him.

Someone in the crowd said, "Shhh!" So, Gloria and I stifled our giggles and listened.

"Yeah, with the first snake, we were both determined, each of us switching from offense to defense until I saw my chance and sliced him right in two." Rudy was gesturing dramatically with his hands to show the slithering of the snake. His audience was captivated.

"The big male snake was so fat that my hoe didn't go completely through him the first time, so when I raised my hoe to strike at him again..." He paused and took a deep, loud breath. The crowd was silent and wide-eyed as Rudy loudly exhaled. "Tsss, tsss, tsss...." Rudy shook the rattle, and all the girls jumped.

"Oh, Rudy!" one girl squealed.

"Your brother's a hero," Blanca said, all jittery and breathless, as she grabbed Gloria's arm.

Rudy continued his awesome tale: "The snake was stuck on the blade of my hoe! He was hanging! Dangling! Just inches from my face. His tongue was flicking in and out...'Tsss, tsss!' I was locked in mortal combat con el mero diablo chingoa!"

"Ahh! Rudy!" Some of the girls jumped back in fright, covered their eyes, and whimpered in disbelief; while the boys laughed at Rudy's antics, teased the girls, and mimicked Rudy's movements.

Soon, all of Tortilla Flats was buzzing with the news of Rudy and the two snakes. Over the next few weeks, it was the biggest story in Tortilla Flats. Even parents came out to hear what had happened.

Rudy was a looker, and he had a charming way with the girls. His new heroic adventure added fuel to the fire. Girls were enthralled. They admired Rudy, and they wanted to get close to him. On the other hand, some of the boys were not exactly thrilled with Rudy's extra leverage—he was an out-of-town rival.

"Rudy, you are such a liar!" yelled Juan. "You're just trying to show off. I bet you're exaggerating and even making things up."

"Oh, yeah?" Rudy replied, shaking the rattles in Juan's face. "Well, then where'd these come from? You're just jealous, Juanillo. Go ahead, ask my mom and dad! Ask my sisters."

"Shut up, Juan! Rudy's a hero, and you're just jealous," said Becky. She smiled adoringly at Rudy.

This was the biggest news around, yet, as usual, there was not a reporter in our midst. Oh, well, who cared? We didn't need reporters or TV cameras when word of mouth was just as reliable, if not better. And, Tortilla Flats was just the place to be any time we wanted to catch up on the latest local news and gossip.

On Saturdays, we worked only six hours—not our usual ten-hour day. The Kids were always happy on Saturday. Not only was it a short workday, but we didn't work at all on Sunday—we had a whole day and a half off. That time away from the fields, time spent with friends, was enough for us.

Finally, we finished the workday. Dad drove up the gravel road leading to the patrón's house. Rudy sat between him and Mom. I was in the back with Gloria, Norma, and Freddy. Parking in front of the enormous house,

Mom and Dad went up to collect our weekly pay, while The Kids waited in the car.

Rudy promptly scooted over to the driver's seat and sat tall, pretending to drive. Then he sat back and pulled out his two rattles. He examined them admiringly and gave them both a shake. Norma, Gloria and I pleaded with him to put them away.

"Rudy, put those horrid things away," I snapped. "They creep me out!"

Norma and Gloria joined in the protest. "Ahhh," Gloria screamed. "I hate those things! I'm telling Mom and Dad!"

Norma agreed. "Rudy, you're gonna get in trouble. Remember what Dad said…"

Ignoring us, he played with his trophies. Freddy climbed into the front seat, always eager to see the rattles and listen to Rudy's tales.

Suddenly, out of nowhere, all hell broke loose:

Upon hearing the snake rattles, the patrón's two huge dogs, barking wildly, attacked the car. Thud! They threw themselves against the car. In a panic, we screamed and tumbled over each other, as we tried to roll up the windows to keep the raging dogs out. As I reached for the window crank, a dog lunged at the open window. I jumped back against Gloria, landing on top of her. Gloria screamed. I jumped off of her and again tried to roll up the window.

Rudy "screamed like a bitch"—as he later recalled—and lost his grip on the rattles, which flew into the air. Landing in the back seat, the rattles only caused more screams and delirium.

The dogs were going absolutely nuts, baring their huge, sharp teeth and growling viciously. Dog slobber flew through the window, into the car. "Gross!" I yelled as the wad of saliva—all sticky and yucky—landed on my face. We were all screaming and scrambling in the cramped confines of the car. In his effort to get the window closed, Rudy accidentally honked the horn. Norma clambered over to the front seat to help Freddy close the passenger window, and Gloria and I fumbled all over the place, trying to close the back windows. Every time I reached for the window crank, one of the huge dogs jumped, thrusting his big body forward, causing me to recoil in terror. With loud, heavy body thrusts, both dogs jumped repeatedly against the car. Their jowls flapped, and slobber went flying all over the place.

Before he could get the car window up, Rudy felt the dog's hot, foul breath on his face. Nauseous and shaking in fear, Rudy wiped the slobber off his face with the sleeve of his old cotton work shirt. Then he pulled off the shirt and furiously wiped his face and neck. With the windows finally up, Gloria and I sat back limply. The vicious, snarling dogs continued to lunge incessantly at the car. We were all shaking and sweating as the interior of the car grew hotter by the second..

"I feel sick," Rudy said slowly. He slumped back in the seat and closed his eyes.

"Are you going to throw up?" I yelled, throwing him the old towel we kept in the back seat. I had already used it to wipe my face. I had rubbed so hard that my cheeks and forehead stung from friction and dried dog saliva.

Mom, Dad, and the patrón rushed out of the house to see what was happening. It seemed an eternity before the patrón called off his raging dogs and had someone take them away.

"¿Que pasó… que está pasando?" everyone wanted to know.

Mom and Dad opened the car doors. We were all panting and sweating. Wide-eyed and silent, Rudy straightened himself up in the seat. Norma, Gloria and I all spoke at once.

"The rattles…"

"The dogs…"

"Rattles scared the dogs… they thought it was a snake!"

"I told him to put them away…"

Dad broke in, "The rattlesnake rattles? Rudy, what's wrong with you? No wonder the dogs are going crazy."

Mom shook her head, adding, "Ay, mi—Rudy, that's why we told you to leave those things…."

At long last, with everything explained, Mom and Dad apologized to the patron and collected our pay. We set out for home. Because he was already pretty shaken, Mom and Dad didn't scold Rudy much, but they left no doubt that they would not tolerate another incident involving those rattles. My sisters and I didn't complain anymore because we didn't want Mom and Dad in a bad mood—it was Saturday, and the last thing we needed was to get grounded. We were anxious to get over to Tortilla

Flats. Zapata—a local rock band—would be practicing, and, man! Those guys were cool!

To put it mildly, it had not been our usual work week, nor had this been our usual Saturday. Rudy had managed, once again, to shake things up just a little.

El susto had us shaken up for a while, but we all bounced right back—except for Rudy. He had seen a rattlesnake flick its forked tongue inches from his face, and he had landed many blows on two rattlesnakes—with just a hoe as his weapon. But the huge, slobbering dog's hot breath on his face was, apparently, the final straw. Maybe it was the element of surprise—and Rudy's lack of control over the situation. Maybe it was just too much happening too fast. Maybe both. But I knew the situation was serious.

Mom and Dad couldn't ignore the trauma Rudy was suffering. Swift action was in order. They knew that a regular doctor wouldn't know how to handle a case such as this. Only an expert could set things right, so an expert it would be. They would take Rudy to a curandero*.

Several of my parents' friends had highly recommended a local legend. Don Juan was well known for his healing powers, and people came from miles around to consult him. He was also known for doing only the work of the lord—and for his refusal to work for el Diablo. Mom and Dad were confident that Don Juan was just what Rudy needed. They had no doubts about Don Juan—his fame preceded him.

It was common knowledge in the Latino community that a true curandero is not in it for the money. Don Juan didn't charge for his services; he accepted donations and often was paid in goods rather than money. He asked only for what his clients could afford.

On the appointed day, Mom called out, "Ready to go, Rudy? Vámonos ya, para no llegar tarde. Just wait and see—you'll feel much better."

"I'm ready, Mom," Rudy smiled. "Dad's outside waiting." Mom patted Rudy reassuringly on the back as they walked outside together.

"Listos, Valentin," Mom said to Dad. "Ready to go. Right, hijo?"

---

* Curandero is a traditional Mexican folk healer. They heal or cure physical and emotional illness. Many use catholic elements, i.e. prayer, holy water, saints. They work through God. This special gift is often handed down through generations.

Dad smiled, asking Rudy if he was okay: "¿Como te sientes, hijo? ¿Estás bien?"

The rest of us waited at home while Mom and Dad took Rudy to see Don Juan. Upon their return, we were anxious to hear all about the experience.

"Rudy, what happened with the curandero?" I whispered, as the rest of The Kids gathered around Rudy.

"What did he do? What did he say?"

"Déjenlo," Dad interjected. He didn't want us bothering Rudy about any of this.

"Si, déjenlo," Mom repeated. "He can tell you later, if he wants to. Rudy, you need to rest," she said, pointing him towards the bedroom.

Rudy looked tired, but he was more than willing to appease our curiosity. He always loved to tell a good story.

"Come on—let's go to the bedroom," I said, "so you can tell us everything." In the bedroom, we all sat on the mattress on the floor and Rudy commenced.

"Okay, so on the way over there, Dad told me to remember my manners and to be sure and shake hands. Mom said not to be scared. She said it would make me feel better and that Don Juan is a holy man." He paused. "So, first thing, Don Juan took me into a dark room. There were just a few candles. I couldn't see at first. Mom and Dad waited in the front room."

"Were you scared?" Norma asked.

"Kind of, but not like I was with the snake!" Rudy laughed. We all did.

"Shh, don't interrupt! Let him talk," I said. "So, what else? What did Don Juan look like? What did the room look like?"

"How come you get to ask questions and we don't?" Gloria frowned.

"Okay, okay," Rudy said, his hands raised. "At first, I wasn't too scared. Don Juan is small and kind of old. He smiled and called me hijo a lot. He was nice. There were a lot of pictures of Jesus and Mary and different saints, I guess, on the walls. I didn't recognize them all. And there was a small altar, with pictures and statues and a big crucifix. The altar was, like, over there," he said, pointing straight ahead. "And," he waved both hands, "everywhere else, you know....All kinds of holy stuff and candles all over the place. It smelled good, kind of like church."

"Like incense?" Gloria asked.

"Yeah, like incense, it smelled really good, and it felt relaxing. He told me he came from Mexico and he was a curandero there, like his father and grandfather...and I don't know how far back they went 'cause I didn't understand that part. Anyway, he said he doesn't do brujeria, just good stuff because he works with God, con Dios."

"Then, he put his hand on my shoulder and told me to sit down on an old wooden chair. He handed me an old black-and-white picture of a little girl. Man, she was totally cross-eyed. And when he handed me the picture, I saw a big ring with a big red stone on his index finger. He told me that the girl had been a really hard case...that she had seen all kinds of doctors and none of them could help her."

"Then," Rudy said, "well, first he held up his hand, showing me the ring and said, 'With this ring, and with some of her personal things, and many prayers....' That he was able to heal her."

"But he said it in Spanish—he said everything in Spanish: 'Con este anillo, con otras cosas personales de ella y con muchas oraciones, logre curarla....' He said, 'logre.' That means he was successful in healing her. I didn't know that word, 'logre,' but I figured it out, and then I asked Mom and Dad." Rudy sat up straight and smiled proudly. He had understood everything Don Juan had said.

"Then, Don Juan showed me another picture of the same girl when she was older and cured. Her eyes in this picture were normal. And get this—when he healed her, she was in Mexico, and Don Juan was here, in the United States. Man! He did a long distance healing, you know?"

"Wow," we all responded.

"But, you guys," I said, biting my lip, "I'm not saying I don't believe him or anything, but, well, someone could take pictures like that and, you know, fake it. I mean, they could, but a real curandero would never..."

Gloria cut me off before I could finish my sentence, and I was actually glad she did. "God, Sally! Don't even say that," Gloria whispered disapprovingly. She looked a little worried.

"Yeah, you know he's a holy man. Mom and Dad said so," Norma added.

I backpedaled. "I know, I know. I didn't mean it like that. I didn't mean that Don Juan… I believe in him."

"Okay," Rudy continued, but he stopped for a moment as he got up from the mattress on the floor to sit on the army cot. We all shifted, stretched, and repositioned ourselves.

Rudy lowered his voice to a near whisper and raised his hands. "Then, Don Juan walked to the back of the room. Slow and quiet. I couldn't even hear his steps. I turned to watch, and he lit more candles. Then I saw it!" He yelled.

"Ahhh!" We all screamed. I covered my mouth, but then I quickly grabbed Freddy as he started to stand up. Gloria had buried her head under the covers. Now she came up for air.

"Rudy!" she scolded. Norma started laughing, and then we were all giggling and rolling on the mattress.

"Quiet!" I warned, "We're going to get in trouble. We're supposed to be asleep."

"Okay," Rudy continued, "I saw a huge rattlesnake skin spread out on the back wall. I didn't really panic, though. I mean, the thing was dead, it was just the skin tacked to the wall. Still, it was creepy, and, yeah, I guess I was kind of' scared. But, it made me think, man! If I had only thought to take the whole snake—to take both of them—to save the skins."

"Oh, Rudy!" Gloria frowned. "You know Mom and Dad would never…"

"For sure!" I said. "Are you crazy? Anyway, I don't think you, or any of us, could have handled that."

With a tired look, Norma added, "No way, Rudy. How can you even think that way? I've had enough with snakes!"

Rudy continued, "I know. So, then Don Juan told me to come to him. He was still in the back of the room by the snakeskin. He said to bring my chair and sit. So I sat, facing him. The snakeskin was on this side of me," he said, motioning with his left hand. "And the altar was on the other side. Then he put a human skull in my hands. I held it in my lap. Okay, now I was scared. I started sweating and getting nervous. I guess I was wiggling around, 'cause he put his hands on my shoulders and told me to relax and be calm. He started praying and kind of' singing—no—chanting, that's what he was doing, chanting. Then he took the snakeskin off the wall and put it across my shoulders." Rudy shivered and so did the rest of us.

"He kept sweeping it, rubbing it, all over me," Rudy said. All of us girls moaned in fearful awe.

Rudy took a deep breath. He looked kind of ashen.

"Hold on. I'll get you some water. Take a breather, and don't start without me," I said. Quietly, I opened the door and peeked out from the bedroom. Everything was dark, so I walked slowly, feeling my way through the darkness to the kitchen.

When I got back, I handed Rudy the glass of water and reported, "Mom and Dad went to bed." Rudy drained the glass and went on explaining how Don Juan then draped the snakeskin on his shoulders and around the back of his neck. The snakeskin was so long that each end, head and tail, touched the floor. Then Don Juan began murmuring and chanting while rubbing Rudy all over with his ruby ring. Rudy broke out in a cold sweat, shivering at the touch of the snakeskin rubbing against his own skin. Don Juan continued to do an all-over sweeping with medicinal plants. He continued praying in a soft, melodic rhythm that soothed Rudy.

"He told me to close my eyes, and, all of a sudden, I felt completely relaxed." Rudy went on, "His hands were soft… remember Mr. Campos's hands? Like that."

We all nodded and whispered. Of course, we all knew Mr. Campos. I couldn't forget how he had massaged and healed my sprained ankle when I was young.

"Anyway," Rudy explained, "Don Juan just made me feel good. Everything about him, I don't know… I guess a curandero just really knows what he's doing. I wasn't scared anymore."

With all of us transfixed, Rudy told us how Don Juan had a soft and gentle, yet firm hand. How Rudy had closed his eyes and let himself drift off as he felt a calmness and warm security envelop him. Rudy explained how Don Juan had intermittently instructed him to strengthen his faith and get closer to the deity. "He kept telling me over and over, to get closer to God."

"Don Juan kept saying, "Acercate mas a Dios," and he said that God is always with us. God is always here, but that it's up to me to believe in

Him, look for Him and ask for His mercy. He said that if I ask God for help, he will always help me."

Rudy paused for a moment, and then he continued, "Here's something else – important. Don Juan told me…he said it in Spanish, but this is pretty much what he said: 'Hijo, do you think you would be here today if God had not been with you? Do you think it was pure chance or luck that nobody was hurt? Yes, you were extremely brave, but you must know that the hand of God was at work. And what about the fact that it was you who encountered both snakes? Isn't that a strange coincidence?'"

We were all captured in the moment as my little brother told us everything. He told us how the medicinal plants smelled fresh and clean and felt good against his skin. How the plants seemed to have a kind of magic, how the ritual seemed hypnotic.

Rudy told us that after his session with Don Juan, he felt rested, refreshed. His initial fear had quickly subsided as the old man continued his ritual. He admitted that he actually felt a pleasant serenity.

"Somehow, I feel safe now," Rudy yawned, "But I'm really sleepy and tired." We were all quiet for a moment, deep in thought of all that had transpired.

"Okay," I said getting up from the mattress. "We better get to bed. Sweet dreams and lights out." I had a good feeling knowing that Rudy felt tranquil and at peace. His session with Don Juan had worked wonders. I felt that all of us, including Mom and Dad, would get a restful sleep tonight, peaceful and secure in God's grace.

It had been quite an unforgettable experience for all of us, but all the more harrowing for my little brother Rudy, who had shown such grace and valor.

I truly admired my little brother. He showed bravery way beyond his years in confronting those deadly rattlesnakes. At the tender age of thirteen, Rudy had earned his manhood through a ritual as dangerous and harrowing as any ancient tribe might have conjured up.

Like Mom and Dad, we were already believers in the powers of a curandero, for we had seen and experienced their work. However, those few days in the summer of 1968 left a strong and lasting impression on all of us. Mr. Campos, Don Juan and even our own mother were figures who had earned our trust and admiration for their curative knowledge and power. I had always somehow known that my mother had a special connection to God, but the events of that summer proved it.

I have no doubt that our spiritual experiences that long-ago summer left a lasting impression on all of us, reinforcing our spirituality and our already-strong faith in God. Don Juan's insistence on the importance of God in our lives had a huge impact on all of us. I also felt that God was sending me messages through Don Juan. God was warning me to cast aside my sinful doubts, and He was offering me redemption and strengthening my faith.

Rudy claimed the rattles of his two slain foe as his badge of honor, and he would rattle them whenever he got the chance, proudly telling his warrior's tale to anyone who would listen. Lots of kids were awed by Rudy's vivid story.

Mom and Dad warned Rudy against taking his trophies; they didn't want him touching the snakes, even when they were dead. But Rudy was not about to give up his well-earned fame as Valentino El Valiente. He carried both rattles in his pocket, careful not to pull them out in front of Mom and Dad, but eagerly showing them off to his peers.

Rudy loved to tell the story of killing the two rattlesnakes. His willing audience was amused and entertained—they didn't have to think very hard about the reality and the danger of it all. Rudy loved to say that, with the snake just inches from his face, he was "locked in mortal combat con el mero Diablo chingoa."

# Chapter 6

Mom and Dad's stories—and Rudy's pendejadas—were our saving grace while we worked in the fields. Rudy's humor kept us in stitches. Mom and Dad often had to reprimand us for being too distracted. They insisted that we focus on our work, but that was okay. We didn't mind their reminders. Mom and Dad were never angry. They knew Rudy's jokes and stories were just a part of our day, and we all welcomed the occasional distraction from our misery. Still, we had work to do.

On Saturday mornings, Looney Tunes cartoons were a big part of our lives, and so Rudy used the term "cartoon series" to refer to anything funny. In the fields, we would beg him to do a "cartoon series." We began to apply the term to all of his antics.

One morning in the beet field, Gloria and I were being distracted by Rudy's "cartoon series." He was a comical sight—wearing one of Dad's shirts, which was way too big to fit him. He put his hoe behind his back, sticking the handle under and up the back of his shirt. Acting as if he were hanging limply from the hoe, he swung his arms, like the scarecrow from the Wizard of Oz. Then he began to sing:

"Nothing to get hung about… Strawberry Fields…"

At that moment Dad yelled, "¡Ponganse a trabajar!"

Startled, Rudy jumped, and in his rush to get the hoe out from under his shirt, he ripped a hole right through it instead. Rudy struggled to gain his composure. The more he struggled, the more tangled up he got. "Ándale, Mr. Macho" I jeered. Gloria and I laughed so hard we almost peed our pants. We accepted our well-deserved scolding and began working faster than ever, hoping we could make up for wasting time. For the rest of the day Rudy wore Dad's tattered shirt, now looking just like the scarecrow he had tried to portray.

Life was never dull when Rudy was around. He never ceased to make us laugh, get us in trouble, or cause some kind of mischief or uproar. As Dad drove the old highway between Grandview and Prosser, Mom and Rudy sat in the front seat, while the rest of us Kids sat in the back. Prosser was even smaller than Grandview—and just as uneventful. We hardly ever had occasion to go there, but, for some reason or other, there we were. I stared out the window, ignoring the Kids' usual backseat ruckus, when suddenly Rudy called out, "Hey, there's the hospital where I was born!" Rudy was, in fact, born in Prosser, but he was pointing to a sign that read, "Prosser Veterinary Hospital."

Cracking up, I managed to spit out, "You animal! I knew it. That's an animal hospital!" The Kids jumped at the chance to poke fun and laugh at Rudy's expense. Apparently, he had just seen the word "hospital" and jumped at the chance to proudly point out the place of his birth. We laughed so hard we could hardly breathe. Mom scolded us, explaining the situation to Dad.

"Settle down, all of you. That's enough. Your brother is not an animal, and this is not funny. Rudy was born in Prosser. He made a simple mistake."

I laughed. "But Mom, he pointed to..."

"I know what he pointed to, and I'm telling you he made a mistake. Now settle down this minute, all of you! Mira nomas Valentin, estos niños estan burlándose de Rudy…"

Chastised, I glanced at Dad. I'm pretty sure he suppressed a little grin. Por supuesto, poor Rudy could never live this one down. Not that he cared. He quickly found it just as hilarious as the rest of us did.

The sweltering heat made it impossible to eat lunch in the car. If we were really lucky, we could have lunch in the shade of trees surrounding the field. If trees were nowhere to be found, we would sit in the little bit of shade the car afforded. We took it all with a grain of salt. What I could not tolerate, though, was that—as inconceivable as it might be—the patrónes did not think outhouses were necessary. None of the fields we worked ever had one, and we were forced to find a secluded spot to take care of business. The indignity of it all was almost unbearable. Imagine a girl or a woman having her period and being forced to deal with this humiliation. Talk about getting kicked when you're down! Such insults were a part of our everyday lives.

My period never failed to cause unbearable cramps. Understanding my pain and discomfort, Mom sent me to the shade to lie down and rest. I had a prescribed medication for the pain, but it did nothing to mitigate my depression and moodiness. The reality of our lives—the injustice, oppression, humiliation and profound hopelessness—increasingly overwhelmed me. I felt an uneasy impulse for vengeance rising within myself.

Every farmworker I knew was Mexican. Pay was minimal. As draining and damaging as the physical, backbreaking work was, the emotional pain was even greater, along with its accompanying resignation. Y pa' 'cabarla de fregar. The patrónes didn't even have the decency to provide an outhouse.

People who are so used to their "status" and privilege have a knack for adding insult to injury without so much as a second thought. I just didn't get this additional humiliation in a long line of indignities. Was there no end? Did they think we deserved such inhumane treatment? Did they think we were less than human, without feelings, without pride or dignity?

The profound confusion in my mind and in my heart gave way to depression, hatred, and despair. My failure to comprehend or understand the complexities of our oppression elicited feelings in me that I despised in others. My pain blinded me to the point that I blamed all white people for the many injustices I had witnessed firsthand. But my hatred also made me feel guilty and hollow. I knew two wrongs wouldn't make anything right. Reverse racism didn't solve a thing, and why should I lower myself to that level of ignorance? Still, I didn't know how to deal with the darkness that consumed me. I was miserable.

So much darkness, so many questions, yet nobody to turn to. All the Christian values I had been raised with were compromised during these dark, depressive moods that I was increasingly succumbing to. And no answers meant no hope.

With no outlet, I continued to dwell on negative thoughts and emotions. I wondered how and why nobody seemed to notice the enormity of the wrongs we suffered. None of us rebelled—or even complained. It was as though we had surrendered—there was nothing to be done. I resigned myself to the hopelessness of it all, sadly realizing that everyone concerned, including my parents, had done the same. We had all given in to our hopelessness. We—and all of the people we were close to—were preoccupied with the simple reality of making a living for our families. Survival was first and foremost. Anything beyond survival was secondary, and anything that might jeopardize a family's livelihood could not even be contemplated. I was powerless. We, as a people, were powerless. I feared that our struggle would never cease.

At the end of the summer work season, Mom and Dad were sacando cuentas and setting aside money for The Kids' school expenses. School supplies, fees, clothes, monthly lunch tickets—so many expenses. They added up quickly, especially when multiplied by five.

We all eagerly looked forward to our annual back-to-school shopping trip to Wenatchee. This was a special event, and Mom and Dad allowed us each to buy a few items of our own choosing. I had learned to manage my money wisely, buying only cool, in-style clothes from the sales racks. I stretched the little money I had, picking out items I could fashionably tailor to maximum stylistic effect. The rest of my wardrobe consisted of the clothes I made, which were also always the latest style.

Rudy and I were slaves to fashion. By carefully attending to what I wore, I had found a way to be cool, different, envied. I reveled in this notoriety and dedicated myself to being fashionably different. My style, my cool clothes, my demeanor—all worked in my favor. Instead of being looked down upon because of my race, I became admired for my cool.

Ironically, this superficial self-preservation technique temporarily enabled me to rise above what I had fought against my whole life. At the time, I didn't realize I was trading in one counterfeit coin for another just as fake.

My junior high school years differed starkly from my childhood years. I went from being a happy, carefree child to a rebellious, moody teenager. I just wanted to escape the cruelty and hardship I saw everywhere, but I could see no way to do this. After some struggle, I came up with my own way to ease the pressure.

I thought, If I am different from the others... Everyone respects and admires what is perceived as cool, above the ordinary.... This awareness was my "ticket to ride,"* my shield—it was one I would wield for some time to come.

Seventh grade was a major change for me. I thought of myself as an adult. How things had changed over the summer! I had worked alongside the adults in the fields, and I now contributed to the family's income. I wasn't in grade school anymore. I was grown up. It was time for a more grown-up look. I assembled my cosmetic arsenal: black eyeliner, pink blush and a big handful of trendy, frosted lip colors. Grape was my favorite. It didn't matter that I had to hide any trace of it from Mom and Dad!

Of course, in order to reflect my new, mature status, my wardrobe also had to change—no more frilly, full-skirted kid dresses. It was time to trade up to A-line dresses, tightly tapered hip-hugger skirts and pants, and stylish, ribbed T-shirts. I made sure my hairstyles completed the look—full, teased tresses and a stylish little flip at the end of my dark, shoulder-length hair.

School was different too. We no longer stayed in one class with one teacher—now we had different teachers and different classrooms for each subject. So cool!

Walking to the cafeteria at lunchtime, my cousin Sylvia grabbed my arm, muttering, "Look at those two holding hands! They can't do that in school—can they?"

"Oh," I replied casually. "That's Becky and Pete. He rides my bus, and they're always holding hands, and kissing too. Man! They do it all the time and in front of anybody. They don't even care who sees."

Oh, yes—we were all grown up now. We didn't know that our naïve, protected little world still held many unpleasant surprises.

---

* From "Ticket to Ride," a song from the Beatles' 1965 album HELP!

Numbers had never been my friends. Third grade math had introduced the wonders of multiplication and division. Mass confusion thus ensued. Adding, subtracting, and multiplying were understandable enough—not fun, but perhaps manageable. However, division was a different ballgame. This was the point when my real struggle with math began.

The teacher didn't try to help me understand the lessons. Instead, the class continued, leaving me bewildered. I wonder now if there were others like me, who didn't understand but were, perhaps, too shy to say so. At any rate, the shameful feelings of incompetence I struggled with helped create a self-fulfilling prophecy. I hated math with every fiber of my being. I resented it for making me feel like a moron. Soon, my fear and hatred of numbers was reflected in my grades. Still, I floundered—adrift and alone. No one came to my rescue.

My seventh grade math teacher, Mr. Wyatt, was short and stocky, an elderly man, with a gruff voice. I was used to female teachers, and I wasn't keen on a male teacher, but Mr. Wyatt—with his gray hair and slow, limping gait—seemed grandfatherly, and, thus, less daunting. His wise, kindly demeanor overrode my bias against male teachers.

It didn't take long for Mr. Wyatt to see that I was struggling. He made an effort to talk with me about getting some additional help. One day, when the bell rang at the end of class, Mr. Wyatt dismissed everyone, but he quickly added, "Sally, I'd like to have a word with you."

"Huh?" I said, stopping abruptly. A few of my classmates bunched up behind me, trying to rush out to their next classes.

"What did I do?" I asked nervously.

What can he possibly want with me? Now I was nervous, sweating. I had never been singled out by a teacher—this couldn't be good.

Mr. Wyatt explained that he knew I was having a hard time with math. He said he wanted to have a talk with me about it. I just stared, openmouthed and thought, Oh, God, I'm doomed.

"I'd like to see you tomorrow so we can discuss this trouble you're having," he continued. I stood there, silent and shaking.

"But, I… I have Home Ec.," I stammered, hoping that he would realize I couldn't spare the time.

"I'll make the arrangements with the office, and you'll be given an excused tardy slip for Mrs. Mowry," he explained, reassuring me I didn't have to worry about being late for Home Ec.

Actually, being late was the least of my worries. I wallowed in fear and anxiety until my meeting with Mr. Wyatt.

I couldn't focus on anything beyond my insecurity and fear. I was embarrassed and ashamed that math was such a foreign language to me. How could I explain to Mr. Wyatt that my mind simply went blank when confronted by numbers and mathematical equations? How could I admit that I was the dumbest person in the entire world when it came to Math? How could I possibly make anybody realize the enormity and hopelessness of my limited mental capacity…without being labeled "retarded"? I wanted a lifeline to pull me out of that horrible mess, yet I was much too ashamed to admit the depths of my ignorance. I was bound to lose this encounter.

Nervous and scared, but mostly ashamed, I sat through Mr. Wyatt's talk, unable to look him in the face, much less the eyes. I desperately wanted help, but I figured I was beyond salvation—that I had, somehow, slipped through my last few years of school in complete mathematic ignorance. Surely, it was too late. At this point, I was beyond salvation.

I supposed Mr. Wyatt took my lack of response as a sign of disinterest. After an awkward silence, he cocked his head, looked at me, and asked, "Sally, are you even listening to me? Do you understand the gravity of your situation?"

I shifted nervously in my chair, hung my head, and shrugged my shoulders. How was I supposed to respond? I didn't know what to say. I knew I was hopeless. Retard! Retard! Retard! I was terrified of the word—and of being unmasked completely.

Mr. Wyatt continued, "Are you just going to live the rest of your life beautiful but dumb? Is that going to be your M.O.?"

Caught completely off guard, I slowly peered up at Mr. Wyatt. Beautiful? For the fraction of an instant, I wanted to ask, "Can you repeat the question?" But I caught myself. This was no joke. Again, I glanced quickly at Mr. Wyatt. I was deeply ashamed to face him, wondering if I was the dumbest student he had ever tried to teach. Yet, all I could think was, Beautiful? Really? Me?

I was beautiful. Wow! Perhaps things weren't completely hopeless after all. My mind was racing. From the depths of my painful insecurity and worthlessness, a tiny ray of sunshine was trying to squeeze through the darkness. I sat up straight and let out a slow sigh. I needed to breathe, but I still felt stifled. Then, my eyes caught his and my shame resurfaced in its entirety. My shoulders sagged just as quickly as they had straightened up. With a sigh of resignation, I concluded that perhaps there was a ray of sunshine in my destiny after all, but it would never be a mastery of math.

"May I be excused?" I said in a low whisper, glancing up at him cautiously. All I wanted was out of that awkwardness.

Sadly, Mr. Wyatt had accomplished nothing with this little talk. Insinuating that I might be "beautiful but dumb" was clearly not the best strategy, but I couldn't blame him for making an effort. He had tried to talk to me. He voiced his concern, which was more than any of my other teachers had ever done.

Ever since then—in school, and in "everyday life"—math has been my worst nightmare. I still panic when confronted by numbers—and, rather than deal with such complexity and confusion, my mind goes directly into a kind of self-preservation mode. That is, it goes blank and shuts down.

Thank God for calculators. My friend Mary recently suggested using a calculator with a mirror. That way, she said, I could master my mathematical equations as I glanced into the mirror, reminding myself that I still had, well—maybe not beautiful, but at least half-way decent looks.

My younger sister Gloria had a similar aversion to math, which, sadly and unforgivably, could only be attributed to her sixth grade teacher, Miss Carroll.

From the very beginning, Gloria was studious and intelligent. She loved school and cherished learning and discovering new things, so when her test scores reflected a high aptitude in reading, spelling and comprehension, she was asked to help her fellow students who struggled in those areas.

"Gloria," Mrs. Nelson said, "how do you feel about helping students who have trouble with reading? All you have to do is act as teacher and help them when they struggle with a word, like I do with our reading group."

Caught off guard, Gloria replied, "Really, Mrs. Nelson? Me?"

"Yes, Gloria, you do so well in reading. Why, you're one of my best students. I've already gotten the permission slip from the office, signed by Principal Dickey."

"Oh, I would love that, Mrs. Nelson. I can help them sound out words and review the reading. Maybe my help will get them to love reading as much as I do." Gloria was thrilled to be able to help other students master such a wonderful skill. She beamed with enthusiasm, pride and self-confidence. Learning came so naturally to her that she had never given it a second thought.

Through the fifth grade, Gloria had excelled in every subject, but in the sixth grade, math was becoming increasingly difficult, and her teacher, Miss Carroll, was moving too fast. Miss Carroll didn't explain the process of solving division problems, and she had a nasty habit of shaming students in front of the entire class. Gloria's confusion increased, as did her fear of being found out. She began to think she wasn't smart anymore.

Miss Carroll wrote a division problem on the blackboard: "100 divided by 25," she said. "Is the correct answer a one?" she asked.

The class answered in unison, "No."

"Is the correct answer a two?"

"No."

Miss Carroll continued, "Is the correct answer a four?"

The entire class answered, "Yes!"

Gloria felt lost, not understanding why one, two and three were No and why four was Yes. None of it made sense. She became increasingly fearful and apprehensive. She sat nervously at her desk, her heart racing. She crossed her fingers, praying she wouldn't be called to the board to solve a division problem. Her greatest fear was to be found out and exposed in front of everybody.

Gloria quit doing her math homework because she simply did not know how to work through the problems. She didn't know what to do or where to turn. Mom and Dad can't help, she thought. They didn't go to school past the fifth grade. Anyway, they're so exhausted after working all day. Oh, God, what am I going to do? I don't want anybody to know, but I can't hide this forever.

The next day, Gloria's world was shattered. "Gloria, go up to the blackboard and divide 250 by 5," Miss Carroll said.

Gloria's heart thumped rapidly in her chest—she feared she couldn't move. She began to shake. She swallowed hard, but her mouth was dry. "Gloria! Go to the board and solve the problem I just gave you," Miss Carroll repeated angrily. The whole class turned to stare. Gloria felt sick. She got up very slowly and walked up to the blackboard. Miss Carroll repeated the division problem, and Gloria wrote it on the board in a trembling hand. She had no idea what the answer was. Still holding the chalk, she squeezed her hand tightly. Feeling a weakness in her legs, Gloria grabbed the chalk tray at the base of the blackboard, steadying herself. She stood there, drenched in sweat and feeling unbearably ashamed.

Visibly irritated, Miss Carroll kept at her. "Gloria, what are you waiting for? We're waiting for you to solve the problem." There was a long, awkward pause. "Gloria! I am speaking to you, young lady! If you can't do it, I'll give you an easier one, although...Gloria!"

Gloria's vision had blurred. She was afraid to move, afraid to turn around and face the class. Suddenly, Miss Carroll stomped toward the blackboard and shouted in a loud, angry voice, "Go sit down!"

Demoralized, ashamed, and hopeless, Gloria turned slowly toward the class. Tears rolled down her cheeks, and her chest heaved as she walked slowly back to her desk.

Miss Carroll's angry eyes followed Gloria to her seat. She thumped her open hand against her leg and grimaced. Walking towards her desk, she grabbed her long wooden pointer. "Thud!" Miss Carroll hit her desk furiously with the stick. Gloria cringed and wiped her tears with the back of her hands. With scared, astonished looks on their faces, the rest of the class sat in silence. The atmosphere was intense.

Frowning in disgust, Miss Carroll pointed her long, bony finger at Gloria. "Some people," Miss Carroll paused as she looked around the classroom, "will never make it in this world because they are too lazy to lift even a finger to help themselves!" She whipped her pointing stick at the blackboard, continuing her tirade against Gloria.

Gloria didn't hear her anymore. She was devastated, sick about what the future could possibly hold for someone as dumb and worthless as she was. In a matter of minutes, Gloria had gone from being a smart, confident young girl to a stupid, hopeless nobody. There was no denying this—hadn't her teacher just said it was so?

I was a sophomore in high school and the end of the school year was approaching. It was a beautiful spring day—sunny and warm. As much as I wanted another school year behind me, I also knew that summer would only bring more grueling farm work.

My cousin Sylvia and I needed money for the annual spring carnival in town. I had already spent all my monthly lunch money, my only real source of income during the school year.

Finally, I came up with an ingenious plan. My older sister, Viola, had a steady boyfriend named Cruz Rangel. Cruz was a well-known musician who also worked in the fields to supplement his income, and he just happened to be working in the mint field about a mile from our house.

I came by this information while tagging along with Viola and Cruz on one of their many outings. Mom and Dad held steadfast to the old Mexican tradition of overprotecting their daughters. We were never allowed to go out with our boyfriends alone, and so I was assigned to be Viola's trusty tag-along.

I didn't understand the reasons for my parents' strictness, and as soon as we could, I eagerly went my way, and Viola went hers. I don't know which of us was more eager to escape the other. Mom and Dad were aware that we had boyfriends and that we met up with them every chance we got. This made me wonder why in the world we had to appear to follow the rule. It felt deceitful. I supposed it was just a smokescreen my parents used to maintain a semblance of propriety.

"We can go work with Cruz," I told Sylvia excitedly. "As much as I loathe field work"—I emphasized the word "loathe," letting it roll slowly off my tongue as I winced and shook my fists—"we can handle one day. If a whole summer of fieldwork hasn't killed us, this will be a cinch. Just think about the reward."

How perfect that Cruz was working with a crew in the mint field so close to home! I was a genius to come up with such a clever idea. As soon as we could, we cautiously approached Cruz with our brilliant plan.

"Cruz, we need your help," I said. "Um, we..."

"Can we go work with you on Saturday?" Sylvia blurted out.

Cruz listened to our scheme in disbelief. We didn't let him get a word in edgewise until we had the chance to reveal our entire ploy.

His puzzled look quickly changed to a scowl, and he exclaimed, "Are you girls ...kidding?"

"No, Cruz," I pleaded. "We're dead serious."

"No, you girls cannot go to work with me. No way. It's not that simple," he argued.

"Cruz, please! We're serious, and we're begging," I insisted. "¿Que te cuesta? It's just one day. Have we ever asked you for anything, ever? Well, have we?" I followed this supplication with a dramatic sigh and slumped shoulders.

It took a lot of begging, but we finally convinced Cruz to take us to work with him on Saturday, the weekend of the carnival. We were thrilled when he finally gave in, especially when he agreed to advance us our wages at the end of the workday.

Cruz had an injured knee, and he walked with a limp, but that didn't stop him from working. He warned us that we had better do a good job. He wasn't going to let us make him look bad.

"You girls have to keep up with the crew. If I take you, I'm responsible for you and the kind of work you do, understand?" Wide-eyed, we nodded. "You'll need to work like you do with your mom and dad. Sally, I know how strict your parents are about work, so I'm going to trust in that."

We wholeheartedly assured him that he could count on us; we wouldn't let him down.

"Cruz, you know I've been working since I was twelve. If anyone knows good work ethics, it's moi." I pointed proudly to myself and bowed dramatically, grinning from ear to ear. Quickly, though, I realized that Cruz wasn't amused by my exaggerated gestures. Composing myself, I added, "Seriously, Cruz."

When Saturday came, Sylvia and I were ready and dressed in our farmworker gear, covered from head to toe, except for our faces, which would be shielded from the sun by our straw sombreros.

We were in the garage getting our work stuff when Cruz arrived to pick us up. He stepped out of his car and walked back to open the trunk. We smiled and said good morning, handing him our hoes, sombreros and lunch bags. Then we were on our way to the mint field, happy in the knowledge that we would soon have money for the carnival after a hard day's work.

"Okay, girls," Cruz said as we arrived at the field. "I'll get the hoes and the water cooler from the trunk. I brought you some Cokes, too. It's going to be a scorcher."

"Thanks, Cruz," I said adjusting my oversized work shirt. "We brought lunch—some taquitos for you, too.

"Yeah, thanks, Cruz." Sylvia smiled.

Together, we started towards the mint rows. Sylvia and I put on our big, clumsy sombreros. Cruz strategically positioned himself between us, saying, "Okay, girls, you know what to do. Sally, you take these two rows to my right, and Sylvia, you're here to my left." As we followed Cruz's directions, I took a deep breath, savoring the invigorating scent of mint. Sylvia and I smiled at each other and began to hoe the weeds. It was a nice change from working in the bean or beet fields.

As was customary, I walked between my two rows, hoeing out the weeds while being careful not to damage the mint plants. We hoed up our rows and then turned around, heading back down the next two rows. This would be our familiar-yet-tedious routine for the entire day.

After a while, I started feeling ill. God, I'm tired, I thought as I winced and tightly closed my tired, stinging eyes. Why didn't we go to bed earlier last night? Taking a deep breath, I straightened up, stretching my back and neck. All the other workers were in front of me, so nobody saw that I was trailing behind. Still, I needed to take a moment because now I really didn't feel well at all.

I leaned the hoe against my body so I could pull off my gloves. What in the world is wrong with me? Oh, my God—maybe I should have eaten breakfast. I looked down at my shaking hands. "Man, I do not feel well. Why do I feel so awful?" I grabbed a bunch of mint leaves and stuffed them in my mouth, remembering that Mom had always said mint was a good remedio for stomach trouble. I chewed on the pungent leaves, which kind of overwhelmed me. My mouth watered and I spat out the half-chewed leaves. "Yuck!" Fatigued and light-headed, I realized that my furtive attempt to make myself feel better was backfiring on me. I pulled my gloves back on in a rush and began hoeing again. "Please God," I whispered, "make this pass—please, let me feel better." Hoeing hurriedly, I thought, Cruz is going to kill me… But I don't think I'm going to make it.

Looking up, I saw Cruz and Sylvia hurrying toward me. Oh, man, they're trying to catch me up to the rest of the crew. Cruz is scolding… something about the need for me to catch up… he should've known better… should've… But I couldn't concentrate. Now my head was spinning.

"Cruz," I whispered breathlessly. "I really…" I was consumed with how awful I felt. Everything was a hazy blur, like the blistering heat waves rising up from the ground. Then, blackness—I had passed out.

Slowly, drowsily I came to. What a bizarre sensation. I struggled to comprehend what had happened. "What…?" I mumbled, blinking my heavy eyes.

I began to realize that Cruz was carrying me in his arms. The awkwardness of being carried that way by a limping man treading over dusty and uneven terrain was a once-in-a-lifetime experience.

"What's…going on?" I said, regaining consciousness. "Ohh, I feel awful," I slurred. Carrying me as his added burden, Cruz hobbled toward the car.

"Sal! Are you awake? You fainted! Sally, are you okay?" Sylvia was hysterical, trotting alongside Cruz and fussing over me. She was always so dramatic.

The whole crew was watching, wondering what was going on.

Syl's hysterics only served to amplify the borlote and, undoubtedly, the chisme that would follow. I was embarrassed and humiliated, but too weak to walk on my own. Cruz quickly took Sylvia and me home, returning to work only after being reassured that I would be fine.

I had been dieting, and I guessed my lack of sustenance had taken its toll, forcing my undernourished body to rebel. Once we were home, Sylvia ministered fastidiously to me. She got me a pillow and a blanket so I could lie on the couch. She patted me lovingly before heading to the kitchen to prepare me some soup and a sandwich.

"I just want to sleep… to rest…" I droned. I was very tired, but Sylvia, now in full motherly mode, insisted I try to eat something first. Aside from being physically sick, I felt terrible about breaking my promise to Cruz.

"Poor Cruz," I said. "Sylvia, we let him down, big time. We promised. Actually, I'm the one who gave my word, and then… I'm the one who failed him. He's never going to trust me again."

"I know, Sal, but it's not your fault. I feel awful about that too. But we could never have known this would happen. Cruz has to know that. I mean, this is serious. You fainted."

"Still…" I said, shaking my head as I took a bite of my sandwich. Mmm! Who knew soup and a sandwich could taste so good? I devoured my food, realizing that I was very hungry. Then, feeling a bit better, I lay back on the couch and quickly nodded off into a deep-but-restless slumber. I was exhausted.

Later that day, I was back to my regular speed. The carnival was in town, and we had been counting on this annual event to break the monotony of our small-town, teenaged lives. So what if we were broke? What else was new? We could still have fun. I assured Sylvia that I was fully recuperated. We both agreed it would be wise not to mention what had happened to anyone. Besides, it certainly wouldn't do any good for us to wallow in our guilt. En fin, que será, será, and life goes on.

That afternoon, we busily began putting together our "look" for the evening. We laid out clothes on the bed, trying to decide on the coolest-looking outfits. Our main concern was to be the epitome of fashion. I had huge rollers in my hair to smooth out my frizzy, natural wave—so much in contrast to the long, straight-haired look in vogue then. Sylvia was lucky. She had much better hair than I did—not frizzy and baby fine, like mine—with more volume. And her hair was jet-black, while mine was mousey brown. Besides, she was good at hair styling, a skill I sorely lacked. But we were both masterful makeup artists—we wore black eyeliner that emphasized the length of our eyelashes; blush that gave our cheeks a rosy-pink glow; and pearl gloss that nicely accentuated our lips. We had "the look" down pat.

Finally, we were as put together as we were going to get. Viola was ready too, so we all tugged on our little skirts and presented ourselves to Mom and Dad. Saying adios, we hopped into Viola's little red Camaro. On our way to the carnival, we chatted excitedly about trivial matters. Of course, Viola would soon hear the whole truth, and nothing but the truth, from Cruz, so Sylvia and I avoided discussing what had happened to me in the mint field. We would let Cruz spill the beans.

Sylvia and I walked around, enjoying the carnival and showing off how cool we were in our miniskirts and barbarian sandals. I noticed some guys checking us out, and I tried to act blasé. I nonchalantly veered toward a jewelry booth, saying, "Get behind me so I can turn around and talk to you. That'll give me a chance to check out those guys over there." Without a word, Syl followed my lead.

"Okay," I said, casually tossing my hair back over my shoulder with a cool, devil-may-care tilt of my head.

"Hmm," I purred, pouting my glossed lips coquettishly and simultaneously glancing at our prey. That was all it took to knock me off of my imaginary pedestal. It suddenly hit me that these were the same guys who had been working with us in the mint field that morning.

"Oh, no!" I gulped, grabbing Sylvia's arm in a panic. "Follow me—hurry!" Sylvia was baffled, so I added, "Never mind. I'll explain later. Just come on. ¡Vámonos!"

Safely in the women's restroom, I explained the situation to Sylvia.

"Sally, are you sure? How embarrassing!" she panted, bringing her hand up to cover her heart.

"Of course I'm sure," I replied. "Don't tell me you didn't check out those cute guys when we first got there. Man! Embarrassing for you? How about me? I'm the fragile fool who fainted."

"Fragile fool who fainted?" she repeated. "You're the FFF!" She laughed.

"Oh my God, Syl, this is no time for jokes. Imaginate, after this morning's commotion they must really be laughing at us—I mean, at me. And I thought they were checking us out," I pouted.

Wide-eyed, Sylvia and I stared at each other. She slowly moved her hand from her heart up to cover her mouth. Raising her long black eyelashes, she stifled a giggle, and then we both started laughing. We imagined what the guys must have been saying:

"Orale, huey, that's the one that fainted in the field today, la guerita," I mimicked.

"Yeah, man, will milagros never cease? She sure made a miraculous recovery though, huh?" Sylvia responded.

"Looks like she's feeling' no pain now, but I think she's allergic to mint fields."

"Nah, I think they're both allergic to work y punto."

¡Que vergüenza, qué escándalo!

# Chapter 7

At long last, the school year was over, and it was report card day. Because she lived close by, Sylvia walked to school. As usual, I took the bus to school with the rest of The Kids. Report card day always felt like a holiday, even if summer was anything but a vacation. Maybe because we didn't want to think about the impending hard work, we were caught up in the celebratory mood of the day.

When the school busses came to take us home, I wasn't ready to call it a day. I don't know what got into me, but neither I nor my little sister Gloria got on the bus home with the rest of The Kids. On that fateful day, I decided she could tag along with me and Sylvia without getting into too much trouble. Como dicen, "Mejor pedir perdón que pedir permiso." (As they say, "Better to ask forgiveness than to ask permission.")

Grandview Park was just a couple blocks away from the high school. Across the street from the park was a popular restaurant and drive-in called, The Greyhound, aptly named for our high school mascot. Everyone referred to The Greyhound as, "The Dog". It was a high school lunchtime hangout which served the best burgers and fries anywhere. The restaurant was owned by a family with two kids—a boy and a girl—who attended school with us. It was our favorite place to buy lunch, when we could afford it. "The Dog" also had a couple of pool tables, and guys were always hanging out there, shooting pool. Some of them were older; some were dropouts—wasting time, instead of working like decent folk (como gente decente). Mom and Dad disapproved.

"They should be working if they're not in school. What business do they have hanging around, looking at girls?" Dad's comments about the place were like a warning running through my head, but I immediately suppressed them.

"The Dog" had a walk-up order window, so we never went inside. But today was different. We went in and sat at the counter. We had no bad intentions—we were just three young girls enjoying a beautiful spring day and celebrating the end of the school year. I convinced myself that Mom and Dad didn't ever need to know about our indiscretion. Anyway, it was not as if we were doing anything wrong.

The three of us decided to share a large order of fresh, hot French fries. As we dipped the steaming, hot and delicious fries into our tartar sauce, we savored every bite, talking and laughing. Umm, they were salty and good!

Suddenly, in walked Mom, Dad, and Aunt Mary! ¡Dios Santo! They had tracked us down. ¡Que verguenza! Sylvia and Gloria hadn't spotted the posse yet, but I was choking on what could easily be my last French fry ever.

Who knew how they had found us? But here they were, and, judging from their faces, they were not happy. Mom gripped my shoulder. "¿Que hacen aqui?" she asked quietly, yet firmly.

"Mom!" was all I managed to squeak out. In the next instant, Aunt Mary slapped Sylvia. Chastised, Sylvia rubbed her reddening cheek. Dad was quiet, as the three of us were marched out of there, our egos bruised, embarrassed in front of our peers.

Aunt Mary was livid, Mom was contained, and Dad had a stern look on his face as he silently drove us home. I ran things over in my mind. Mom and Aunt Mary must have talked on the phone when the three of us were nowhere to be found. They must have convened an all-out search party. Well, at least we had a full summer to live down this humiliation before we saw any of the kids from The Dog back at school.

I was sure it was Aunt Mary who had initiated the search, and Dad, in an effort to appease his sister, had folded. I was pretty sure that my parents had acted out of peer pressure. They never would have caused such a public display on their own. Aunt Mary was even more old-school than Mom and Dad. Nevertheless, punishment was in order. Poor Sylvia had been slapped in public—and it was a slap that all three of us felt.

Por lo contrario, Mom and Dad would dole out the appropriate sentence in the privacy of our home. This was a capital offense. We were guilty as charged. It was not a debatable issue—we had been caught red-handed, in a pool hall! We had committed our crime in public.

The Areagas, close family friends, lived right next door to The Dog, and I know that Mom, Dad and Aunt Mary were all the more concerned and upset because the Areagas—la comadre Lola, y el compadre Cuco—had very likely witnessed our scandalous behavior as it unfolded. But it was even worse that Aunt Mary was involved. Seeing what we had done from her straight-laced perspective made our crime all the more shameful. I guessed that Mom and Dad had to live this down, just as much as we did. ¿Que dira la gente? ¡Que escandalo!

In an age when mini-skirts and knee high boots, skin-tight pants and midriff tops were the rage, I drove my pious, old-school parents crazy. They were always concerned about what people might think, or, worse yet, what people might say about the family. Out of their eleven children, I was, hands down, their biggest headache. Being part of such a highly respected and spiritual family meant that my longing to be different, cool, and in-style was an incredible hardship on all concerned.

In our small community, it seemed that people were always looking for opportunities to criticize and find fault. An attack on the family was a powerful assault on what was most valued and dear. I gave my apprehensive parents more than enough to worry about and to defend.

As far as I knew, my dad never cussed or used swear words. Mom almost never did either, but sometimes the situation just merited more than what could be expressed in everyday speech. I have to admit that I was most often the cause of her use of forbidden expletives. For instance, one time I knelt backwards on the couch to look out the big picture window. Gloria and I were just hanging out and talking when Mom entered the room and sat next to me. "Hija, sal a regar las flores. Andale, they haven't been watered for too long. They're starting to wilt."

"Water the flowers? Oh, Mom. Why me? It's too hot. Tell the boys to do it. They're always outside anyway."

"Andale MiCeli, haz lo que te mando."

"But Mom! I don't want to. C'mon, Mom, 'get off of my cloud.'* 'Cause I'm a true nature's child, born to be wild.'"*

* "Get Off My Cloud": Song written by Mick Jagger & Keith Richards (The Rolling Stones). It topped the charts after its release in 1965.

* "Born to Be Wild": Song released by Steppenwolf in 1967.

Knowing full well that I was really pushing it, I slowly got up while delivering that last utterance. As Mom got the gist of my words, she snapped, "¡Si, cabróna!" She didn't appreciate my lame attempt at humor, or my disrespect.

In an effort to redeem myself, I ran outside to do as I had been told, but my sister, Gloria, who watched the events unfold, shuddered at my bold insubordination. Of course she would—little goody two shoes that she was.

When we later recalled that event, Gloria said that Mom slapped me (¡Tas!) but I begged to differ. I knew I had run outside, and Mom could never catch me when I ran. I think Gloria imagined Mom slapping me because that is what I deserved.

In Jr. High school, Cousin Sylvia and I were still best friends and always together. I envied Sylvia's slender physique, which was quite fashionable. Twiggy was the rage with her emaciated look—skinny chicken legs and all.

I had some meat on my bones, and I saw myself as fat, or at least overweight. I didn't know that what I perceived as fat were actually curves. The fact that Real Women Have Curves* had not yet been established.

In the 1960's, schoolgirls wore nylons whenever we could get our hands on them. But they were expensive, often beyond our means. We also wore the long-legged, lightweight spandex girdles that were "in" then. They came in beautiful pastel colors, edged with pretty lace at the bottom of the leg. I didn't know why they were called "long-legged"—the legs were only about an inch long. They fit perfectly under our miniskirts.

Among those of us who were proud owners of this lacy undergarment, it was no dishonor to show a little lace, but only if we could get away with it. Thus, we did what we could to avoid being caught and disgraced by a puritanical teacher or some other adult authority figure.

Black eyeliner pencils, mascara, and frosted lipstick or gloss were also essential for any self-respecting, vanity-ridden, junior-high girl. Anybody

* Real Women Have Curves is a 2002 movie, starring America Ferrera.

who was anybody had her little make up stash, carefully hidden from the adult world.

I had to apply my makeup on the bus or in the school restroom, and I had to be sure to remove all traces of it before returning home. I also left the house in what appeared to be proper attire, but by the time I reached the bus stop—some distance up the road from the house—my skirt was already rolled up, and my lipstick was on.

I was usually prepared to sleep over at Sylvia's, but one day I stayed over without bringing clothes for school, so Sylvia lent me an outfit to wear. Because I was a little curvier than Sylvia, the little skirt she lent me was tighter and, consequently, shorter on me. Evidently, I filled out the outfit a little too well—or too much—depending on whom you asked.

Our school counselor, Mrs. Mowry, was also my Home Economics teacher. I should have skipped her class that day, but I had never even entertained such a thought. Anyway, no amount of tugging and pulling on my little skirt was able to save my hide.

In a huff, Mrs. Mowry reprimanded me in front of the class. "This is completely unacceptable. I've had it with you, young lady. I've told you repeatedly not to wear your skirts so short. Enough warnings—come with me. We're going to the principal's office."

Like a stunned deer caught in the glare of headlights, I looked at Sylvia. She, too, was caught off guard, and she could only offer me a concerned look as she mouthed the words, "Oh no!" Off I went with Mrs. Mowry, silently shaking in my boots. I followed her down the hall as she continued scolding me. On and on she rambled, ad nauseam, as my thoughts wandered off to Mom and Dad and how they would react to this, their wayward daughter's latest escapade.

I felt sick to my stomach. Mrs. Mowry threatened, "Since I haven't been able to impress upon you the importance of following the rules, you've left me no alternative. You'll be getting some well-deserved hacks."

Wait a minute! Hold everything, I thought, stopping abruptly. A surge of defiant energy shot up my spine as I straightened my shoulders and stood at my full height. Mrs. Mowry turned to see me standing motionless, with a smirk on my face and a hand on my hip. "Well, come on, we... are...going...to...the principal's office," she said slowly, emphasizing each word.

I tilted my head slightly and raised my eyebrows. "Oh, no you don't. Nobody touches me, except my mom or my dad." Well played, I thought. I am brilliant! Our eyes were locked in anger, and I savored my short-lived defiance.

Mrs. Mowry's response, though slow in coming, knocked me for a loop. "Well, then, I'll just take you home—where your parents can handle the situation."

Oh… no! Oh my God! I'm a goner. My heart surged. I felt like a fly, reeling after being swiped at with a fly swatter. But I was determined not to give her the satisfaction of seeing me squirm. I was really scared, but I tried to act indifferent. I cocked my head again and with the most defiant look I could muster, I just glared at her. I felt my nostrils flare and my chest heaving up and down. I felt weak.

Mrs. Mowry turned away and we continued walking, but now I trailed behind, trying to hide the fact that I felt like a dog with my tail between my legs.

Cool it! I told myself. Don't show defeat; don't let her think she's won. Relax. Calm your breathing.

Following Mrs. Mowry to her car, I felt my ears buzzing—all the outdoor sounds were muffled. She opened the passenger door without a word, and I scooted into the passenger seat. As she walked around to the driver's side, I quickly raised my butt off the seat and pulled on my little skirt in an effort to cover my exposed legs. It was an exercise in futility.

As Mrs. Mowry settled into the driver's seat, I casually spread my jacket over the books on my lap. Whew, that's better—my bare legs are covered. We sat in silence on the drive home, but I was sweating bullets under my devil-may-care facade. I stared out the car window at the open fields, railroad tracks, trees, and buildings—all flashing by in a blur. It was the same scenery I had seen thousands of times before, but this time I knew I was fast approaching my doom. Everything seemed surreal. My mind was fuzzy, but I was determined not to crumble in front of the old hag.

Realizing that my whole body was tense, I slowly relaxed my jaw and seized the opportunity to casually wipe my mouth with the back of my hand. Oh, geez, I realized, I didn't have time to take off my makeup. ¡Ay! Lord have mercy. Lowering my right hand, I slipped it under the jacket covering my bare legs and grabbed the hem of my little skirt. I couldn't pull it down any further, so I relaxed my clenched hand and nervously tapped my index finger on my leg, telling myself that although I faced impending doom, I would never let Mrs. Mowry see my fear.

Finally, we pulled into my driveway. I sat silently, staring straight ahead and waiting for Mrs. Mowry to make a move. She opened the car door, stepped out and walked over to open my door. I had no choice but to get out of the car, which I did very cautiously, slowly tugging on my miniskirt. She backed away from the car, and I got out, deliberately slamming the car door behind me. Mrs. Mowry glared at me, and I shifted my books and jacket from my right arm to my left, smoothing my little skirt with my right hand. I made all of these unnecessary movements in order to appear preoccupied and thereby avoid her cold stare.

Not a word had passed between us since before we left the school. "Well?" she said as I again smoothed my skirt. I straightened up, tossed my hair over my shoulder, and looked at her with my eyebrows raised. I smirked and cocked my head slightly, as if to ask, "What?"

Clicking her tongue and shaking her head in disgust, she said, "Come on—let's go." Reluctantly, I followed behind her as she approached and then knocked on my front door. I knew only too well that I was a dead girl. I fidgeted with the crucifix around my neck. This time I had truly gone too far. How had things gotten so out of hand, so quickly? Why did I have to open my big mouth? I could blame no one but myself. I wished I could turn things around because now a few hacks suddenly seemed like a slap on the hand.

What a disgrace! What a dishonor! My smart-assed ways had backfired on me, and now I had left my parents no choice but to kill me.

When Mom answered the door, I lingered nervously, fidgeting and tugging on my little skirt as I stood behind Mrs. Mowry. I was scared out of my wits. Mrs. Mowry proceeded to explain to my mother why she had been forced to bring me home. I had left her no alternative; I had been repeatedly warned, etc., etc.

Mom listened, allowing Mrs. Mowry to speak her piece without interruption. An awkward moment of silence followed, during which I cautiously peered around Mrs. Mowry to look at my mother. She was looking at Mrs. Mowry, nodding as if to say, "I see."

Mom looked Mrs. Mowry up and down and very calmly told her, "You know, for a woman of your age and position, you don't set a very good example. Look where your skirt is."

I gasped. My eyes felt as though they would pop out of my head. I swallowed the lump in my dry throat, not daring to show any kind of expression. But I was so proud of my mother!

Mrs. Mowry took a step back as I brushed past her and stood behind my protective mother. Finally, the encounter was over, and Mom had thrown us all for a loop. Mom closed the door, and we waited as Mrs. Mowry walked safely out of sight. I knew my time had come. Mom stood in silence for a moment. Then, she calmly reached toward the coatrack behind the front door. She took a belt off the rack and turned sternly to me, saying, "¡Y tú cabróna!"

Whoa! Hell hath no fury like a mother defending a wayward daughter…a daughter who has brought down shame and disgrace like hell fire! My survival instincts kicked in as I let out a muffled shriek. I turned so fast that I felt a muscle in my side about to snap like an overstretched rubber band. Oh, the pain! Running up the stairs, I narrowly escaped the belt's reach as my mother swung it at me. I felt my little skirt hike up even more as I climbed each step, and I knew Mom could see all the way up to my butt. Ay, ay, ay!

Mom didn't bother to follow me up the stairs, but she yelled out a warning: "You wait, just wait till your father gets home!" I locked myself in the girls' bedroom.

Apparently, Mom wasn't going to bother with me just yet. She would wait for Dad to get home so they could kill me together. I dreaded facing them both at the same time.

I didn't dare emerge from my room until the next morning. Waking up, still full of dread, I looked in my closet for the longest skirt I could find. Not an easy task. Timid, but ready for the worst, I went downstairs, passed Mom in the kitchen while faking a muffled cough, and slipped into the bathroom. Okay, I had managed to pass by, seemingly unnoticed. But by the time I exited the bathroom, I was ready to face my mother.

Mom acted as if nothing had happened. She seemed preoccupied with Norma and Freddy. Dear God, this is serious. They're making me wallow in my fear and anticipation. Maybe they plan to wait until after school to kill me? Not knowing was agonizing.

I kept waiting for my punishment, but neither Mom nor Dad ever mentioned the subject. Knowing what a serious offense I was guilty of, I kept trying to figure out their silence. I could only conclude that perhaps they thought I was beyond redemption, so why beat a dead horse? Maybe I was just destined to be their hopeless daughter, and maybe they considered themselves lucky that all their other children were good. Out of eleven, only one bad child is actually pretty darn good.

I never really figured it out. ¿Quien sabe? Who knows? One thing was crystal clear, sin duda, my parents knew what they were doing. I always knew that I was the greatest challenge to them. I had gotten into trouble for things my older sisters would never have dreamed of doing. Yet, Mom and Dad never wrote me off as hopeless, although my guilt often made me think they should.

As much as I kept being a very difficult teenager, they somehow had a sixth sense. They knew that I was worth saving. They enforced their discipline, and I had to admit that they were doing an amazing job, although it would be a while before they reaped the rewards for all their efforts.

During my difficult junior high school years, I discovered Edgar Allan Poe. I was fascinated by his morbid melancholia. I admired his power to keep the reader enthralled through not only his storyline, but by his unique and intricate vocabulary, rhyme, and use of repetition and imagery.

Poe was a genius whose writings I had stumbled across at a most crucial time in my life. He ignited my fascination with the macabre—and with the twisted, psychotic, neurotic mind. Evenings after school, while The Kids watched TV, I read Poe's stories and poetry and became lost in his world. Poe had a style that drew me in and mesmerized me. I was there, in the midst of each story, as it unfolded before me.

I was Annabelle Lee. I was the lost Lenore. Poe held me captive through the magic of his words, and he provided me with an escape from reality that I badly needed. I imagined myself being as creative a genius as he. What it must have been like to have such talent, to be someone who could make a difference and have such an impact in the lives of so many others! What it must have been like to actually be somebody.

Through his songwriting and music, Bob Dylan fought for social justice and human rights. He fought against war, oppression, discrimination, and all such worldly evils. Between these two heroes, I felt a glimmer of hope. Bob Dylan was bringing about a much needed awareness and he was popular enough to make people listen.

I listened to Bob Dylan singing his words of hope. I wrote my own poetry and lost myself in Edgar Alan Poe. I reveled in sci-fi horror movies, fantasy and mythology—outlets that provided a great escape from my own reality and teenage angst. I believed in happy-ever-after fairytales, knights in shining armor, and wishes upon stars.

My favorite song was Jiminy Cricket's "When You Wish upon a Star" because I believed in magic, and I liked to imagine all sorts of fantasies with happy endings. I believed that somehow, someday, things would be better. It was logically reassuring to know that conditions do improve through hard work, faith and circumstance. I only needed to look at my own family—at how each generation had built upon the hard work of its forebears to make our lives better. There was hope… we always must have hope!

Dad never let anyone drive his car, but in the spring I needed to be at graduation practice in the afternoon, and he decided to trust me. I had completed my Driver's Education course and learned always to be on the alert and extra careful, especially after all the imaginary manslaughters I had committed while learning.

"Pull into that driveway," my driving instructor, Mr. Tucker, said.

I put my left turn signal on, slowed down, and carefully pulled in. Stopping in the driveway, I put the car in park, pulled up the emergency break, turned off the ignition, and pulled out the key. Smiling, I looked at Mr. Tucker.

"Very good," he nodded. Now, pull out of the driveway and continue driving on the street around the park."

"Okay," I responded proudly. I was doing well that day. I felt excited and confident. As I proceeded to back out of the driveway, Mr. Tucker suddenly yelled, "Oh no!"

Startled, I hit the brake, yelling, "What?"

"You just killed a person," he replied.

"No, I didn't!" I shouted. "I checked all my mirrors!"

"You didn't turn your head and look back," he said somberly.

"But..."

"No buts about it, young lady. You can't skip a step. That's how important it is to be alert and cautious; it could mean a life or other serious consequences."

"Mr. Tucker," I said biting my lip, "How many people can I kill and still pass this course?"

"I haven't decided yet," he answered.

"Okay, but let's just say I scared this one. I didn't kill him."

Even if it was scary, driving was exhilarating and it was such a necessary skill. Grandview High School was only a couple of miles away. I was confident that I would do fine. After all, I was ready to graduate. I was grown up.

My classmates and I were caught up in the excitement. We had a great time and graduation practice was a cinch. Afterwards, some of the seniors wanted to celebrate, but I wouldn't even consider it. I had to prove that I was mature—I couldn't betray my parents' trust. Besides, I wasn't given permission for anything but practice. I would be in big trouble if I didn't take the car back to the house.

I drove straight home without incident, and all was well. Feeling grown up and optimistic, I parked the car in the back and sighed in happy relief. I was going to graduate! I was an adult!

Then it dawned on me that maybe I should put the car in the garage so Dad wouldn't have to bother. He always took such good care of his car. Yeah, that's the least I could do. Dad preferred to park his car in the garage, so I would do him a favor and carefully align the car just right. I had never done this before, and there wasn't a lot of space, but how hard could it be? I felt puffed up and full of confidence, like those exotic birds that displayed their puffed-out chests. Yep, I was good. Dad would be glad that I was considerate with his car. Just go in very slowly and perfectly straight. No problem.

For a moment, I thought about just leaving well enough alone. But on second thought...no, I wanted to do things right. Sitting tall in the seat, I said to myself, "Okay now, slow and careful."

I inched my way forward. Suddenly, "Screech!" The metal molding on the passenger side of the car was scraping against the garage door. My heart was pounding, my body stiff and stretched up as high as I could sit. I froze. I couldn't react! The sound was awful as the molding tore away from the car. It seemed like I was moving in slow motion. Finally, I was able to gather my senses, and I hit the brake.

"¡Dios Santo!" Somehow, I finally managed to back up and try again. This time I got it right. I turned off the ignition and sat there in the driver's seat, not wanting to move. Slowly, I opened the door, stepped out, and walked around the front of the car to look at the damage. I stared in disbelief, thinking, Oh no! How could this happen? I was trying so hard to be careful and responsible. "Oh, God, get a hold of yourself. I have to go in and tell Mom and Dad," I whispered to myself.

I decided to tell Mom first so she could help me figure out how to tell Dad. I found her in the kitchen. I wondered if I should just blurt it out. She was in good humor. She smiled, saying, "¿Como te fué, hija?" I just didn't know how to start; I couldn't get past my fear. I simply replied to her question.

"Oh, uh, it was good. I have to be first in line 'cause I'm short, but that's okay. Sylvia's as short as I am, but she had higher heels on, so they let her be second. We have to go in pairs, a boy and a girl—and guess who my partner is?" I knew I was rambling.

"¿Quien es? I don't know him, do I?" Mom asked.

"It's Marvin James," I said. "You know Norma's little friend, Patricia James? Marvin's her brother."

"Oh, mira que bien," Mom replied. "La muchachita me cae muy bien."

The car, I thought. Confess. But how? Instead, I kept putting it off.

"Yeah, Marvin's really nice too, but he better not get any ideas, just 'cause we have to be partners. You should've seen his face light up when they called my name as his partner."

Just then, Rudy and Freddy burst in, panting and thirsty. Mom became distracted, and I kept thinking, the car! The car!

As evening drew near, Mom and Dad got all dressed up to go out. Oh No! It was Wednesday, Mexican movie night at the Grandview Theatre. Mom and Dad never missed the Mexican movies. I stood in the dining room as they got ready to leave.

"We'll be back later," Mom said over her shoulder.

"Se portan bien," Dad added, and they walked out the front door. I braced myself, knowing Dad would be coming right back in to question and reprimand me.

I waited. Nothing happened. I ran to look out the window in time to see the car leaving our driveway.

"What's wrong, Sally?" Viola asked.

"Um…nothing…."

Mom and Dad hadn't seen the damage. They were on their way to the movies. My stomach churned as I contemplated what would happen. I knew that, as more time passed without their knowing what I had done, I would be in even bigger trouble! Oh, God! Now what? I had to go to bed without the blessed relief that came with confession. Tossing and turning, I slipped in and out of disturbing dreams in which demons chased me relentlessly. Every time I found what I thought was a good hiding place, it suddenly transformed into an obvious open spot, and I had to keep running. I ran myself ragged all night long. With the devil at my heels, I tried to scream for help, but I had no voice. I woke, drenched in sweat—the shame and fear of my sin hung heavily over me.

The next morning, I dragged myself out of bed, exhausted from the long night I had spent running in my dreams. Looking in the mirror, I said to myself, "Ugh! You look as bad as you feel." Running my hands over my hair, I called the rest of The Kids. "Time to get up. Come on. Mom's already called us twice. Up!"

As I started down the stairs, I tried to be quiet. I dreaded what I had coming. Mom stopped me in the kitchen before I could slip by. Very calmly, she said, "Sally...." There was an awkward pause as I froze in my steps.

"Huh?" I answered nervously, knowing exactly what was up.

"Stop biting the inside of your cheek! Why didn't you tell your dad what you did to his car?"

I hung my head. "Mom, I tried, but I was scared," I replied meekly.

My mother continued, "Sabes muy bien como es tú Papá con su caro. How do you think he felt when we got to the movie theater and saw what you had done? Y lo peor... you didn't say a word to us. Why?" My mother's face showed utter disappointment. "Go get ready for school. Ándale," she said, breaking an egg into the skillet.

Oh, Dear God. I felt horrid. I wanted to scream, "Why don't you just beat me? I deserve it!" I deserved a beating. I could tolerable a beating. But this horrid feeling... I wanted to cry. I was so guilty and so ashamed. Even worse was my failure to take responsibility and face the consequences, which was precisely why my mother was so disillusioned with me. I knew that only too well.

My poor father never mentioned the incident, and it was forgotten with time. But I would never forget my parent's disappointment and calm resignation. I was a lost cause. "No tienes remedio," I told myself. I felt ashamed and disgusted.

In the New Year of 1970, the holiday season was over, and we were back at school when a momentous announcement came over the school's public address system. I didn't know it then, but this announcement would forever change the course of my life.

Recruiters from the University of Washington's Minority Affairs Office in Seattle were scheduled to visit Grandview High School in two weeks to address minority and economically disadvantaged students. I rarely paid attention to these announcements—they were usually irrelevant to my everyday life. But on that day, I stopped fumbling with my notebook and sat up, straining to hear every detail.

"Whoa, minority recruiters," I repeated. "I can't believe it." I was anxious for the end-of-class bell to ring so I could rush over to the bulletin board and read the announcement for myself.

It was my senior year, and I would graduate in June. I couldn't wait for the recruiters to come. Not that I thought my attending the university was even a remote possibility, but I still looked forward to the event. I wanted to see the recruiters and hear what they had to say. This was very exciting.

It was common knowledge—a fact that simply went unmentioned and unchallenged—that the Mexican kids were never counseled or encouraged in the public school system. I had never met with a counselor to discuss or make a plan for my future. I wasn't even aware that such planning was the counselor's job. But I learned from the recruiters that I could be accepted to the University of Washington through the Minority Affairs Educational Opportunity Program. The program had been developed for this very reason—to help students of color such as me, my family, and my friends.

The 1960's saw the emergence of a new age when people fought for equality and basic human and civil rights. Minority Affairs was but one fruit from this struggle. I now realized that, as a minority, I was being given a chance to succeed. The roadblocks had been pushed aside. I could find a remedy for my high school deficiencies, and I could get help to succeed—financial aid, academic advising, counseling, and tutorial services.

For the first time in my life, I had hope for a better future. The people and resources I now encountered could make all the difference in the world. The mere fact that there were educated, professional people who believed in me was more than I had ever dared to hope.

The UW recruiters' presentation included a slideshow that left me breathless. The Educational Opportunity Program had been carefully designed and geared towards success. I saw Mexican and other minority students and counselors smiling and working together, sitting in classes, learning. I had never seen so many different "ethnic" people. "Diversity," as it turned out, was a great selling point for the University of Washington. This great educational institution was actually proud of being diverse and multi-cultural. I was blown away.

The immense and beautiful campus with its stately Neo-Gothic architecture enthralled me. I imagined myself in that wondrous, magical place. Did I dare follow the Yellow Brick Road? The big city of Seattle was a place I had dreamed about and yearned to return to since I had visited there when I was ten. Thus far, returning had only been a fantasy. Yet, here and now, a whole new world had opened up before me, and I was being handed a special invitation.

The recruiters emphasized that, although special help was available to compensate for our lack of college preparation, we would be required to maintain a good G.P.A. and compete with every other UW student at the university level. This was most certainly not a free ride. Plain and simple, it was a way to make up for how the public school system had failed us. An opportunity was now being afforded to those of us who had been discouraged, denied, and derailed along the way.

The required tools would be provided, but I understood that I alone would bear the load. Could I possibly be up to such a challenge? There had never been a reason to try before. Due to our economic and social situation, I had always thought my future was preordained: I would graduate from high school, get a job in town, get married, and have kids. Life held no other prospects, and I accepted this reality. I had never even dared to question, much less challenge, such a scenario before.

We had no money; college was something I had always imagined was for families who had the luxury of financial security—i.e., my White peers. But suddenly, out of nowhere, things had changed. My stomach fluttered with anticipation and excitement. I felt giddy. I felt hopeful. I felt happy. Was it really possible—me, not just in college, but at the prestigious University of Washington?

How could I pass up such an opportunity? I simply had to give it my best shot. Yet my hope was also, paradoxically, ominous. The excitement and disbelief that came with so great a gift were accompanied by an unimaginable fear. Did I even dare to believe that there might be more to life than just working in the fields and struggling to make ends meet? Did I dare embark on this journey without an ounce of preparation? Did I dare even allow myself to think that life as I knew it could possibly change? I was overcome with questions and doubts: I didn't even know how to study; I had never done it before, never had a reason to. Throughout my public school education, my only concern was that I pass. Why should I have cared about grades? They wouldn't show on my diploma, and that diploma was all that mattered.

The only things I liked about school were my English classes. I loved good literature, and I liked to write. Other than that, I didn't care about any of it. In my other classes, I had never even opened a book to study. I did all of my homework in study hall, and I managed to pass by paying attention and taking good notes in class—that is, I had simply gotten by without doing any real homework.

My mind raced: If I could do average work without ever studying or even trying, imagine what I might be capable of if I really tried. Surely, I couldn't be that dumb if, without really trying, I had managed never to fail a class. Now that I had something to work for, I would read and study, and maybe I could make it. At the very least, I would never have to regret the fact that I hadn't tried. Maybe all my hopes and excitement were as futile as my Jiminy Cricket wishes on a star, but, somehow, I had always really believed something more was possible, and I had to believe now, more than ever.

Most of the teachers and other high school staff thought the whole thing was a big joke. Mexican kids being allowed into college? What a laugh! To them this was a big waste of money, time, effort and resources. Some of them didn't even bother to hide their disdain.

Were they really so blind, or did they just pretend not to realize that they were the ones responsible for our learned lack of effort, for our acquired complacency? It was, indeed, mind-boggling to think that our very teachers and counselors had programmed us for failure and had made sure we stayed on that grim track.

It had been over a week since the UW recruiters' visit. I was now constantly preoccupied with the possibility of attending the university. Both my cousin Sylvia and I were excited, thinking more clearly than we ever had as we imagined our futures. On our lunch break, we sat outside in front of the school, chatting with friends.

Standing up, I said, "I'm going in. I've been carrying this UW application with me since the recruiters were here. I'm going to fill it out."

"So why're you going' in now? Where are you going?" Juanita asked.

"I'm going to sit in the classroom. It's empty now, so I'll use this time to get going on my application.

"Sally, you're really going to do it? Are you sure you want to go? It's a major step," Juanita added.

"I've thought a lot about it and I'm positive," I replied. "Syl, are you sure you don't want to go?"

"No, I'm going to beauty school. That's what I really want to do."

"Well, I haven't said a word about this to Mom and Dad," I confessed, "but I'll cross that bridge when I come to it. Okay, I'll see you guys later."

Running up the stairs to the second floor, I quietly walked into Mr. White's empty classroom. I pulled out my University of Washington application and started to fill it out. Unaware that he had even entered the room, I was startled when Mr. White walked up silently behind me. Peering over my shoulder, he asked, "What do you have there?"

I gasped and clutched the paperwork to my chest. Turning to face him, I lowered my eyes and responded timidly, "I'm filling out my application to, um, the University of Washington."

He snorted and walked away, shaking his head. Then he laughed facetiously and sneered, "You'll never make it."

I sat there, holding my breath. I should have been used to this by now, but somehow I had never gotten used to being kicked down, time and again.

He had caught me completely off guard. I didn't know how to respond, so I didn't. I just turned back to face the front of the classroom, and I sat there. My chest heaved as I struggled to calm my rapid breathing. Placing both of my hands on top of my paperwork, I admonished myself, Stop it! Get ahold of yourself. Oh, how I hated this uncontrollable, heavy breathing! It always happened when I got nervous or upset.

Mr. White was now at the front of the room, and he stood with his back to me, writing on the blackboard.

This is my chance to sneak out of here, I told myself. Still trying to calm my breathing, I very quietly put away my application. I felt humiliated. I knew my grades didn't reflect college aptitude, and for that reason I was deeply ashamed and embarrassed. Still, why had he found it necessary to be so mean?

Biting the inside of my cheek, I stared at his back as he wrote on the board. Mr. White stood at least six feet tall, and he was wiry and skinny. He had perfect posture, which might have made him appear stately if it weren't for his pinched nose and thin, frowning lips, which reflected his arrogant and callous nature. He reminded me of the big bullies on the playground who got off on beating up other helpless kids. I bet he has been a bully all his life, I thought. Ugly, arrogant son of a bitch!

I felt hot all over, and I knew my face was beet red. I glanced at the clock on the wall. There was plenty of time before class, so I quietly slipped out of the classroom. Once in the hall, I ran down the stairs. I rushed into the sanctuary of the girls' restroom and headed straight for the sink. Splashing cold water on my face and forehead, I mumbled, "Oh, God! Why?" How I dreaded going back to Mr. White's classroom! But, despite the deep humiliation I felt, I had no choice.

Clenching my jaw and taking a deep breath, I looked at myself in the mirror. I stared intensely until my vision blurred. Images of my family working in the fields flooded my mind, bringing back the hardship, suffering, pain, and sacrifice.

Wiping away hot tears, I said under my breath, "I'll show you. I'll show you and everybody else." I took another deep breath, exhaled slowly, closed my eyes, and slowly cocked my head from side to side to relax my neck and shoulder muscles. Suddenly, my quiet moment was interrupted as a couple of other girls entered the bathroom. I realized it was getting close to class time and soon the restroom would be crowded.

Shaking my head I thought, Okay, go ahead. Think what you want, but someday I will prove you wrong. Then and there I made up my mind. There was nothing more to think about. I would attend the University of Washington.

I quickly brushed my hair, freshened my makeup, and walked out of the restroom. Indomitable and resolved, I returned to Mr. White's classroom. I entered the room—proud and straight, with my head held high. Students filed in along with me. Taking a seat in the front row, I looked straight at Mr. White. I knew he could feel my hard stare, but he never even glanced my way.

Coward, I thought. Slap me down, and now you can't even face me. You don't scare me anymore. You can't hurt me anymore, 'cause "The Times They Are A-Changin'."*

---

* "The Times They Are A-Changing" was released Jan. 1964. It was Bob Dylan's third studio album & his first album to contain only original compositions—mostly ballads concerning issues such as racism, poverty, and social change.

The "someday" I had vowed to "show him" did come a few years later, when I returned to visit Grandview High School as a recruiter for the University's Minority Affairs Educational Opportunity Program. I used myself as an example to emphasize the success of the program and the fact that it could enable the success of young Latino students just like me. But I didn't look for Mr. White to exact my revenge, as I had once planned.

Finding myself back in my old high school, looking at my image in the same bathroom mirror that had reflected my shame and despair a few years earlier, I realized that I no longer felt the need for vengeance. I was such a different person, with a confidence and security I had so sorely lacked those years before. I actually pitied Mr. White and his twisted, narrow-minded views. As I looked at my reflection, a little smile appeared as I thought, I don't have time for such ignorance. My mission here is clear, and it doesn't include senseless retribution.

I felt confident and invigorated as I met my fellow recruiter in the hallway.

"Ready?" I smiled.

"You bet," he responded.

"I'll take the lead," I said. "This is my school."

The summer after I graduated from high school, I didn't work in the fields as usual. Mom and Dad had decided to give me a break from field work because I was now eighteen and would soon be on my own anyway. Because my sister Lydia's second child, David, was just a year old, I was sent to spend the summer with her so I could help out. I was thrilled. I stayed with Lydia—the oldest Cantú sister—in Othello, another tiny Eastern Washington town.

Lydia was beautiful—tall, thin, and elegant, with a stunning natural smile accentuated by her perfect teeth and big dimples. I loved and envied Lydia's smile. It lit up her entire face and made her beautiful, dark eyes sparkle. No matter how much I practiced in the mirror, my smile always looked fake and forced.

Lydia was the only girl in the family who wasn't short. Her complexion was flawless, and her long legs perfectly shaped. She always looked impeccable. Along with her physical attributes, she was bubbly, outgoing, and full of energy.

Lydia was also a strong advocate for education. She insisted that the five of us younger Kids grow up with English as our first language and that we complete our education. Without her and Viola's intervention, Mom and Dad would never have allowed me to leave home to attend the University of Washington in Seattle.

Lydia's husband, Jack Heath, was Caucasian and one of the handsomest guys I had ever seen. Jack was a carpenter. His skin was deeply bronzed from working outside. He had deep blue eyes with long, curly eyelashes. His face was perfectly chiseled, revealing deep, handsome dimples whenever he smiled. He could easily pass for a movie star or TV celebrity. Best of all, he had a wonderful personality and was great with us Kids. He often took time to play with us, take us to Dairy Queen for treats, or tell us jokes that kept us in stitches. We all loved him.

"Hey, Sally," Jack called out over his shoulder.

I was riding in the back seat of his car while he took me and Lydia for a drive.

"Huh?" I answered, leaning forward to see through the gap between the front bucket seats of his little red convertible.

"See that?" he asked, pointing to a huge smashed bug on the windshield.

"Yuck! That's a big one," I responded.

"Bet he doesn't have the guts to do that again," Jack laughed.

"Ha! Good one!"

Lydia just said, "Oh, Jack." But Jack and I were laughing so much we got her laughing too.

Days later, I was still laughing every time I thought about it. Jack was good-natured, with a great sense of humor, always making people laugh and helping others. It's no wonder Lydia and Jack married. They were a perfect match.

Wednesday was Lydia's grocery shopping day, so on that day I would stay home and take care of my nephews, Johnny and David. I was good at that. Johnny had recently turned six, and David was a baby, so he slept a lot. Although I had never been crazy about children, I liked being with my nephews. David was the cutest blond-haired baby I had ever seen, with his mom and dad's big dimples and good looks. Johnny was adorably cute and such an intelligent and self-sufficient child. He didn't often need to be disciplined or require much attention from me, especially when he was focused on something. I guessed that he had been used to being an only child.

As cute as my beautiful nephews were, there was something about them that I found a bit ironic. Johnny looked completely Mexican, while David looked just as completely Caucasian. Of course, they were an equal mixture of both, but the difference in their appearance struck me as odd. Still, who really cared? They were both beautiful.

I loved to engage Johnny in conversation because he was very smart and perceptive. He often picked up on things and asked interesting questions, such as, "Why is your shirt so small? It doesn't cover your tummy. Don't you have a bigger one that fits?"

"Yeah," I laughed, "I have bigger shirts, Johnny, but I like this one 'cause it's in style, and it keeps me cool."

One day, while I was walking to the store with Johnny, I reached into my pocket to pull out some money. I was counting the change in my hand and happened to drop a dime. When I stopped, so did Johnny. "Johnny, can you pick that up for me, please?" I asked.

He looked puzzled and asked, "Why? Are you going to have a baby?"

"What? Why did you ask me that?" I said, taken aback by his question.

He answered, "When my mom was going to have a baby, she couldn't bend over either."

"Oh, Johnny, you're so funny! No, I'm not going to have a baby. I guess I'm just being lazy." We both laughed.

When they heard that story, Lydia and Jack got a big kick out of it.

On another day, Lydia had gone out to do some errands. Little David was sleeping soundly, and Johnny was playing in the living room.

"I'm going to get the mail, Johnny," I yelled, opening the front door. The mail drop was just outside the door, and I grabbed the envelopes quickly, not wanting to let the hot summer air into the air-conditioned house.

"Phew! It is hot out there," I said, sorting through the mail. "Oh, here's one for me. Yay! It's from the University… Financial Aid. Hmm." I grabbed the letter opener. Slowly, neatly, I slit open the envelope. Containing my excitement and anticipation, I carefully took the letter out of the envelope, smoothed it on the table, and then picked it up with both hands.

"Oh, my God!" I moaned. I stared in disbelief at the huge sum of money the letter said I had been awarded. My hands were shaking. "Oh!" I said again, folding up the letter as fast as I could and returning it to the envelope. I clasped the letter to my heaving chest, and I rushed to the bedroom. I pulled open a drawer and stuffed the letter underneath some T-shirts. Still breathing heavily, I slammed the drawer shut and closed my eyes.

"What am I going to do?" I asked myself. Slowly opening the drawer again, I pulled out the letter. I read it once more. "Student Loan. Student Grant. Work-Study," I read slowly. The dollar signs and numbers entered after each category knocked me for a loop. "Loan… Student Loan," I repeated.

Having no concept of large amounts of money, I read the letter over and over, devastated by the fact that I was sinking into debt and my education had not yet even begun. In my mind's eye I saw huge bundles of paper money in stacks and piles, and I thought about how the loans would grow larger every year.

How would I ever repay such huge amounts of money? The idea dominated my thoughts and had me scared and overwhelmed. "This is ridiculous. It's impossible," I exclaimed.

Walking over to the bunk beds, I plopped myself down on the bottom bunk. "What in the world was I thinking?" I mumbled. Oh, yeah, financial aid. I knew darn well financial aid didn't mean free. But, I hadn't really stopped to think about the reality of this. Okay, calm down and think. I don't have to go. It's not like I signed a contract or agreement or anything… yet. My decision to attend the UW had been made under a kind of duress; it was rather impulsive. Thinking back, I had to admit that at the time of my snap decision what I wanted most in the world was vengeance, retribution—to show todo el mundo that I could be more than they had ever given me credit for. Okay, I still wanted that, but most importantly I wanted a better chance in this life; I wanted a bigger, better, brighter future… I wanted the future that only a university education could procure. My thoughts raced, and I said loudly, "I want… never… to be a farmworker again…." The end of my sentence trailed off as I shut my eyes and tried to calm myself.

After just a few minutes, I heard Lydia's car drive up, so I hurriedly jumped off the bed and hid the letter. Walking into the living room, I said, "Johnny, your mom's home. I'll go help her with the groceries."

"Hey," Lydia smiled, "how are the kids? Everything okay?"

"Yeah, good, same as always, never any trouble. Johnny's playing and David's sleeping. Go on in. I'll get the bags."

As I carried in grocery bags, Lydia started putting away the groceries, saying, "I just saw Birdie at the store. She invited us over for a BBQ and swimming. How about that, Johnny? Wanna go swimming?"

"Yes!" Johnny and I both answered in unison.

"Oh, good. That'll be fun," I added, trying to conceal my inner anguish. I was happy for the invitation—it would serve to keep me distracted.

Birdie was one of Lydia's best friends, and she had a huge, beautiful house with a swimming pool. She was a good-natured person and always fun to be around, just like Lydia. I knew there would be games and laughter, fun, and great food. "Just what the doctor ordered," I smiled. Everyone always had fun at Birdie's.

I continued to worry and weigh my options about attending the University. I needed time to think, but the immediate and most crucial issue was that I could never let my parents—or anyone else—find out that I was getting myself into such debt. Oh, what a heavy secret to harbor! I felt like a naughty child doing something wrong, especially when I thought about how Mom and Dad would react if they knew about my loans.

One of Lydia's neighbors was an elderly lady who lived in a huge, old, two-story house on the corner. Her grandson, Marc, had come to spend the summer, so there were always teenagers next door. One of them said hi to me one day as I walked by. We talked, and before long I became friends with all of them. I was happy to have a bunch of friends just down the block.

After spending some time with them, I felt a bit intimidated and concerned because they did things I had never thought of doing, things I hadn't even been exposed to. Cigarettes and alcohol—especially beer and what they called "cheap wine"—were readily available, and they always smoked and drank freely. They didn't seem to care about the time. It was never too early or too late to drink.

How strange, I thought as I observed their transformation—from being straight, to being tipsy, and sometimes to being downright drunk. Other than on television, I had never seen anyone drunk. I didn't understand the appeal. Alcohol smelled and tasted nasty. I couldn't get past the rank smell of beer. Being drunk just meant being out of control and usually acting stupid. I had enough trouble just being my normal self—I was often inhibited and uptight, always worried about my public appearance and actions. I figured this was probably a good thing because I was not about to let my guard down. My need to be in control pretty much ruled out any chance of me ever becoming an alcoholic.

My new friends always offered me something to drink, but I politely declined. It made me especially nervous the first time they offered, but I soon learned that I could be myself because nobody ever insisted or tried to coax me to indulge. What a relief—I didn't even have to come up with an excuse.

Although Marc occupied the basement part of the house, I wondered how his grandmother could be so blind to all of the partying that went on. I had never seen her, not even once. In fact, I wondered if she even existed.

One evening at dinner, Jack asked, "So, Sally, how's your Othello summer vacation going? Are you bored yet?"

"No way," I answered. "Not working in the fields is a real vacation. Johnny's no trouble at all; he's such a good kid. Aren't you, Johnny?" And I love Lydia's cooking and Birdie's swimming pool. I've got it made this summer."

"Great. I thought you might be missing your family and your friends," Jack smiled.

"She's made some friends next door," Lydia added. "Mrs. Riley's grandson is here for the summer."

I smiled, nodding my head.

"So, that's why all those kids are always around over there. I wondered about that," Jack said.

"Hey, by the way," I cut in, "I've never seen the grandmother. Do you guys know her?"

"We've met her, but we don't see much of her," Jack answered.

Lydia added, "I've seen her working in the yard and tending to her flowers. She's really friendly. I stop and talk to her sometimes, but she mostly keeps to herself. It looks like she has someone over to help her every Thursday, though. And I did give her our phone number, a long time ago, in case she ever needs anything."

"Well, that's good to know," I replied. "Her grandson, Marc, doesn't seem much interested in her. He's forever busy with his own thing." But that's all I told Lydia and Jack. No way was I going to tell them about the drinking and smoking that went on over there. I didn't want to be banned from the place.

I made it a point to walk every day. Since I was not working in the fields, I figured I had better get some exercise. One day, Lydia asked me to stop by the drug store for her while I was out on my walk. Passing Marc's place, I stopped to say hi. Everyone was excited as they piled into the back of a van. Somebody yelled, "Come on! You're just in time! We scored some acid!"

"Oh, sorry," I said. "I'm running errands for my sister." I waved and yelled, "Have fun." Watching the van disappear around the corner, I stared blankly, with a forced, fake grin on my face. I felt dazed. My eyes stared intently into the distance. I tried to process what I had just heard… Slowly, I put my hand across my mouth as if to wipe the fake grin off my face. I was frozen in time and space. My open hand, still over my mouth, bunched into a fist. I bit the upper part of my index finger as I closed my eyes in disbelief. Everything seemed to be in slow motion. I opened my eyes and looked down at the sidewalk. I replayed the previous scene over and over in my mind.

We scored some acid? We scored some acid. We-scored-some-acid? I couldn't believe what had just transpired and how it had all happened so fast.

I muttered, "Am I dreaming? Oh, man."

Real acid? As in LSD? What in the world are they doing with drugs? I knew it was illegal, but wasn't it also really dangerous? In fact, hadn't I just read somewhere that it can kill you or screw you up for life?

My mind raced back to a film about drugs that I had seen in junior high school. Seeing the ugly, hopeless lives of drug addicts had left a lasting impression. The film did its job quite well—and not just on me, as was evident from the looks on the faces of my classmates. It was terrifying to think that people could end up that degraded, and inconceivable that all their misery could have been avoided by simply staying away from drugs.

I shrugged and shook my head before continuing on my way. But I couldn't shake the eerie feeling that had come over me. I was in shock. I thought about how awful it would be if those kids got into any kind of legal trouble when I was with them. How would I ever clear my name? What would happen to me? Mom and Dad and the rest of the family would be disgraced forever.

After that, I kept my distance for a while. To avoid passing the house, I walked around the block. But because I didn't have any other friends in Othello, I soon missed their company. I started walking by the house again. Sometimes I just said hi; other times I stopped and talked for a few minutes.

When they invited me to Black Lake, I really wanted to go. I had heard so much about Black Lake and how much fun it was. Everyone loved the place. So, after some deliberation, I asked Jack and Lydia if I could go, and they consented.

The trip was great. No one mentioned drugs, and I was elated to be there. Black Lake was a beautiful spot, and even though I couldn't swim, I had a wonderful time. I hoped the acid thing was just a fluke—a one-time thing.

On the drive home, I sat in the crowded back seat with three other people. We all sang along with the radio as The Who belted out their popular hit, "Summertime Blues":

Well, I'm a'gonna raise a fuss
An' I'm a'gonna raise a holler.
I've been working all summer
Just to try and earn a dollar...
Sometimes I wonder what I'm a'gonna do
'Cause there ain't no cure for the summertime blues...

We all cheered as the song ended. Everyone prattled on excitedly about different things. I grew silent for a moment as the song's lyrics lingered in my mind. I thought, Wow, these kids don't have a clue about my summertime blues. They have it made. They do whatever they want. They don't work. I felt a sudden pang of guilt. Here I was, enjoying my summer and having fun while my family worked in the fields. I didn't want to think about that. What good would it do? Anyway, I would soon be attending the University of Washington, and that was a step towards the betterment of not only my own future, but my family's as well. I tried to rationalize my guilt away.

Back in town and not far from home, we passed a house with Mexican people in the yard. The scene caught my attention—it was obvious from their appearance that they were just getting home from working in the fields. They were dressed in dusty, loose-fitting work clothes, and they carried sombreros, hoes and water jugs. I saw the fatigue in their faces, their slow movements. Man! How I could relate to their pain!

At that very intense moment, Danny blurted out something about "those beaners." Completely taken aback, I slid myself forward, grabbing the back of the front seat. In disbelief, I asked, "What did you say?" As he repeated his racial slur, I was sick. I trembled with fury. In an instant, I was transformed—I unleashed my outrage:

"Where do you get off calling names and looking down on them?! What makes you think you're better? And the rest of you think it's funny? Is that how you all get your kicks? Does it make you feel superior?"

"Whoa," Deb said with a startled look on her face. Everyone was shocked—not at what Danny had said, but at my reaction. Marc, who was driving, looked back at me with a furrowed brow in open-mouthed surprise. Quickly, he tried to make light of the situation, "Oh, come on, Sally, he didn't mean..."

Jenny put her hand on my outstretched arm. "Sally, let it go. It's okay," she said, rubbing my arm. Then she looked at Danny, saying, "Stupid!"

"Oh…I…man!" Danny said with a confused look, but then he just shut up and sat there, shaking his head.

"Okay? How can it be okay? What is wrong with you guys?" I snapped back. "You're not better than they are. You couldn't measure up to them if you tried. And just what do you think I am? If that's what you think of Mexicans, then I'm a beaner too! What the hell are you doing hanging around with me?"

Someone interjected, "Oh, no, but you're different."

"You bunch of fools!" I yelled. "Stop the car. Now! Let me out!"

"But, we're not home yet. Sally…."

They were all stunned. They had never seen me like this—my Mexican side, my enraged side. Por lo contrario, I was always so quiet and mild-mannered.

Finally—after I continued angrily to insist—Marc pulled over and stopped. I didn't even wait for the person next to me to get out of the car. Instead, I scrambled right over him, sneering, "You guys really need to be more careful who you hang around with. You might be seen fraternizing with a beaner. I mean, what would people think?" I slammed the door.

I rushed off in a huff as they trailed behind me in the car. Marc was saying, "Sally, get in. Come on—everything's cool."

I turned towards them, shaking my head—a disgusted, indignant look on my face. I felt such a burning anger—a violent, raging fury. Turning sharply away from them, I walked faster. They were all trying to apologize, to justify themselves.

"Sally, we're sorry… I didn't mean it, honest…."

"But what's the big deal? You're nothing like those people."

I cringed. That one really burned—it stabbed right through the heart.

"Just shut up! – shut UP! Leave me alone!!" I screamed. Closing my eyes and taking a deep breath, I covered my ears with my clenched fists. I wanted to scream out my rage like a crazy person.

Abruptly, I stopped in my tracks, turned slowly, and walked up to the passenger window of the car. My hands were balled in such tight fists that I felt my long red nails digging into my palms. I tried to maintain a semblance of composure.

"Don't—you—ever—bother me again!" I yelled. "All of you. Get it into your retarded, red-neck heads—you ignorant White trash. I never want to see the likes of any of you, much less be seen with you!" I continued yelling. I hit the car with my fist and shouted, "Get lost!"

When I finally reached my sister's house, I was relieved to find nobody else home. I couldn't stop shaking, and my heart was still racing. Safely in my room, I plopped face down onto the bed. I was exhausted, in a state of utter disgust and disbelief. I hit the bed with my fist, yelling, "Stupid! Stupid! You're a fool!" I rolled over onto my back. I grabbed the teddy bear from the pillow, curled up in a fetal position, and tried to slow my rapid, ragged breathing. I focused on each breath, breathing in deeply and then slowly exhaling. Soon, my shoulders relaxed, and my head rolled to the side.

I woke to my sister calling me for dinner. As we ate, I could not hide the fact that something was wrong. Jack told me I looked tired, but I brushed it off, saying, "I am tired. We walked and climbed a lot out at the Lake, and it was so hot."

"I told you to take a baseball cap or something," Lydia said. "You know the sun's too strong to be out there unprotected."

"Yeah, I know. I have a bit of a headache. Anyway, it's nothing; I'll just take some aspirin."

"I'll put the food away. Just leave the dishes," Lydia told me.

"No, no, I can clean the kitchen—then I'll go to bed," I insisted.

I continued to dwell on the incident. I was still furious. I was glad I had told them off, but ultimately disappointed that I had lowered myself to their level by calling them ignorant White trash. How smart was that? I needed to be better than that.

After I did the dishes, I started writing in my journal. Writing always served as an outlet for my emotions. In order to deal with the whole situation, I needed to write out my feelings. I was not happy with my impassioned response. Reverting to ignorance and "reverse racism" simply wouldn't do. I didn't want to turn into the type of person I despised, and I didn't want anybody to think of me in that way.... But I couldn't help but be glad I had said what I said and had put them in their place. They deserved it... and more!

I didn't know if I was as mad at them as I was at myself for being stupid enough to think that I had been accepted into their elite White group in the first place. "I know some of those idiots thought I was White," I wrote in my journal. "That's the only reason I was so readily accepted into their group, while those who knew or suspected I wasn't White were okay with me as long as I passed for White. They said I was different. Goes to show how little they know me, as if I want to be different, want to deny my own people, my true heart and soul. They actually thought they were doing me a favor by accepting me as one of them, but only if I was willing to be a sell-out, to turn my back on my own people. NEVER! What makes them think that I could accept them after discovering their true colors?"

I thought about the irony that I hadn't worked in the fields with Mom and Dad and The Kids that summer. I would soon be starting a whole new phase in my life, and what a great start I was off to! Maybe those White kids had done me a favor, teaching me to always keep my guard up, to never forget where I had come from and who I was. More importantly, I needed to be mindful of who I was dealing with—to always be wary of the proverbial snake in the grass.

It would not be an easy task—how would I distinguish? I had had no idea about those kids. I had thought they were my friends. Well, the University of Washington, I hoped, would be the source of a real education for me—not just from books, but from the bigger world outside of Grandview and Othello. I had never been out on my own, never been away from the watchful eyes of my family, who had always kept me safe and secure. I knew nothing of the world. I had great expectations, and my vision of the future was more than scary, but it was also exhilarating. I hoped I wouldn't crash and burn.

*Mom & Dad Wedding—
Valentin Cantu
and Beatrice Cavazos*

*Mom & Dad*

*Seedless Hop Ranch Labor Camp in Grandview, WA.*

GRANDVIEW LABOR CAMP

Lydia Cantú 1953

*Lydia*

*Cousin Mary Aguilar & friend Olivia at Grandview Labor Camp*

*Bridesmaids - Viola & Lydia*

*Dad with Baby Sally*
*at Grandview City Park*

*Gloria & Sally*
*hop harvesting machines & La Kila in background*

*Sally, Imelda, and Gloria*
*In front of La Kila*

*Efrain*

*Sally, age 15*
*Picture Dad saved from garbage*

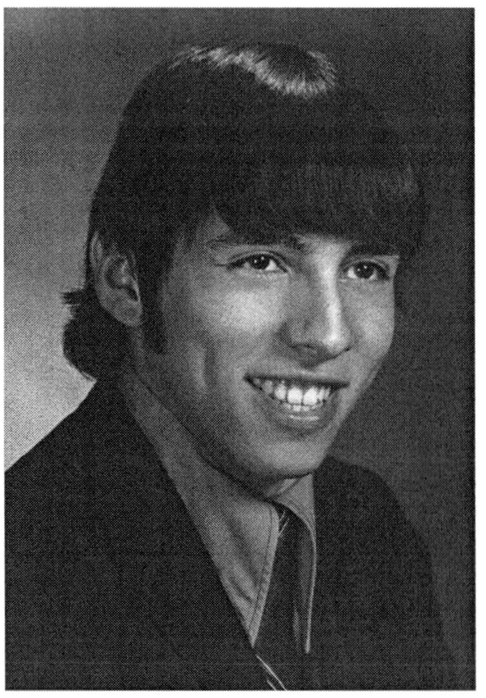

*Rudy*

*Gloria*

*Norma*

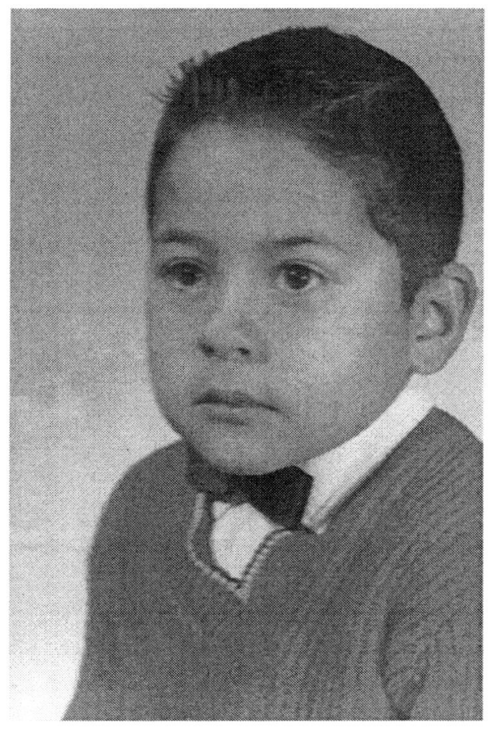

*Freddy*

*UW Anti-War March / Sally Cantu holding Brown Beret sign*
*Photographer: Antonio Salazar / Chula Vista Media*

*UW Anti-War March / Sally Cantu between Esteban Zambrano & Hector Gamboa*
*Photographer: Antonio Salazar / Chula Vista Media*

*Sally, Norma, Gloria. - Freddy, Rudy, Hector & Efrain*

*Mom & her seven daughters -*
*(Standing) Norma, Elida, Imelda, Viola & Gloria (Seated) Sally, Lydia & Mom*

*Mom, Norma & Gloria, Making Tamales*

*Gloria, Sally & Norma*

# Part III

# Chapter 1

In the fall of 1970, I began attending the University of Washington in Seattle. "A dream within a dream,"* one might say. It all seemed so surreal. I had not been prepared for college—I had never had the luxury of educational counseling, and my grades were clearly not up to par. But, by the grace of God, I was at the right place at the right time—and especially in the right era. Affirmative Action was in full force.

I was fortunate to be in a position to reap the benefits of the civil rights activism of the 1960's:

- The 1964 Civil Rights Act outlawed racial discrimination and mandated equal opportunity for women.

- The Higher Education Act, passed in 1965, provided need based financial assistance for all students.

- The "Open Admissions" movement maintained that all high school graduates should be allowed to pursue higher education.

My student file at UW reflected high school deficiencies and average grades—as a result, my academic progress would be carefully monitored. The university would take measures to prevent me from falling through the cracks. My counselor would follow my progress, and I was well aware that this was my one and only chance to prove that I could succeed, that I was worthy of the great opportunity being afforded me. I could not fail. I would not fail.

---

* "A Dream Within A Dream," Poem by Edgar Allen Poe published in 1849. It questions how we can distinguish between reality and fantasy.

I arrived a week early for the Minority Affairs Orientation. Viola drove me to Seattle, and we arrived Friday evening at my brother Hector's house. On Saturday morning, Hector drove us to the University District, where, following the map and written instructions I had received in the mail, we located Lander Hall. I signed in at the registration desk and received instructions to settle into my dorm room in Terry Hall, which adjoined Lander. It was 8:30 a.m. The clerk instructed me to settle into my dorm room and return by 10:00 a.m., when orientation would commence.

Apprehensively, I unlocked my dorm room door. We all walked in, carrying my things. "Wow," I exclaimed, "such a small room."

"And you'll have a roommate," Viola added. "I'm sure you'll get used to it. You'll be fine."

"Geez, I don't know. It's almost claustrophobic," I frowned.

"Being a university student is going to be very different, Sally, but you will be okay. You'll be busy with your classes and studies. You won't even think that much about your dorm room. Really," Viola reassured me.

Hector had left the room after putting my stuff down, and when he returned, he said, "Hey, there's a big lounge room over there. It's even got a small kitchen. Pretty nice."

"It's a big dorm," Viola smiled. "You won't be spending so much time in your room. It's really not a bad room at all."

"Thanks for bringing me," I smiled at Viola. "And, Hector, thanks for everything."

We said our goodbyes by the elevator, and I returned to my room. I wondered if my roommate would come for orientation. I was really hoping she wouldn't come until later. I hoped I could have some time to myself in the room. It would be the first time I didn't have to share.

"Oh, boy," I said, glancing around at the room. I walked over to look out the window, which ran the entire width of the small room. I liked having the big window and the natural light coming in. I was on the eighth floor. "Pretty high up," I said, looking down at the street far below. I didn't have much of a view, but that was okay. The important thing was the natural light coming in. There was a sill big enough to serve as a good-sized counter or shelf at the base of the window. I leaned on the counter, looking out. Then I turned to view the room. Both sides were identical. On each side, a desk stood next to the window, against the wall. Above the desk was a bookshelf, and underneath the shelf, a study light that extended over the desk, which had three small drawers and, of course, a chair.

Next to each desk was a twin bed, the length of which was aligned against the wall, like the desk. The head of the bed touched the desk. Right at the foot of the bed stood a stack of drawers built into the wall. The top served as a high shelf with a mirror above it. "Great," I said, standing on my tiptoes in front of the drawers as I tried to look in the mirror, which was mounted too high on the wall for me to use. "I'm glad I brought my new make-up mirror," I said. "It will have to go on the desk, and the top desk drawer can hold my cosmetics."

Next to the drawers was a small closet. That was it—pretty spare furnishings. I opened the closet door and saw that it was more spacious than it appeared. The back of the door had a rod and hooks for hanging clothes, hats, and accessories.

There wasn't much distance between the beds. Very close quarters—too close for comfort, given that two strangers would be housed here. "Oh, well," I sighed, plopping myself down on the bed. "Hmm, do I want this bed or…" I said, getting up and plopping myself down on the other bed. I went from bed to bed, sitting, stretching myself out, and curling up on my side. Then I tested the chairs and the desks, finally deciding to occupy the left side of the room.

"Okay, I pick you," I said, looking down at my bed. I took my alarm clock out of my suitcase and placed it on my desk. Then I took out a pen and notebook and walked out of the room. I had better not lose this key, I thought as I locked the door. I headed back to Lander Hall for orientation. I wanted to be early.

At the end of the day, I asked about my roommate and found out she would be arriving later because she was not a minority. Yay! I would have the room to myself for the whole week.

On the day my roommate showed up with her parents, I was in my dorm room, with the door open. They were loaded down with her luggage and bags. Wow, she's got tons of stuff. I haven't brought much myself, I thought, but then I really didn't have a whole lot. In high school, I often wore Viola's clothes. She was the only older sister who had graduated from high school, and although she had a steady boyfriend, she still hadn't gotten married. She had a good office job and cute, stylish clothes that fit me to a T.

Seeing my new roommate enter the room, I sighed, thinking that my carefree solitude was over. Oh, well. I smiled, confirming, "Yes, room 807—this is it. Hi, I'm Sally," I said, holding out my hand.

She put down her suitcase and, with a big smile on her face, shook my hand. "I'm Chelsey Smith, and this is my mom and dad."

We briefly exchanged pleasantries, and I said, "Well, make yourself at home. Oh, Chelsey, I've chosen this side of the room, if that's okay with you." Then I glanced at the clock, saying, "Oh! I'm sorry to have to rush off, but I have an appointment." Trying to act cool, I left the room with a smile and a wave. Once I was safely alone in the elevator, I breathed a sigh of relief. Hitting my forehead with my open palm, I said, "I am such a liar."

As I walked out of the elevator on the first floor, I decided to take another trial run to where my classes would be.

A couple of hours later, I returned to my dorm room. Chelsey was busy, arranging her things. Because I had been alone in the room all week, I had left some pamphlets and paperwork on the windowsill counter between our desks. I noticed she had pushed my papers over to my side. I walked over to the papers, picked them up, and placed them on my shelf, above my desk.

"These rooms are so small—we need to be careful not to invade each other's space," she said as she drew an imaginary border in the air. I was caught off guard by her remark.

I just answered, "Yeah, of course."

A few minutes later, she announced that she was going to "dress for dinner." Pretending to be engrossed in my reading, I ignored her.

"Are you going to dress for dinner?" she asked, standing in front of me.

"Um, no, I ...actually, I have to go...do something," I replied.

Grabbing my purse, I rushed out the door, thinking: What in the world!? "Dress for dinner?" I'm wearing new jeans, for heaven's sake. What more does she want? I was tempted to tell her, just in case she hadn't noticed, that we were not at the Ritz. Oh, well, best leave her to her idiosyncrasies.

"Okay, calm down," I told myself. I can't be leaving abruptly every time... Who the heck "dresses for dinner" in this day and age? And why is she being so overtly territorial? She's just weird! I thought. ¡Catorce, hombre! Now what?

Every night, Chelsey would start preparing for bed at 8:30 p.m., and by 9:00, it was lights out. Things were just not working out, between us. I couldn't go to bed so early, especially when my first class wasn't until 10:30 a.m. I got a lot of studying done after dinner, in the lounge, not in my room.

After a few weeks, I went to the front desk to ask if it was possible to get a single room. The girl behind the desk looked at me quizzically and said, "I'm sorry, but we just don't have the space. You can apply for one, but priority is given to previous residents."

"Well, can I change roommates?" I asked.

She gave me a puzzled look, saying, "It's just way too soon to request a roommate change. We do ask that you give it some time. Do you have someone in mind you'd like to room with?"

"Never mind," I said with a sigh as I turned and walked away, feeling stupid. How could I ask for a roommate change when I didn't even know anybody here? And it was likely that I wouldn't like the next roommate, either—the simple truth was that I didn't want to share such close quarters with a stranger. But, from the looks of things, I had no choice.

No amount of time was going to make me and little Miss June Cleaver compatible. I avoided my room as much as possible. It was awkward and uncomfortable when we were both in the room. I was sure the feeling was mutual.

I did a lot of my studying at the university's Suzzalo Library. Entering Suzzalo was like being beamed into another galaxy, like teleportation on Star Trek. It was an enormous, threatening building. I felt inconsequential inside its vastness. So many books, so much knowledge—so fantastic.

Before long, I began to find comfort and refuge at Suzzalo. Besides tables to sit at, the library had an array of comfortable furniture. I could always find a discreet spot where I could spend hours reading, writing, and studying. In Suzzalo, I immersed myself in other worlds, and for a while, I escaped my feelings of emptiness.

I was lonely and miserable. I didn't know anybody, and I missed the commotion of family life. Here I was, in the big city, missing my own backyard. Flashes of Dorothy from the Wizard of Oz came to mind. The Kids had watched it every year for I don't know how long, and now, for the first time, I could really relate to the story.

"Yeah" I told myself, "you're not in Grandview anymore." As people often said, be careful what you wish for. On the bright side, I was doing well in my classes. In fact, I was surprised at how easy school was. I never even used the free tutorial services that were available—mostly out of pride and determination—but I really didn't need them. The problems weighing me down were depression and loneliness—plain and simple.

Every now and then, I called home in the evenings and talked to Viola. Of course, I used one of the dorm pay phones. Mom and Dad were working in Othello, as they did every fall and winter. They wouldn't return home until after the potato harvest. Hearing The Kids and the TV in the background, I hung up, feeling empty and alone.

I spent almost all of my time studying because I was determined to succeed. Studying also served as a distraction from my burdens. I couldn't turn back now, not after borrowing so much money. It might as well have been a million dollars. I almost felt as if I had traded my very soul for this opportunity to go to school. Knowing it was so far beyond the family's means, I was consumed with guilt and fear—feelings I had to work hard to keep bottled up inside.

I couldn't believe that the hard part about school was not my classes. Who would have guessed that loneliness would be my biggest obstacle? Accustomed to being around my big family, I now found myself completely alone. My roommate and I hardly spoke to one another—we were from different worlds. She was an only child and she came from privilege. It was obvious, her parents had money. I was miserable. I didn't know how much more I could take.

Just as I began to entertain the idea of giving up in despair, my Minority Affairs counselor paid a visit to my dorm room. Luckily, my roommate was out, and we were able to have a heart-to-heart talk. The visit was unexpected; I was grateful for the company, but nervous just the same.

Eventually, I confessed that Seattle and the UW were overwhelming me. Raised in the small town of Grandview by my strict, protective parents, I had lived a sheltered existence, and I was not prepared for life in the fast lane, in the big city of Seattle.

I told her that my crisis had nothing to do with my classes. In fact, I didn't understand why I had only been allowed to take two classes—the academic advisor had signed me up for Spanish and English and said it was a full load. But the classes were way too easy. The Minority Affairs counselor explained that for my first quarter I was only allowed to take ten credits because I was in the Educational Opportunity Program, and they wanted me to ease into the transition without becoming overwhelmed.

"Okay, I get it," I said. "But anyway, I feel obligated to acknowledge my failure. I just don't think I can handle all this. To be perfectly honest, I'm dying of loneliness. That's the part I can't handle. And I'm so concerned—well, actually, scared—about borrowing so much money. How will I ever pay it back? Especially if I'm not able to do this?"

My counselor took it from there. She explained how the academic loans worked. Repayment didn't start until well after graduation—until the student had found secure employment. Even then, the payment schedule allowed for one payment every three months.

Soon, I knew all the Minority Affairs staff, all of whom were readily available to help students. Minority Affairs—the Chicano Division in particular—became my safety net. Over time, I became acquainted with Chicano Professors and T.A.'s, other Chicano staff, and Chicano students. Before long, I had become part of the close-knit Chicano community on campus.

I surprised everyone, including myself, by getting A's every quarter of my first year. As a result, I was offered an academic scholarship from one of the sororities during my second year, as well as admittance to the University of Washington Honors Program. It was all so unreal—was I dreaming?

"Congratulations Sally. We're all very proud of you," my counselor smiled, handing me the scholarship letter, along with documents for the Honors Program.

"Wow" was all I could muster as a response. I stared at the documents in my hand and wiped away tears of disbelief and joy. Dumbfounded, I accepted the sorority scholarship but politely declined the invitation to join the sorority house and attend their dance.

"I am infinitely grateful for your most generous scholarship gift," I wrote. My letter ended, "Thank you so much for inviting me to the Black Tie Gala and for your offer of an escort for the evening. However, I must convey my regrets, as I will be out of town."

I always took advantage of any ride offered by my fellow students to go home to Mom and Dad's for a weekend. Like me, many of my Chicano peers had been recruited from the Yakima Valley.

I also declined the invitation to join the Honors Program, fearing that it would be too demanding and stressful. I thought that earning all A's had been just a fluke. My first year had been much too easy—I was being carefully monitored, and I had not been allowed to carry a more challenging load. Still insecure, I couldn't accept the fact that I might actually be smart. There's no way I can do that again, I thought. I hadn't yet learned to believe in myself.

I had made the right decision in deciding against the Honors Program. Although I continued to do well in my classes, I knew the Honors Program would not allow me the freedom I so critically needed to pursue my political activism. It was the height of the Chicano Movement, and I was involved in all of it.

Later, I managed to graduate from the University of Washington with a 3.3 G.P.A. Not too shabby for the Mexican farmworker kid who had been deemed predestined for failure.

I joined the Latino student groups on campus. First was MECHA (Movimiento Estudiantil Chicano de Aztlan), the main student movement group. Then I joined El Teatro del Piojo, the Chicano theatre group, and Las Chicanas, the Chicana woman's group. Finally, some of my fellow Chicano students and I established the Seattle/UW chapter of the Brown Berets. I was appointed Recording Secretary.

We modeled our group after The Brown Berets who were going strong in California. They fought for the dignity and basic rights of Chicano/ Latino people. Racial discrimination, education, the farmworkers' plight, police brutality, and the Vietnam War were major issues addressed by the Brown Berets.

The Brown Berets at UW were instrumental in the occupation of the Beacon Hill School, for which we fought the City of Seattle. As a result of our struggle, the old school was converted into El Centro de la Raza, which now houses one of Seattle's most prominent civil rights and social service organizations.

We supported our hero, Cesar Chavez, founder of the United Farm Workers Union, in all his efforts to organize the farmworkers and fight for Chicano civil rights. Now, finally, thanks in large part to Chavez's heroic efforts, I had the opportunity to make a difference in redressing the very injustices my family had suffered and that I had felt so hopeless and resigned about. Cesar Chavez was my biggest inspiration. Here was the answer I had long prayed for—a powerful, yet humble leader who had built a strong movement within the larger fight for justice, dignity and equality for our people. My activism served to reinforce the importance of my education. It was crucial, something I could not consider giving up on. How could I be a part of this struggle, how could I hope to make a difference—if not through education and awareness?

Before I found the Movement, I had long since given up on ever seeing a better world for farmworkers and other disadvantaged people. I thought God had abandoned me and my people, that God had not heard my prayers. But now I knew better. I immersed myself in political activism even as I submerged myself in my studies. How I managed to do both can only have been through divine intervention!

I was present for anti-war demonstrations; to boycott stores that funded oppressive interests and/or discriminated against consumers; to challenge farmers or companies who abused their workers or sold non-union goods. My Chicano compadres and I disseminated information in the Yakima Valley to help educate and bring political awareness to la Raza. I brought posters and information home for The Kids. I wanted them to know about our Mexican heroes and be proud of them. I wanted them to be schooled in social justice and political activism. Mom and Dad attended events and public forums sponsored by the United Farm

Workers Union, and Cesar Chavez himself sometimes made the trip north to address the people and answer their questions.

The times, they were a-changin', and I was intensely proud of being a part of the Chicano Movement. My life during this time was busy but fulfilling—I knew my efforts were making a real difference. Although people were reluctant because of their fear of reprisal from the patrónes, they were interested. They wanted the changes the United Farmworkers Union was fighting for.

My grades were good, sometimes exceptional. Still, I was amazed every time I saw my good grades—it was extremely difficult for me to accept the idea that I might be smart. I had not forgotten the vow I had made in the high school bathroom after my teacher, Mr. White, humiliated me by laughing and saying I would never make it at the UW. No longer did I feel humiliated by that memory—on the contrary, I now felt empowered.

After my first quarter, I moved from my dorm room in Terry Hall, where I was miserable, to the adjoining Lander Hall—the eighth floor of which mainly housed Chicano students. Lander Hall was common ground for us, and we used the big lounge for various gatherings, meetings and social activities.

Later, we fought for—and were eventually granted—the recognition of the eighth floor of Lander Hall as "Chicano House," complete with our own Chicano floor advisor.

I finally belonged and had a real purpose. It was exhilarating to be politically involved in efforts that would bring about change and social justice.

Throughout my twelve years in the public school system, I had always considered myself not just mediocre, but actually dumb—and thus insignificant. I was never motivated in school, never encouraged by counselors or teachers. But despite this, my older sisters, Lydia and Viola, showed faith in my ability. Now I needed to make my family and my parents proud.

Lydia and Viola knew the value of education. They smoothed things over when I left for the UW without Mom and Dad's consent. My parents thought I had no business moving to Seattle. A girl does not leave her parents' home until she gets married. I was educated, I was a high school graduate—what more could I ask for? They thought that, like Viola, I should get a good job in town, y punto.

After a while, Mom and Dad accepted both my decision to attend UW and my political activism. They, too, believed in what I was fighting for, and they supported my efforts. When Teatro performed in Grandview or Sunnyside, they attended our shows. Mom and Dad knew that my political activism was for good, and they were proud, but they were also worried. They knew very well that fighting for Chicano rights stirred up much controversy and racist opposition. My parents had been victims, and they had witnessed the verbal abuse and violence that broke out when people fought for basic rights. They were scared by the violence they watched on the TV news, and they feared for my safety. Yet, the struggle continued.

Later, with work-study as part of my financial aid package, I was hired by the Minority Affairs Chicano Division to recruit other young Chicano scholars. Just like the recruiters who had come to my high school, I now had the opportunity to visit high schools and address students. I knew that my former teacher, Mr. White, was aware of my presence and my purpose at Grandview high school the day I returned to recruit others like me. Grandview high school was small, an event such as UW recruiters coming to recruit minority students was very controversial.

In the summer, our recruiting trips included visiting Mexican households, where we spoke to parents and prospective students—addressing our beloved community face to face and disseminating information.

I coordinated workshops to help prospective students fill out admissions applications, financial aid forms, and housing paperwork. Back in the office, I followed up on paperwork, correspondence, and phone calls. I was so good at my job that the rest of The Kids also ended up at UW!

Through my involvement in the Teatro, I discovered my passion for singing. Although I had no training in voice or music, when it came to singing the Mexican corridos of the revolution, I felt the music in my heart and in my very soul. I enjoyed the actos, or skits, that we performed, but my real passion was singing. More than everything else I had experienced in my short life, this was where I felt completely consumed and fulfilled.

In California, El Teatro Campesino had been performing since 1965. When I joined the UW's teatro in 1971, El Teatro Campesino had already won awards and toured internationally. When they came to perform in Seattle, I was thrilled to play a part in hosting their visit. We performed for them, and later enjoyed our discussions about politics and dramaturgy. For me, working together with this legendary theater group was a once-in-a-lifetime opportunity.

However, when they invited the members of my group to join them, I realized that I was not prepared to give up the materialistic life I was accustomed to. For even with their awards and celebrity status, they were starving artists. Thinking that I might very well regret my decision later in life, I continued to focus on my initial goal. I made the common-sense decision to stay put until I graduated from the University of Washington.

I might still have had years to go before earning my degree, but it was my main purpose. So, perhaps, I missed my calling. ¿Quien sabe? I would never know.

During my third year at UW, I officially declared my major in English, Literature and Advanced Writing. My unofficial minor was Chicano Studies. Later, I applied for and was accepted by the UW School of Education.

When I started school at UW, I had no idea what I would major in. In my first years there, I made up my deficiencies and completed my pre-requisites. In the process, I discovered that I had a knack for writing, and I was encouraged by many of my English professors. By default, English became my major. Later, when I couldn't imagine what to do with my English degree, I decided teaching was the professional choice.

But teaching elementary school was definitely out. I was not good with children. I discounted junior high school teaching as well. I knew first-hand the angst and rebellion of that age group. I figured high school would be the best fit. As I searched for my assigned classroom on my first day of classroom observation at Chief Sealth High School in Seattle, I walked the quiet, empty hallway. Its lockers and shut classroom doors were a little intimidating. Suddenly, the bell rang, the doors flew open, and the hall was flooded with students rushing past me.

Thinking I was now grown up, educated, and mature, I was annoyed at the group of boys checking me out. "Hey, new chick in school!" said one. I ignored them, thinking, Oh, for heaven's sake! I'm your teacher. I wanted them to respect and admire me as an adult and as a teacher, but I hadn't fully thought this through.

It turned out that I found my classroom observation extremely boring. All I did was sit in the back of the room. I was not allowed to interact or take part. My observation only made me realize that I would never be happy teaching in the public school system. What I really wanted to do was teach college-level ethnic literature and writing, but I also knew I couldn't afford graduate school. Maybe someday, but not then.

As so often happens when we put things off, my someday never came. Looking back now, I know that, if I had it to do over again, I would continue my education, but it's not something I dwell on.

Through my senior year in high school and my years at the UW, my boyfriend Hector and I had a rocky relationship, often breaking up, but then making up again. It was the classic can't-live-with/can't-live-without relationship. Hector was from Sunnyside, just a few miles from Grandview.

I was living with roommates in a big, two-story house in the University District. My room was upstairs and we often all gathered in our huge living room.

"Sally and Hector broke up again," Gwen warned the roommates. "She's all sad."

"Again?" Sylvia responded. "They'll get back together. They always do."

"Yeah, I don't know who is worse—Sally and Hector, or me and Danny," Olga laughed.

"Well, she's pretty upset; she said it's for good this time," Gwen added, "but I bet those two end up getting married someday. Anyway, she's pretty down."

"Oh, sorry. I didn't mean to make light of it. Let's go talk to her," Olga said.

"Sally, come downstairs!" Sylvia yelled up from the bottom of the stairs. "Come on—it's Friday night. Don't stay cooped up in your room."

"Okay," I yelled down. "I'm coming."

As I walked into the living room to join the girls, the radio started to play "This Time (We're Really Breaking Up)." Everybody froze, and all eyes fell on me. I stood there in disbelief. Gwen rushed over to turn the radio off, so I said, "No, leave it."

This time there'll be no goodnight kiss

This time is forever

This time I find that I'm

Really losing you.

As my friends predicted, from prior experience, Hector and I did make up, as usual, and after our stormy six-year relationship, Hector and I married in 1974. We had stood side by side at demonstrations and on picket lines. We shared the dreams for social justice and basic civil and human rights. Hector was one year older than I. I was twenty-two and in my last year at the University when we married.

Our marriage lasted six years before ending in divorce. At the beginning of our marriage, much to my amazement, Hector mentioned having children—I had never entertained the idea. Mistakenly, I didn't take him seriously and brushed off his question, saying, "Kids? Why do you want kids? You never mentioned them before."

"Of course I want kids," he replied. "Everybody wants a family. Don't you?"

"Well, we never talked about it. I really never even thought about it. We just got married, Hector. We need time to ourselves; we can think about having kids in five years or so."

Right then, five years was a lifetime away to me. We dropped the subject, and life went on. My thought of having a child lasted less than five minutes. I completely forgot about it, but before I knew it, Hector was reminding me of my "promise."

I was in shock. We had been married for five years. How had time flown… so fast? Had Hector really taken my words so literally? Had he actually waited patiently over the previous five years? An anguished fear shot through me. I felt guilty and selfish, but I was not ready to make good on words I had uttered in passing. How awful! How could I have been so thoughtless? I had said "five years" as a kind of tentative placeholder—I hadn't meant it literally.

From that point, our marriage began to deteriorate. I had to face the harsh reality that a child was the last thing in the world I wanted. The more pressure and guilt I felt, the more I knew that I simply could not have a child. I had no desire to be a mother, and I had no idea how to be a good one. God! I was consumed with guilt, questions, and fear.

Yet, in ambivalent desperation, I resigned myself to the fact that I didn't have a choice in the matter. I had been raised to believe that having a child was my obligation—and my duty—as a woman and as a wife. Regretfully, I stopped taking birth control pills and waited for the inevitable.

"Yes, I did stop taking birth control pills months ago," I told Hector's mother on the phone.

"Oh, Sally, I didn't know that. I'm so happy. What are you hoping for, a girl or a boy?" she asked.

"It really doesn't matter," I responded halfheartedly. I was desperately trying to sound enthused, but I felt despicable. What a horrible person I was! I simply did not want to have a child. I was worthless, useless; I should never have gotten married.

When nothing happened within a year, I took it as proof that having a child was just not meant to be, and I made up my mind that I would never be a mother. Predictably, our relationship soon deteriorated to a point of no return.

I felt abandoned and betrayed. Unable to think clearly, I concluded that if my husband really loved me, I would be enough to make him happy. If all he wanted was a child, a family, he could have that with any other woman. He didn't love me, or we wouldn't be in this mess. Clearly, I could only see things from my own perspective. I had no idea how much Hector must have been suffering. Only in retrospect have I come to realize that he felt just as betrayed as I did, and with good reason. I had broken my word and shattered his dream.

I was young, naive, defensive, and stupid. Feeling that one of us had to make a move, I ended the relationship. I left due to my own insecurities. He was a good man. I hoped that he would find the happiness that he deserved and that I had denied both of us. In an effort to ease my pain—and my guilt—I found myself thinking that, just maybe, I had done him a huge favor. Now he was free to find a better person, someone more deserving of his love.

In lonely desperation, I moved into an apartment by myself. On "auto-pilot," I robotically went to work and came home, night after night. Nothing outside of work held my interest. I was now working as a counselor for the UW Chicano Division of Minority Affairs. My work kept me busy, and I attended campus events related to my work and student mentees. I remained politically active, but the emptiness that filled my lonely days and nights was becoming unbearable. Nights were the worst. Still, I told myself that I shouldn't worry about Hector. I truly believed he was better off without me.

Night after night, I lay awake, wondering what would become of me. I didn't have, nor did I want, a social life. Terribly insecure, feeling alone and unworthy, I felt that I would die. But, of course, I didn't. Life went on, and time invariably healed the wounds I had suffered.

I graduated from the University of Washington in 1975—an accomplishment beyond my wildest childhood dreams. My family was proud, and I was ecstatic, until I realized that I didn't know what to do next. I couldn't find a job, and I didn't know how not to be a student. Before my anxiety got the best of me, I found that UW was offering a new Bilingual Education Teaching Program.

I immediately made an appointment with the director and completed my financial aid paperwork. By the time I was accepted into the program, my financial aid award was also secured. Relieved beyond words, I felt safe again, knowing that this would enable me to postpone my entry into the real world. At least for a while, I again enjoyed the safety and security of my role as a student. How I wished I could be a professional student and never leave the University that had become my home and my life!

The University of Washington, that unattainable dream of my youth, was now my entire world, my safety net, my comfort zone. This beautiful academic setting was all I longed for; it was all my dreams come true. Was it any wonder that I didn't want to leave it?

Yet, I had to face the fact that someday I would leave. Approximately a year later, as I was contemplating this harsh reality, I got an unexpected telephone call. It just happened that the University of Washington, Chicano Student Division, was in need of a permanent, full-time recruiter. Was I interested in applying? La pregunta es necia; por supuesto, I would apply!

Gracias a Dios, I got the job. Within a short period of time I became a full-time counselor. Not only did I enjoy my job and the security it afforded me, but it meant I didn't have to leave my safety zone.

My youngest sister Norma was a student at the UW when I was a counselor. This was a great bonding opportunity for both of us.

Norma was sitting in her Chicano Studies classroom, waiting for class to begin.

"Did you finish the assignment?" she asked her friend, Irma, thumbing through the pages of their assigned book.

"Yeah, but there's..."

"Good Morning, class," the professor announced. "Let's get started with this book," he said, holding up Chicanos – Social and Psychological Perspectives by Hernández, Haug, and Wagner.

All of a sudden, Norma jumped out of her seat, yelling, "My dad! Hey, it's my dad! In this book!" All eyes were on Norma as she looked around excitedly. Her friend, Irma, startled by Norma's yelling, had jumped out of her seat, and she stood there with her hand over her heart and her mouth open.

"Sorry, professor, but my dad's in this book," Norma repeated.

"Oh, girl, you scared the crap outta me!" Irma said, sitting back down. Everyone was laughing. Irma's face turned red.

"Seriously, my dad's in the picture on page seven of the Introductory section," Norma said, showing the page to the class. "Right here, behind this lady," she smiled proudly, pointing out our father.

That's how the rest of our family found out that dad's picture was in the book. It was just a random shot of the audience at a United Farmworkers forum. We probably would never have seen that photo if it hadn't been for Norma and her Chicano Studies class.

The movie Urban Cowboy hit the box office in 1980, and it soon set style trends in country music and western fashion. My girlfriends and sisters had been trying to get me to go out with the girls since my divorce, but I was not interested. Finally, in 1982, I succumbed to their pressure and reluctantly promised to join them, but only because they were honoring my 30th birthday. I was divorced, and I saw myself as "over the hill." I wasn't interested in much of anything.

We decided upon The Longhorn Bar & Grill in the University Village. The bar was featuring live music by The Silver City Ramblers. I might be over the hill, I thought, but I'm still a slave to fashion. I spent all afternoon at Nordstrom's. By the end of my shopping spree, I had an entire cowgirl outfit, except for the gun, of course. Hadn't I always wanted to be a cowgirl?

From the moment we entered the club, we had guys approaching us, asking us to dance. I wasn't interested. One disappointed and rude cowboy asked me, "What did you come for, then?" I gave him an icy look and replied, "Certainly not to dance with you." The girls told me to lighten up. I knew I was putting a damper on things. I thought, Why did I come? Why did I go through all the time, expense and trouble to get all decked out just to give off an arrogant attitude when someone simply asks me to dance?

We finally managed to get a table right up front. The lead singer kept looking our way, and the girls all teased, "Sally, he's looking at you. He likes you."

With a disinterested shrug, I muttered, "Yeah, right. He's looking our way, but there are a lot of pretty women at this table. Knock it off, you guys. Like I care anyway." I was trying to act indifferent, although I had noticed he was good-looking—and he did keep looking our way.

"I wonder what nationality that guy is," Carmen said, nodding her head towards the stage. "He looks Latino, maybe Puerto Rican."

"Could be Mexican, but nah, I don't think so. Hmm...," Norma added, furrowing her brow. "I don't know—you got me."

Jessie held her hand up, counting on her fingers. She said, "Not Mexican," pointing to her index finger. "And definitely not White," she said, pointing to her middle finger.

"I'm guessing Italian," I said, looking towards the stage. "Definitely Italian," I repeated, looking at Jessie and pointing to my ring finger. We all laughed in agreement.

"Yeah, Italian," Norma said, holding up her glass. "Happy Birthday! ¡Salud!"

"¡Salud! ¡Salud!" We all laughed and clinked our glasses in a birthday toast. I was drinking Diet Coke, but I had the waitress give me a cocktail glass—for effect, of course.

On his next break, the lead singer approached our table. "Hi, ladies! Mind if I join you?"

"Not at all—please, have a seat," Jessie said as we all smiled.

He grabbed a chair from another table and set it next to mine. Looking at me, he said, "Thanks. I'm Tony."

"I'm Sally," I replied. "And these are Carmen, Jessie, and my sisters, Norma and Gloria." After the formalities, Tony asked if we were enjoying the music. Everybody agreed it was great.

"We're celebrating tonight," Carmen added with a big smile. I cringed, thinking, No, don't say it's my birthday, and don't say I'm thirty. Thanks a lot, Carmen. Sure enough, my secret was out. Tony made a toast, and before we knew it, his break was over.

He joined us again on his next break and I found his beautiful smile contagious. I also noticed that he had beautiful green eyes and long, curly eyelashes. Before I knew it, his break was over. He walked onto the stage and sang me a song in Italian, or so I thought. He looked at me the whole time, smiling and winking. I was smitten!

When he returned to our table at the end of the night, we asked him about the song. He explained that he had just made up the words on the spot because he only knew a few real words in Italian. Nevertheless, it was my song, and it was how I took the bait.

I didn't know it then, but on that auspicious night I had met my future husband, Tony, lead singer and bass player for the Silver City Ramblers. He simply reeled me in. We started seeing each other regularly, and soon we were in a committed relationship.

"Don't you think he's cute?" I asked Gloria and Norma.

Gloria replied, "He's okay, I guess, but he's a little chubby."

"Well, I'm not going to marry him," I snapped.

We were married in 1984, and we had a beautiful wedding and a wonderful, fairytale marriage. During our first year as husband and wife, Tony's band decided to change their name to The Wayback Machine and feature exclusively 50's and 60's Rock 'n' Roll music. We had a blast with that band. Every place they played was jam-packed with people rocking and rolling.

When my sisters, friends, and I went out for a night of old time rock 'n' roll, we lined up in front of the stage and danced ourselves ragged. We declined offers to dance—we were having way too much fun being the band's go-go dancers. I had the perfect excuse to decline a dance offer: "Sorry, I'm married, and I'm with the band."

I didn't drink or smoke, and I certainly never touched drugs, but we were all high on adrenaline and music. Drenched in sweat, we invariably tied our damp hair in clips or ponytails. When we got too hot, we would slip out the back door for a bit of cool air. Dancing kept us very much in shape. It was an absolute blast.

My fairytale marriage, however, harbored a secret problem—a total lack of communication. We never talked things out; we both acted like everything was always great. I was so busy pretending that my life and marriage were perfect that I never dared to upset the picture. Twelve years was a very long time to pretend. Although our marriage was mostly good, a lot was missing. We never talked things out. Things started to fall apart in 1993, and by 1996 we were officially divorced. Strike Two!

Upon joining the working class, I tried to help Mom and Dad financially, because they were now elderly and trying to get by on a fixed income. My brothers and sisters also helped out when they could, but we were also trying to stay afloat—we had our own living expenses to deal with. Still, we all made an effort to ensure that Mom and Dad had a good television set, VCR, microwave, etc.—small luxuries that would make their lives a little easier. And a little extra money also helped.

"Sally, I was home visiting Mom and Dad last week end," Lydia told me on the phone. "Mom and Dad got your check in the mail Saturday.

Dad was so happy that he put on his hat right away and drove into town to cash the check. Mom told him to stop at Red Apple to buy some sugar-free sweets."

"Oh, poor Dad," I replied, "He loves sweets so much. How awful that he has become diabetic in his old age. Oh, hey Lil—you know how I started buying lotto tickets just because Dad likes to buy 'em? Well, we made a deal that if either of us wins, we'll split it. I just won $38.00 the other day."

"You did?"

"Can you believe it? It's not much, but it'll be fun sending Dad the money. How cool is that?"

Now that The Kids had grown up, Mom and Dad were "empty nesters". We all went home for holidays, and we also coordinated our visits for other family festivities. It was always great to be together again—at home with la familia. Waking up in the morning to the smell of fresh coffee and bacon, papitas, tortillas, and pan dulce took me back to my childhood, when my life was so carefree and simple.

After eating breakfast and clean-up, all the sisters would sit around the big dining table, platicando (conversing) and applying our makeup, as the new generation of kids ran in and out.

My brother, Hector, loved to tease us. "Why is it," he asked, "that you girls make the ugliest faces while trying to beautify yourselves? Look, look at Sally. Close your mouth before you catch a mosca."

"Very funny. Knock it off, and let us finish. Don't you have something to do someplace else?"

"Maybe," he laughed, "but this is more entertaining."

My niece, Cristy, Viola's oldest child, loved to watch her mom and aunties as we transformed ourselves from plain-Jane sleepyheads into ravishing beauties. Ah, the wonders of make-up!

Gloria, who had a knack for hairstyling, combed Mom's hair and all the girls took Mom shopping. My mother loved to show off her successful, beautiful daughters. She made sure we all said hello to any of her comadres whom we encountered downtown.

Later, at home, sometimes we would have a big BBQ, and the boys tended to the meat as the girls brought out salads, side dishes, tortillas and pan. Regardless of what we did, it was always wonderful being together. We never ran out of things to talk and laugh about. I usually managed to get out of cooking, which automatically put me on the clean-up committee. A lifelong position, I might add. Old habits die hard.

With the whole family at Mom and Dad's for the long Thanksgiving holiday, the kitchen bustled with activity as the delicious smell of stuffed turkey roasting in the oven lingered throughout the house. Pumpkin and pecan pies were lined up on shelves in the back porch/storage room. "Stay out of the pies! Go on—get outta here!" Viola scolded Rudy and her son Joey as she snapped her dishtowel at them. "Stay out of this room! You have no business here. Muy buen ejemplo, Rudy."

"Aw, come on Mom," Joey whined even as he obediently left the forbidden zone.

"Caught in the act," Rudy laughed. "Come on, kid—let's beat it."

After our Thanksgiving meal, the whole family sat around talking, laughing, sharing.

"Is anybody ready for desert?" Mom yelled from the kitchen.

"No, Mom, let's wait. We're all so stuffed," Elida said. "Come and sit down! Don't worry about the kitchen—we'll clean it in a while."

"Yeah, Mom, come and join us. Come and relax," Imelda added.

Mom walked out of the kitchen, wiping her hands on her apron. Viola patted the seat next to her. "Here, Mom, sit here."

"Iba a hacer un cafécito, hija," Mom said, sitting down.

Getting up from her seat, Lydia said, "I'll make the coffee, Mom."

Mom joined all seven of her daughters around the dining table. We talked and laughed, while Dad and the guys sat in the living room, watching football on T.V.

❧

Before we knew it, Christmas was upon us, and the family had gathered once again at Mom and Dad's. Christmas meant homemade tamales, which I always tried to get out of making, but for some reason that just didn't fly, for the most part. Mom cooked huge pans of beef and pork, deliciously and perfectly seasoned with freshly ground spices, whose mouth-watering scent lingered in the air and then drifted out through the cracks of the house, into the cold. Anyone who entered our front door had the same comment: "Oh, it smells so good in here. You can smell it all the way outside."

"Nobody can cook like Mom," one of us responded. We all smiled and continued our assembly line work, chatting and laughing as we did.

The corn husks were soaked in a big, old-fashioned metal tub in the middle of the kitchen floor.

"Mom, how long do the corn husks have to soak?"

"Until they're soft, así suavecitos," Mom responded. "Then take them out and dry them with paper towels or a secador."

Mom also prepared the masa, adding all the required spices, lard, and boiling water. One of us would knead the masa by hand in the same manner that tortilla dough was kneaded. Then Mom would add spices and hot water to the bowl. When the masa was ready, we spread a fistful about halfway up on each damp cornhusk, and then added meat mixture. After all of the ingredients had been added, the entire tamal was rolled and the top, empty part of the corn husk was folded over. Now it was ready for cooking. After we had rolled many piles of tamales, we put them into big pots to steam.

Our homemade tamales were an incredible amount of work, but we managed just fine, and had a good time while making them. We made enough tamales to last through the Christmas season—and plenty more to freeze for later. Making tamales had become an annual tradition and an important part of our winter celebration rituals.

Christmas, the most special time of the year, as well as my dad's favorite, always came with tons of snow. As a child, I loved our real, hand-cut Christmas tree and the excitement of Christmas morning—with all five of us Kids scrambling under and around the tree. Our Christmas stockings bulged with fruit, nuts, and Christmas candy. Later, when all of us were grown and out of the house, Dad would bring out an artificial tree and all of our old decorations. He knew that each special holiday would bring most of his kids home. As the holidays neared, Mom began her Christmas baking and looked forward to her children's return. By the time the family was gathered at home, the house was decorated inside and out. A neat snow path from the driveway to the front door had been shoveled to welcome all holiday guests and visitors.

Mom yelled to Dad, "Valentin, metete, esta muy frío." Closing the door, she turned to us girls, complaining, "I just don't know why your dad has to be out in the cold so much. It's freezing, and he thinks he has to keep shoveling snow every single day."

"Oh, Mom, you know Dad," I said. "He can't sit still. He likes the exercise, and Rudy's out in the back shoveling too. They'll be in soon."

"Well, if your dad gets sick...." Mom walked back into the kitchen, shaking her head and wiping her hands on her apron.

Soon, Rudy and Dad were at the dining table, blowing on their steaming bowls of porridge, while their wet boots, coats and scarves hung in front of the big oil heater in the dining room.

Christmas Eve was a huge celebration at our house. The big punch bowl sat in the center of the table, surrounded by food, appetizers and special homemade sweets. We all dressed up for this special occasion. Grownups and kids alike were in an excited, festive mood. This was our biggest and most special fiesta of the year. Even the neighbor kids dressed up and came over to join in the fun. We exchanged and opened gifts—except for those that Santa Claus would bring to the little ones. This most special of nights culminated with the adults attending Midnight Mass, Misa de Gallo, to keep us mindful of the true reason for our celebration.

# Chapter 2

"Hey, Mom," I said, "remember you said you'd tell us about Grandma's brother, Tío Chále?"

"Ah, si hija, tú Tío Chále." Mom began her story, telling us that her uncle, Chalé (Charlie) Johnston, was considered a successful businessman in his community because of the thrift shop he owned. He did well, but, by no means was he rich.

"What did he look like, Mom?" asked Gloria.

"Well, Tío Chále was tall, thin, and very light-complexioned, con ojos claros (light eyes). All the Johnston's are very light-skinned. Parecían Gringos pero son de sangre mezclada," Mom explained.

"¿Gringos?" I repeated. "Are we part Gringo?"

'Yes, we're mixed," Mom continued. "Mejicano, Gringo, Español, Indio."

She went on telling us what a generous and good natured man Tío Chále was, always smiling and in a good mood.

The town of La Villa, Texas, respected and loved Tío Chále for being such a good-natured and benevolent member of the community. He was a strong advocate for education and helped the neediest families in La Villa by providing shoes and school supplies for their children. Over the years, he continued his charitable acts—and many families brought him their children on the first day of school. It became his annual ritual, and because of his generosity, needy children in La Villa no longer had to attend school in bare feet.

"Mom, did our family get shoes and stuff for school too from Tío Chále?" Gloria asked.

"Oh no," Mom answered. "We weren't poor."

"Then how come we're poor now?" Norma interjected.

"Normita, we are not poor. These families were very poor. They had no shoes and only a few ragged items of clothing. Besides, before you were born, when we still lived in Texas, we were better off. We had a nice house and your dad made good money," Mom explained.

"I remember," Lydia added. "We were definitely not poor, but there were a lot of families who were very poor."

"I don't get it. Then, why did we leave Texas?" I asked. "Mom, we left all that to come here and live in a labor camp?"

"No, Sally," Mom replied, shaking her head. "We did not come here to live in a labor camp. We came because life here was supposed to be so good and there was plenty of work. The stories made it sound like we were coming to the Promised Land. How could we know that all the stories weren't true? And we certainly had no idea about labor camps."

"Wow, unbelievable," I said. "This is like Steinbeck's novel, The Grapes of Wrath. We should've written that book!"

"What?" Mom said, looking confused. "What book are you talking about?"

"Oh Mom, it's a really good book by one of my favorite authors. It's about migrant workers who leave their homeland." I paused and sighed. "Well anyway, the story is much like ours. It won all kinds of prizes."

# Chapter 3

In early 1991, I faced the worst hardship of my life. Dad was eighty-five years old. He was diabetic and had heart trouble. He had seen several doctors, but the verdict was bleak.

"I'm so sorry," Dr. Toutour said, "but without surgery his heart can't last very long, and if we undertake the surgery, it's highly likely that he will not survive due to his diabetes and his age. I cannot, in good conscience, recommend the surgery, but it is an option to consider."

Mom translated for Dad and then asked, "What should we do, doctor?"

"The other option is to simply control and ease the pain through medication," the doctor replied.

"But, doctor, how long will his heart hold out? Does this mean that he only has… how much time, doctor?"

"I don't know. There's no way of telling, but Valentin's diabetes has always been controlled. He eats well and is in very good shape for his age. The fact that he remains active is a plus. He may live a good amount of time yet—perhaps a year or so—but, I am sorry; we must consider that whatever time he has left is borrowed time."

Devastated, Mom took her husband's hand and explained the situation. She was gripped by fear and could not bear to look into his eyes.

"No te preocupes," Dad said, squeezing her hand and rubbing her arm. He took the news with dignity and grace. "Ya tengo ochenta y cinco años y la vida no me ha tratado mal," he told Mom. "¿Que mas puedo pedir? Dios sabe lo que hace."

Dad made it very clear that he was, indeed, grateful for the life God had granted him and that he saw no reason to try and interfere with God's plan.

We all resigned ourselves to the inevitable fact that this would be Dad's last year with us. It was a devastating blow to the family. We might have all privately mourned the news in our own internal ways, but we went on with life, cherishing our remaining time with Dad.

During his last year, my father lived as fully as he had lived his entire life. He spent more quality time with his family, and we all did what we could to spend as much time as possible at home with Mom and Dad. By taking all my vacation and sick days as well as family leave, I was blessed to be able to spend the entire summer of 1991 at home.

Although the girls' bedroom was upstairs, I took to sleeping on the couch to be closer to Mom and Dad, who now slept in separate bedrooms downstairs. At the slightest stirring from either bedroom, I woke in an instant—in spite of the fact that I had always been a very heavy sleeper.

Dad worked in his garden, as he had always done. He had hardly slowed down at all. He looked great, and we had good times and laughs together. But I also could not forget how, at night, his bedroom light often went on—and that somehow I would wake in an instant and be at his side.

"Apá," I whispered, grabbing his medicine bottle and handing him a pill. As Dad popped the pill in his mouth, I stood ready with the glass of water that we kept on his bedside dresser. Then, sitting at his bedside, I waited, watching the pain in my father's agonized face.

"Dear God," I prayed. "Please ease his pain. Please give him a restful sleep. Lord, do not forsake us." I was wide awake—sitting alertly at my father's side, waiting and watching for any indication that his most intense pain was subsiding.

Sometimes, I asked too soon, "¿Apá, se siente mejor?"

If he was still in a lot of pain, he held his hand up, palm facing me, as if to say, "Hold on—not yet." Seeing that his eyes remained closed, I knew he was still suffering intensely. After a bit, Dad's eyes would open slowly. "Ya estoy mejor," he assured me. "Vete a dormer, hija. No te tienes que levanter cada vez." Always, he was apologetic as he told me to go back to bed, not to get up, not to lose sleep. And so went our nightly ritual, with Dad not wanting to bother me and me reassuring him he was not a bother at all.

What I couldn't bring myself to tell him was that I wanted to be near him. I needed to be near him. The fear inside me never waned. It was constant and ever-present. Somehow, the light of day and seeing Dad awake and active eased my dread. I could pretend that everything was fine and normal—even as the fear persisted within.

In the summer of 1991, Dad and Mom proudly attended their granddaughter, Cristina's, quinceañera.* Another granddaughter, Barbara, had delivered Mom and Dad's first great-grandson. Dad looked great. He was fourteen years older than Mom, but, incredibly, he didn't show his age, and they always looked great together. They were both fastidious about their appearance and always dressed nicely. Mom accessorized her outfits, and Dad didn't leave the house without his trademark hat.

My father had a beautiful German shepherd named Apollo. Por supuesto, Apollo was bilingual. Dad spoke to Apollo in Spanish; Mom used both English and Spanish; and we, The Kids, always communicated with Apollo, as with everyone else, primarily in English. Now that we were all grown and out of the house, Apollo had taken to sneaking off to visit the Mexican family across the street—he liked to play with the kids over there. Still, he knew that leaving our property was prohibited.

It was so funny to watch when Dad caught Apollo trying to pull one over on him. Apollo would go around to the opposite end of our house and walk slowly towards the gravel road. He would run a few steps, stop to look around, and, if it seemed that the coast was clear, he would make a mad dash towards the Garcias' house across the way. When Dad caught him, he would yell, "¡Apollo! ¿Dónde crees que vas? ¿No te dije que te quedes en casa? Andale, sin vergüenza." Apollo would stop abruptly, hang his head in shame, and slowly turn around, trotting to the back of the house.

---

* Traditional coming out party when a girl reaches age 15, consisting of a Mass, reception and dance. It is a reaffirming of one's faith and commitment to family, community and church.

"Miralo," Dad would say with a wink, "¿Que te dije? Sabe y entiende muy bien pero cree que se puede escaper. Y muchas veces si lo hace." (Look at him, what did I tell you? He knows and understands very well, but he thinks he can escape. And many times he does.)

Minutes later, all would be forgotten, and Apollo would join us in the front yard as if nothing had happened.

Apollo was part of our family for many years, but when Dad passed away, Apollo started getting a bit too overprotective. He would not allow anyone onto our property. He had even bitten a couple of people, one of whom just happened to be the homeowner's insurance agent. Mom heard Apollo barking and someone yelling, "Get! Get! Aaahhh!" She ran outside. "Apollo, stop! Ven, right now! Get over here!" Mom yelled as Apollo chased down the man in our yard. Obeying mom's command, Apollo stopped, but the damage was already done.

"Mrs. Cantú," the man said, rubbing his right wrist. "I'm Gordon Blair from State Farm, your homeowner's insurance."

"I'm sorry, Mr. Blair," Mom responded, standing next to Apollo with her hand on his head. "Are you hurt? You shouldn't have gotten out of your car with Apollo barking at you."

"I'm all right, but I wouldn't have been if you hadn't called him off. I'm afraid you're going to have to get rid of that dog. He's dangerous and vicious, just too much of a threat."

"Well, I'll tell you what, Mr. Blair," Mom responded sternly. "Apollo has never been aggressive. He's grieving, just as I am, over my husband's death. Apollo is only being protective. Now, with your permission, I need to get back to my work." She turned as if to leave and then hesitated. "So, if you, or anyone from your company, needs to speak to me, please call and make an appointment." With that, Mom turned and led Apollo toward the back of the house. She was devastated and upset. How dare this man come to her house without warning and start making demands? She mumbled apologetically to Apollo, but her mind was uneasy.

Mom didn't want to get rid of Apollo. He was Valentin's dog and had been part of the family for a long time. But Valentin was not here anymore, and everything was falling apart.

Knowing she had no choice, Mom considered the matter over the next few days and came up with an idea. She knew just the family that might want to give Apollo a good home. Mr. and Mrs. Torres and their children visited often, and they loved Apollo. While the adults visited, the children never got tired of running and playing with Apollo. When Mom explained the situation to them, they were more than willing to give Apollo a chance.

It turned out that Apollo had found a good, loving home, with children to run and play with. I wondered what went on in Apollo's mind. What did he know? It remained a mystery to me. What I did know was that my father was as kind, gentle and loving to his faithful dog as he was to anybody, which is why he was loved and respected by all. It's incredible, I thought, how we take so many things for granted in our lives, or how we so easily forget the value of the many things we have. In my youth I so often took my family and—most of all—my parents for granted.

Once, during my teenage years, I was in a dark and moody disposition. I answered a knock at the door. Mariano Vargas, who was part of La Familia Vargas from up the street, was over for a visit. Mariano was my older brother Hector's, age and they were good friends.

Because I was the one who answered the door to let Mariano in, he addressed his question to me. "Hey, I just ran into your dad outside," Mariano said. "What's wrong with him? Is he okay?"

"What are you talking about?" I replied rudely.

"Well, he's not himself. He seems to be, like, in a disturbed mood. That's not like him. He's always so good-natured, but there's something up today."

Immersed in my own teenage world, I was irritated by the untimely interruption. I grouchily responded, "He's always in a bad mood... Who cares?"

To my surprise, but mostly to my shame, Mariano stood firm in his disapproving admonishment, saying, "Sally, you should be ashamed of yourself. You know that's not true, your dad is one of the nicest and most good-natured people I know. He's always so good to you guys. You couldn't ask for a better father."

The truth of Mariano's words stopped me cold. There was no disputing them. In my shame, I couldn't respond. What he said had really hit me, and it bothered me for a long time that I could be so thoughtless. Shame on me! And good for Mariano! He had held up a mirror and forced me to look at my own selfishness.

I thought about the fact that Mariano's father, Juan Jose Vargas, was brutal and violent towards his family-especially when he was drunk, which was often. Mariano, along with his mother and siblings, often felt El Viejo Vargas's wrath. Their suffering had endowed them with a true admiration and respect for my father.

But Mariano's mother, Tilana, didn't let that, or anything else, affect her funny, dynamic disposition. Everyone loved "Texas Tilly," as Rudy had nicknamed her. She was a character to be reckoned with—always firm, yet constantly making all the neighborhood kids laugh.

The Vargas family was almost as large as ours, but we had more girls, whereas they had more boys. Texas Tilly was rough and tough, and she had a sailor's flair for the fittingly obscene turn of phrase, which her boys were used to hearing. For us Kids, though, her colorful, salty language was always a hoot. We weren't used to hearing such language at home. Rudy would come home after play and report to the rest of us Kids any of Texas Tilly's new antics or words. We got such a kick out of it. We pitied—yet loved and admired—that woman for her strength, humor, and good nature.

I had always felt a special bond with my dad. There are a lot of old pictures of just me and Dad together. I was a toddler, probably between one and three years old, and we lived in the labor camp in Grandview, Washington. I imagine that the slew of pictures of me and Dad that year was most likely because the family just happened to have a camera at the time. Who knows? Whatever the case may be, I am delighted that there are so many pictures of just me and Dad.

As I got older and became a rebellious teenager, I was always being scolded by Mom. Sure, Dad scolded in Spanish, but more often he complained to Mom, who in turn scolded us Kids, always saying, "Your dad says, this…," as she interpreted for him.

Remember, the five of us younger Kids grew up in Washington, speaking English. The older siblings from Texas grew up speaking Spanish, and my dad did not speak English. Dad spoke to us, The Kids, in Spanish, and we answered him in English and broken Spanish. Although we always managed to communicate, I think this language barrier bothered me much more than I realized—probably because I always felt a special connection to my dad. I believed that we understood each other, as if we were just connected somehow—in a special way, where words were not always needed. Still, I wonder if something between us might have been lost in translation.

In 1991, Dad's last year with us, I had a significant dream. In the dream, I was out back, behind Mom and Dad's house. Stairs led down—from the back porch door to the ground—and in my dream, the railing was broken. I decided to fix it and began looking through a pile of wood for the right-sized boards to use.

Suddenly, Dad was there, working next to me, and my older sisters, Lydia and Viola, were also out in the back. I thought to myself, Why is Dad working? He's sick—he needs to rest. In the dream, I was upset with my sisters for allowing Dad to work in his condition. Why weren't they at least helping?

I have to be very clear that this part of my dream makes no sense at all. Lydia and Viola helped both Mom and Dad more than anyone will ever know.

The next thing I was aware of was that I had started to reach for just the right board I needed to fix the railing, when Dad suddenly held the same board in his hand. He placed it exactly where I had intended it. Not a word was spoken during the entire dream, yet Dad and I always knew exactly what the other was thinking because we were both thinking the same thing—we were on the same wavelength. We shared the hammer, the nails, the boards—and we both knew exactly where things needed to be. We were so in tune to each other that we didn't need words.

When I woke, I remembered the details of my dream and knew exactly what it meant. It was so good to know that the connection between me and my father was so real and so special.

When I was fifteen years old, there was a school picture taken of me that I didn't like. I thought it made me look ugly, so I tore it in half and throw it in the garbage. Later, I found that the same picture had been pieced together with scotch tape and placed on the dining room table.

My sister, Gloria, was sitting there, so I asked, "Where did this come from? What's it doing here? I threw it away."

She responded, "Dad saw it in the garbage, so he took it out."

"How do you know?" I asked.

"I saw him taping it back together and asked him what he was doing."

I contemplated what Dad had done. I was surprised that he had bothered to salvage the picture. To be more precise, I was deeply touched.

I was also surprised that I didn't get a scolding for my wasteful deed. I smiled when I realized that Dad had rescued my picture. It made me feel good.

Years later, I came across that picture among a bunch of old pictures in a shoe box. Immediately, I got the same good feeling all over again, fondly remembering my dad and his sweet gesture. Holding up the picture, I smiled as I thought of Dad taping it back together. The picture is very special to me. I look at it now and feel emptiness and longing for my parents—yet, simultaneously, I feel warm and happy. And I say to myself, "I was so darn cute! How could I have thought I was ugly?" To me, it is a beautiful picture, a true reflection of my youth and innocence at the tender age of fifteen. I love that picture and the good feeling and memory of Dad that are so much a part of it.

My Father passed away in September, 1991. Appropriately, his funeral was on September 16th—Mexican Independence Day. He had finally laid down his earthly burdens and entered the Kingdom of Heaven, where he had earned his place. My brother Rudy once gave Dad a plaque that read,

"The true measure of a man's worth is in how much his children love him."

The plaque reminds us all that my father, Mi Apá, was absolutely priceless.

With Dad gone, we started bringing Mom to Seattle to spend the winter months, because she was now alone at the house in Grandview. Although she didn't want to leave her home, we convinced her that it was too difficult, not to mention dangerous, for her to spend the harsh Eastern Washington winters on her own. Reluctantly, my brave mother acceded to our wishes.

I lived in Seattle, as did my two younger sisters and two brothers. Mom spent her time in Seattle in Gloria's beautiful, split-level home. She had her own room and TV, and the rest of us regularly visited her. Still, life wasn't easy for her. Mom and Dad had been married for almost sixty years, and Mom would never get used to being without him. Sometimes, out of the blue, she would say something about Dad or indicate in one way or another that she was thinking of him.

Once, I was driving down the street in Sunnyside with Mom in the passenger seat. It was a beautiful spring day, and we passed an elderly gentleman who was out walking. He was small and neatly dressed in slacks, a well-pressed jacket, and a hat, just like the one Dad used to wear.

Mom looked thoughtfully at the man and then said, "Mira, se parece a tu papá." I acknowledged that he certainly did look like Dad and that, like Dad, he was smartly dressed. Even before Mom said anything, I had noticed him as well. Hearing what she said, I felt my heart ache for her. I knew that as painful as losing Dad was for me, her pain must have been a hundred times greater. I could not begin to imagine her loneliness and overwhelming sense of loss.

Mom's first Christmas in Seattle was difficult because we all greatly missed Dad and our traditional gathering at our home in Grandview. We did our best to keep up the holiday tradition at Gloria's house—tamales and all. The celebration was great, but never quite the same. Not all the family could gather in Seattle, and the holiday rituals—such as the tamal-making assembly line—were downscaled considerably. We tried to preserve as much tradition as possible, but there was no denying that Mom was getting old. She had various health problems, and, worst of all, Dad's absence had left a void that could not be filled—for Mom or the rest of us.

Losing Dad and the special bond that we shared hit me harder than I could have ever imagined. It took a lot of psychotherapy—both before and after his death—to get me through the deep grief and loss I experienced. I had always dreamed of someday being rich and getting Mom and Dad a new house, a new car—everything they could ever need or want. I knew then, just as I know now, what a ridiculous fantasy that was. Yet nobody could take that dream away from me. My greatest wish was for Mom and Dad to be financially secure for the rest of their lives, to know, finally, what financial security felt like. They spent their entire lives working and doing for their family, providing for and taking care of us, worrying about us, praying for us. They deserved so much, yet they received so little. I felt such guilt and resentment, such a feeling of failure. My whole world crumbled when Dad died, and I would never again be able to quite put all the pieces back together. Certain losses cause irreparable damage.

Not realizing it at the time, I tried to build a protective shield around myself after losing Dad. In my selfish despair, I pulled away from Mom and the family. Subconsciously, I reigned in my vulnerability. I had no intention of going through such a painful, hellish nightmare ever again.

How in the world a supposedly intelligent, grown person could be so incredibly stupid is beyond me. But there I was, trying not to be too close to my mother, knowing that the inevitable pain of losing her was beyond my control.

Death was not something I ever really thought about before losing Dad. But now, there was no escaping it. I wanted to prepare and protect myself from suffering this kind of pain ever again. How could I know that I was making the biggest mistake of my life? And, worse yet, how could I be so selfish?

Nine years later, in the year 2000, we lost Mom unexpectedly. Thus, I got my just deserts, unworthy daughter that I felt I was. We had endured several medical crises with Mom, but in August 2000, she was in the hospital for heart surgery. All of us were there, and we each said a few words to her before she was wheeled into the operating room. I didn't know about anybody else, but I was unprepared. It had not even occurred to me that she might not survive the surgery. Holding her hand, I said,

"I'll see you when you get out, Mom." Those were my last words to her. Not "I love you," not "I'll be praying...," just "See you." How could I know that I would never see her again?

Como puede ser (How can it be), that for all my education, for all my supposed intelligence, I could be so incredibly stupid? There was no justifying, no rationalizing... no tengo perdón (I have no forgiveness). I disregarded my mother's last nine years on this earth instead of relishing them. When I should have been there to help her through her great loss, I was, instead, self-absorbed, wallowing in my own misery, and overindulging my instinct for self-preservation. I couldn't go back, couldn't make up for my neglect, and couldn't be forgiven for such insensitive and incredible stupidity.

When I look back on my life, I have many regrets. There are things I would do differently. I would change many things if I could. All of my regrets are born of my own shortcomings, my own faults. However, there is one thing I would not change for anything in the world—Mi Familia, and, most of all, my parents. With all the evil, perversion, and abuse in the world, I consider myself extremely fortunate to have had such wonderful parents and such a good family.

Through all our suffering and hardships, we have always prevailed and never lacked love, food, shelter or unity. My parents were remarkable people. They had eleven children, yet they somehow managed to make each one of us feel special. Each one of us has reason to believe we were the favorite. How did Mom and Dad manage that? What an incredible accomplishment!

No, they weren't flawless. They were only human. They had failings. Yet, they did the best they could in the best way they knew. They worked and sacrificed their entire lives for their family, and they taught us to be good, honest, respectful and trustworthy.

They instilled a powerful and undeniable faith, good morals and values, and they provided a home full of love, safety and comfort. They didn't show a lot of hands-on affection. But, as we started leaving home and my parents grew elderly, we all began to display more physical affection.

Age has a way of bringing out appreciation and gratitude for our many blessings in life. Throughout the hardships, the common times, bad times and the best of times, we always shared a strong bond of unity, love and respect, and an irrefutable belief that family is first and foremost in life. I will always be eternally grateful to my parents and to my siblings for our exceptional family.

FIN

The End

Illustration by Raul Cortés Monroy

# Acknowledgements

*Thank You to my wonderful family* for your help, encouragement and faith in me.

Meagan Douma, Thank You for starting and teaching our St. Mary's writing group. Thanks to you, I started writing my story.

Thank You to my St. Mary's writing group who became my fellow supporters, friends and writers. Thank you all for your constant encouragement and for believing in me.

Thank You to my wonderful teacher, Tara Hardy. Thank you for your faith in me and my story. For your constant encouragement, support, generosity and faith. And thank you for making me promise you that I would see this story through to publication.

Thank You to University of Washington professor Erasmo Gamboa, for your encouragement and for being such a positive role model and influence in my life, especially throughout my University of Washington days.

Thank You Antonio Salazar/Chula Vista Media, for allowing me to use your photographs and for taking an active role in our fight for social justice and equality. Thank you for capturing the essence of those days in your excellent photos.

Thank You Raul Cortes Monroy for your impressive and most appropriate sketches.

Eric Nelson, Thank You for being my editor, advisor and friend. Without you I could not have forged ahead on this project. Thank you for all your hard work.